Jim Mor

Secret Teac.
of the Occu

"Paul Wyld's new book, *Jim Morrison, Secret Teacher of the Occult*, is a fascinating read that delves deep into the stormy rocker's more mystical motivations. Wyld's vividly interpersonal research reveals a side of Morrison that few have considered, one with tremendous relevance to our tumultuous times. This book is not only for fans of The Doors but for anyone intrigued by the spiritual aspects of rock music—a primal force that has impacted global culture in both overt and esoteric ways. Wyld's compelling work sheds light on Morrison's hidden influence as occult preceptor which echoes to this day."

CASEY RAE, AUTHOR OF *WILLIAM S. BURROUGHS
AND THE CULT OF ROCK 'N' ROLL*

"Anyone who has listened to The Doors with any attention knows that they were something more than a rock band. Their music hit some deep, primal spot in the archetypal layers of consciousness and sent their listeners off on journeys of mystery and discovery. From reading Paul Wyld's account of the mystical, magical, and esoteric influences on Jim Morrison and his music, one gets the impression that the infinite was never far from his sight. It's no surprise that he wanted to 'break on through to the other side'—and that the 'other side,' whatever it might be and whatever might inhabit it, wanted him to do just that."

GARY LACHMAN, AUTHOR OF *THE SECRET TEACHERS
OF THE WESTERN WORLD* AND *MAURICE NICOLL:
FORGOTTEN TEACHER OF THE FOURTH WAY*

"As a teenager, Jim Morrison's poetic irrationality and The Doors' psychedelic explorations ignited a deep catharsis within me. Jim's words and musical genius activated something primal—lighting my fire and transporting me to another world. Now, reading Paul Wyld's deeply revealing account of Morrison as a secret teacher, I understand the profound effect The Doors had on my budding spirituality. Wyld has given readers a specialized chronicle of Morrison's spiritual development, rich with modern and historical voices about art, the occult, mysticism, and consciousness. On a journey of vast imagination and creative insight, Wyld reveals a picture of Morrison that transcends the popular vision of him as a sex object, beyond the drunken and lewd performer. We see Morrison as the mystic he was, attempting to shake his audience out of complacency into a state of profound aliveness. Wyld evinces the complexities of Morrison's vital existence as a poet, shaman, mystic, and sage, and at the same, a Dionysian maelstrom struggling against tides of cultural conformity. *Jim Morrison, Secret Teacher of the Occult* is more than a biography of an idiosyncratic artist; it is a guidebook for those experiencing the unavoidable crises that accompany spiritual awakening."

MARLENE SEVEN BREMNER, ARTIST AND AUTHOR OF
HERMETIC PHILOSOPHY AND CREATIVE ALCHEMY AND
THE HERMETIC MARRIAGE OF ART AND ALCHEMY

"Paul Wyld reveals Jim Morrison's true nature and his much-deserved place among the many who have journeyed to the other side to see beyond the limits of a society mired in materialism. In this extensively researched work, Wyld weaves Morrison together with the great poets and travelers in an undeniable story of the deeper spirits he served. His poetic gift, which resonated with so many of his generation, is a torch that is relit in this new telling of the life of the Lizard King."

MAGICK ALTMAN, AUTHOR OF *MAGICK TAROT:*
A JOURNEY OF SELF-REALIZATION

Jim Morrison

Secret Teacher
of the Occult

A Journey to the Other Side

Paul Wyld

Inner Traditions
Rochester, Vermont

Inner Traditions
One Park Street
Rochester, Vermont 05767
www.InnerTraditions.com

SUSTAINABLE Certified Sourcing
FORESTRY
INITIATIVE
www.forests.org
SFI-00854

Text stock is SFI certified

Cataloging-in-Publication Data for this title is available from the Library of Congress

ISBN 979-8-88850-080-4 (print)
ISBN 979-8-88850-081-1 (ebook)

Printed and bound in the United States by Lake Book Manufacturing, LLC

The text stock is SFI certified. The Sustainable Forestry Initiative® program promotes sustainable forest management.

10 9 8 7 6 5 4 3 2 1

Text design by Virginia Scott Bowman and layout by Debbie Glogover
This book was typeset in Garamond Premier Pro with ITC Avant Garde Gothic Std, Kepler Std, and Matric II OT used as display typefaces
Artwork by Georgia Papworth

To send correspondence to the author of this book, mail a first-class letter to the author c/o Inner Traditions • Bear & Company, One Park Street, Rochester, VT 05767, and we will forward the communication, or contact the author directly at **paulwyld.com**.

Scan the QR code and save 25% at InnerTraditions.com. Browse over 2,000 titles on spirituality, the occult, ancient mysteries, new science, holistic health, and natural medicine.

for Margot,
Elizabeth Marie,
spiritual seekers everywhere,
& in memory of Kevin Cahill

*I hope it is true that a man can die and yet not only
live in others but give them life, and not only life,
but that great consciousness of life.*
—JACK KEROUAC

Contents

PREFACE

1717

I think you're the same as me
We see things they'll never see.

—"Live Forever," Oasis

From the very beginning, Jim Morrison's spirit has been with me. I was born on October 7, 1970, in the Doctors Hospital at the University of Miami, just a few miles from the Dade County Courthouse where Jim Morrison's criminal trial was wrapping up. I heard The Doors for the first time one night in 1983 at a weekend bonfire party off the Rickenbacker Causeway and was stoned out of my mind while listening to "The End" and staring at the bonfire flames. I was a thirteen-year-old kid falling in love with rock music. My first rock concert was Van Halen's *1984* Tour at the Hollywood Sportatorium in Pembroke Pines, still my favorite show of all time. Now in The Doors, I'd found yet another L.A. rock band that I could sink my teeth into. I soon discovered the 1980 Jim Morrison biography *No One Here Gets Out Alive* and stayed up all night reading it. From a very young age, I've had a great love for reading and reverence for good books and writers of all kinds. So, like many others, I'd found a hero, a mentor, and a guide in Jim Morrison.

After my parent's contentious and violent divorce, I was placed in a children's home in Central Florida. My counselor, a soft-spoken man named Ted Saunders, was genuinely sympathetic to what I was going through with my family. During one of our sessions together, I confided in him my love for The Doors and Jim Morrison. The next time I saw Ted, he surprised me with a gift, *Weird Scenes Inside the Goldmine*, a compilation Doors album he'd owned since its release in 1972. Ted also revealed that he had been a student at George Washington High School while Jim was in attendance. Ted remembered Jim well from their frequent interactions during a shared class. I'll never forget gazing at the psychedelic watercolor of Jim's image on the cover as Ted told me this, a kind gesture and a fond memory during a difficult and lonely time.

I bonded best with friends in high school who shared a love for The Doors. I was fourteen when I first dropped acid with my friend Jimmy—the first of what would be many LSD trips during my high school years—on a bright and spectral autumn afternoon in suburban north Atlanta. We'd both read Aldous Huxley's *The Doors of Perception* and were quite curious and excited to discover psychedelics. We listened to "The End" as the LSD began to kick in. All we did was laugh and laugh; everything was just very funny. After walking around the Chattahoochee River jumping rocks while peaking—an experience that changed our lives forever—we ended up at a movie theater watching *A Nightmare On Elm Street* where we cracked up even harder. Once in college, I dove into studying great authors, poets, and philosophers, inspired in part by Jim Morrison's example. My senior thesis was a comparative analysis of Friedrich Nietzsche and William Blake—"Philosophy moving towards poetry and poetry moving towards philosophy" as my thesis advisor Dr. Jason Wirth put it.

My conscious awareness of the angelic realm, of the other side, didn't begin until the fall of 2002 when I was living in Santa Cruz, California, and began to experience my first number synchronicity, 333. It became so frequent I couldn't shake the feeling that someone or something was trying to communicate with me. I left Santa Cruz on March 3, 2003—03/03/03—completely unaware that my spiritual awakening was just beginning. In the summer of 2015, while living in Jamaica Plain, Massachusetts, 222 and 888 suddenly began to capture my attention. Finally, in Nashville, Tennessee, in April 2016, all numbers from 000 to 999 were showing up with that mysterious frequency that prompts you to pay attention. This kicked off what was to become for me a seven-year dark night of the soul which more or less ended around April 10, 2023, when I completed writing this book. I've experienced numerous synchronicities of all kinds, but the most healing one in my life so far occurred a few months after I began writing. I was living in Sebastopol, California, in 2020, kipping it in my sleeping bag behind the community wellness center so I could write full time while living as cheaply as possible. The pandemic struck in March 2020 when I began writing in earnest. A surreal time followed as Sonoma County went into lockdown along with the rest of the world. As the terrible summer of 2020 began to unfold following with George Floyd's death, Sonoma County and much of the Bay Area had also become engulfed by wildfires. One morning I awoke to a thick haze of smoke and an unforgettable sight just above the trees. The sky was almost too eerily fantastic to be real: deep, dark, smoldering red low-hanging clouds that instantly made me think of the nightmarish backdrops to Bosch's paintings of Hell. But it wasn't all bad. At night during that time, I got to know the movements of the raccoons as they passed by on the hill above where I slept. Fortunately, I never had an encounter with a skunk.

All the cafés in Sebastopol were now shuttered (a real bummer as this beautiful small town has many good ones), so I spent much of that spring, summer, and fall of 2020 taking the bus into Santa Rosa. Luckily, I'd found a café with an outdoor seating area that was open for business with one available outlet to plug my Mac into. I was deep into trying to make sense of Jim's time in Venice in 1965, back when he used to hang out at a soul food restaurant called Olivia's Place. The café had a music rotation of contemporary rock that featured just one classic rock song, "Soul Kitchen," which gave me the feeling that I was on the right track as well as a fun sense of the creeps.

Still, one evening while heading back into Sebastopol after a day of writing, I asked the Universe for a sign that this project wasn't a waste of my time. For several days leading up to this point, I had begun to notice the house number 1717 while walking to the café. I was far enough along in my spiritual awakening to realize this number was popping into my line of sight for a reason. It was also during this time that the range of angel number synchronicities had expanded from three to four-digit numbers such as 1010, 1212, 1222, 1234, and 1717. Along with new number sequences showing up, I was finding lots of dimes and feathers, was suddenly noticing lots of butterflies while out and about, and was also having extraordinary visitations with red-tailed hawks. My habit by this time was to explore each angel number's meaning by reading every website and watching every video I could find about these numeric symbols. I was soon convinced that this number synchronicity phenomenon must be one of the most significant things that's ever happened to humanity.

The following day I received in the mail Frank Lisciandro's book *Friends Gathered Together*, a collection of revealing interviews with those who knew Jim personally. Flipping through its pages, I was immediately struck by the address of one of Jim's boyhood homes in Alameda, California, an old Victorian house located at . . . 1717 Alameda Avenue. It seems my having placed so much attention on Jim's spiritual person was causing my consciousness to reach out and grasp for things that were meaningful to my project, such as noticing the number 1717. But here was my confirmation from the Universe that my decision to write this book was a good one, and I was grateful for this impactful sign. That night I read Fud Ford's account of his childhood friendship with Jim, and learned that a dying boy—Richard Slaymaker—had lived next door to Jim. Jim and Fud would sometimes visit the boy and comfort him.

A week later, I borrowed a friend's car to drive down from Sebastopol to Alameda. After walking around the house and the surrounding neighborhood (there's a New Age bookstore right around the corner), I saw an old man with a long white beard drive up and stop in front of Jim's house. I walked over and asked him if he was here to check out "the Jim Morrison house." He said he used to live next door, that he was Richard Slaymaker's brother, and that he now lived in Sacramento and drove to Oakland once a week for acupuncture treatments. He made it a habit to stop by the old neighborhood which he said hasn't changed a bit since the 1950s. I told him that I'd read about his brother just a week ago. Sensing my disbelief, he produced his driver's license to show me his last name while stating that he remembered well Jim, Fud Ford, and Jim's father, "the navy man," as he was stationed close by at Naval Air Station Alameda.

We don't know if Jim ever felt that his home address in Alameda had spiritual meaning and instruction. What we do know is that while Jim was living there, he discovered and came to identify with poets and writers like Jack Kerouac who saw the divine spark in everyone and everything while doing their best to live in a world with those who will never see the light. In American film director Terrence Malick's 1998 film *The Thin Red Line*, we meet a defiant character who is much like Jim the secret teacher, Private Witt, played by American actor Jim Caviezel. Witt possessed the secret teacher's ability to perceive the invisible realms. In the film's beginning, Witt confides to 1st Sergeant Edward Welsh, played by American actor Sean Penn, that "I've seen another world. Sometimes I think it was just . . . my imagination."[1] Sergeant Welsh replies, "Well, then you're seeing things that I never will."[2] Towards the end of the film, in light of all that the war had put them through, Sergeant Welsh asks Witt with admiring, somewhat jealous wonder, "Still believin' in the beautiful light are you? How do you do that? You're a magician to me."[3] Witt accepts Sergeant Welsh's compliment and tells him, "I still see a spark in you."[4] Angel number 1717 signals new beginnings as the angelic realm sees a spark in you, putting you on notice to become more independent and in charge of your life. Great change is coming your way. If you're seeing 1717 repeatedly, it generally means you're a person with much inner wisdom and knowledge to offer, someone with a strong inner light, and you should tap into your wisdom to achieve your dreams while helping others to awaken to their divine spark. This is the number Jim saw almost every day of his life for over two years.

I spent the rest of the afternoon visiting Jim's first high school, the beach close by where Jim and Fud used to go swimming, and the navy facility where Jim's father was stationed. I discovered the USS *Hornet*—the aircraft carrier from which Doolittle's famous raid was launched—and spent some time alone walking the length of the dock gazing upon this awesome relic of American history. I thought about Admiral Morrison and his having commanded an aircraft carrier of his own, how Jim must've looked up to him while at the same time feeling quite different and alienated from him, and how complicated it all must've been for both Jim and his father. My own stepfather was a U.S. Air Force reserve officer and commercial airline captain. He made it clear that he disliked The Doors and Jim Morrison. I had the feeling my stepfather had long ago stifled the vital part of himself that loved rock music, as he once told me he had formed a rock band in high school. Maybe he once had rock and roll dreams. Whatever the case may be, the Dionysian sense of life I possess was not felt nor understood by my stepfather just as Admiral Morrison considered himself to be "a very poor interpreter" of his son's art.[5] But for myself, through writing this book, the anger at being misunderstood and shunned by my stepfather and family, being seen as "the naughty one" and "the weird one," was at long last beginning to dissolve into forgiveness and understanding. Some synchronicities are just so breathtaking there's no sense in trying to wrap your mind around them. Forget about attempting to figure out their meaning, just feel them. I walked back to my friend's car that afternoon fighting back tears and then losing the battle once I realized what was happening. In this mysterious meeting with Richard Slaymaker's brother, I felt the healing touch of Jim's generous spirit. Deep wounds unhealed for far too long seemed to begin to close up. For the first time, I felt like I could just move on with a confidence that can only come from feeling an authentic sense of self emerge; this being my strong desire for cosmic consciousness, spiritual enlightenment, artistic pursuits, and inner peace. It's a day that I will not soon forget as it spurred me on to tell a different story about Jim's life as I embarked on changing my own.

Acknowledgments

The best part of writing this book was researching all of the remarkable and fascinating primary source material that, at the same time, aided me through my own dark night of the soul and spiritual awakening. Being able to reach out to these incredible authors and to receive their kind and encouraging responses as well as their support was something I didn't expect. I'm eternally grateful for the positive, healing effect that their communication and books have had on my life.

The initial inspiration for this work, and a life-transformative reading experience that awakened me as no book has ever done, is Gary Lachman's 2015 work *The Secret Teachers of the Western World*, an in-depth and wide-ranging history of the Western esoteric tradition. Lachman's book showed me a completely different way of looking at life and history through a tradition that I never knew existed. Reading about the life stories of its secret teachers, what they dared to stand up for, and what they went through to remain true to themselves, reignited the divine spark within that I was aching to bring back to life. Twentieth-century American poet T.S. Eliot once asked in his 1934 poem "The Rock," "Where is the Life we have lost in living? / Where is the wisdom we have lost in knowledge? / Where is the knowledge we have lost in information?" *The Secret Teachers of the Western World* not only helped to bring me back around to who I truly am but focused my attention on how I can begin to live Eliot's important questions.

It wasn't long before Jim Morrison began coming to mind while reading Lachman's book, and I found myself writing "JM" next to more and more paragraphs. I concluded Jim Morrison was not only a secret teacher but one of the brightest lights in the Western esoteric tradition. Relevant quotes and passages from *The Secret Teachers of the Western World* as well as Lachman's biography on twentieth-century British author Colin Wilson, *Beyond the Robot: The Life & Work of Colin Wilson*, form the basis of this book. This new envisioning of Jim Morrison's life would not have been possible without the incredible breadth and understanding that's been brought to the Western esoteric tradition by Gary Lachman's writings.

In the early summer of 2020, I found author Jean Shinoda Bolen MD's enormously revealing *Gods in Everyman: A New Psychology of Men's Lives & Loves* in a town park. As I read *Gods in Everyman* with rapt attention, many things about my own life became clear, and to my great relief, forgiveness was suddenly possible. *Gods in Everyman* became the key source in presenting Jim Morrison's Dionysian archetype in relation to the mystical and shamanic sides of his person.

Another miraculous find was Christina and Stanislav Grof's clear and concise study of spiritual awakening, *The Stormy Search for the Self,* which explores the extraordinary challenges of experiencing a dramatic change in consciousness. This book was the beating heart of my research. *The Stormy Search for the Self* allowed me to see Jim Morrison's spiritual awakening as an arduous one that he began as a young teenager. This edition of *The Stormy Search of the Self* featured a bright, fiery red phoenix bird on the cover. As there was a large mural of a phoenix being painted across the street from the bookstore in Santa Rosa, I felt this was a sign of the book's importance not only to my own awakening but also to Jim Morrison's story. *The Stormy Search for the Self* is still perhaps the best book yet written on the complicated and mysterious subject of spiritual awakening.

In the early winter of 2023, yet another unexpected grace was discovering painter and author Marlene Seven Bremner's bold and beautiful *Hermetic Philosophy & Creative Alchemy*.

I immediately got in touch with Seven, who in the months that followed was of enormous help during this book's rewriting phase. Passionately devoted to the study, practice, and artistic expression of what Seven views as "the old, old, path," Seven is a wonderful new secret teacher, as well as an incredible painter, and her enthusiasm to see this book published was a tremendous boost of energy at a time when I most needed it.

I want to extend my deep thanks to Bill Cosgrave, author of *Love Her Madly: Jim Morrison, Mary & Me,* an invaluable personal account of his friendship with Jim Morrison and his college sweetheart, Mary Werbelow, and to James Riordan, co-author of *Break on Through: The Life & Death of Jim Morrison,* who always answered my questions and concerns with prompt and helpful replies. Thank you to Magick Altman, author of *Magick Tarot: A Journey of Self-Realization,* who, during a reading one afternoon in Sebastopol in the late spring of 2020, prompted me to focus my purpose and get serious about writing this book.

A huge thank you to Lori Austin for always brightening my day with her fun, friendly, and warm presence in her gorgeous art gallery in Sebastopol during the dark days of the pandemic, and for putting me in touch with London artist Georgia Papworth.

I would also like to convey my sincere appreciation and gratitude to Rocco Ingala, owner of Angel City Books in Santa Monica, for his support over these past years (and for receiving my mail!), as well as all the love and encouragement from Elizabeth Marie, Gabrielle Scarpelli, and to everyone at Inner Traditions & Bear & Company for their belief in this book and their hard work, special thanks to Jon Graham, Jean Levitan, and in particular to Emilia Cataldo.

Finally, I would like to express how thankful I am for the treasure chest of vital ideas contained in the nearly one hundred and fifty books that Colin Wilson left us. In the early part of 2022, I found a new edition of Wilson's classic tome *The Occult* at a bookstore in Pasadena. I intuitively felt *The Occult* was important to Jim Morrison's life story, so I took a deep dive into its many pages. *The Occult* was indispensable in rounding out my presentation of Jim Morrison as a secret teacher. In some ways, Wilson is the British counterpart to Jim Morrison. Had the rock music explosion of the 1960s occurred in 1950s England, Wilson might've seized upon the opportunity to become a rocker himself.

Artist: Georgia Papworth @georgiap.art.

This Is the Strangest Life
I've Ever Known

Jim Morrison's life *was* strange, as he sings in bewildered earnestness at the end of The Doors' song "Waiting for The Sun." Jim Morrison was a great entertainer and lead vocalist for The Doors, as well as a brilliant poet, lyricist, and experimental filmmaker. But this polite, generous, artistic, intelligent, and super fun rock star warrior-poet also possessed the immense transpersonal nature of the secret teacher as presented in *The Secret Teachers of the Western World:*

> For those who have a sense of this invisible, other reality, the answers to life's mysteries offered by modern science are inadequate and unsatisfying. They are unable to accept them and they find themselves seeking something else.
>
> For the esoteric tradition, the physical world available to the senses that science affirms as the only reality is only a small part of a much greater reality, an invisible, inner reality, that informs the outer world and gives it life and meaning.[1]

Esoteric means *inner* and *secret*, and the search for this "invisible, inner reality" has been the pursuit of every secret teacher reaching back to Ancient Egypt and beyond. Jim Morrison felt, as have all past and present secret teachers, that our survival depends on reestablishing contact with the invisible realms:

> *Reality is what has been*
> *concealed from us*
> *for so long*[2]

Secret teachers tend to be loners and so was Jim Morrison. They prefer living in the margins of society where they can be left alone to experience their ecstatic states of cosmic consciousness and respond to them meaningfully through poetry, music, literature, and art. These intense moments of ecstasy are what twentieth-century American psychologist Abraham Maslow termed *peak experiences*. Maslow described peak experiences as being:

> rare . . . exciting, oceanic, deeply moving, exhilarating, elevating experiences that generate an advanced form of perceiving reality, and are even mystic and magical in their effect upon the experimenter.[3]

> [These] mystical experiences [are] characterized by the dissolution of personal boundaries and a sense of becoming one with other people, with nature, the entire universe, and God.[4]

One of our great secret teachers—German philosopher, Christian mystic, and Lutheran Protestant theologian Jacob Boehme (1575–1624)—described in his unfinished 1612 work, *Aurora: Dawning of the Day in the East,* his life-changing peak experience, also sometimes called *unitive consciousness*:

> In this light my spirit suddenly saw through all, and in and by all the creatures, even in herbs and grass, it knew God, who he is, and how he is, and what his will is; and suddenly in that light my will was set on, by a mighty impulse, to describe the being of God.[5]

All of us have peak experiences, what twentieth-century American author John Steinbeck called in his 1952 novel *East of Eden* our "glories," describing them as: "a lonely thing" [that] relates us to the world—It is the mother of all creativeness, and it sets each man separate from all other men."[6]

Peak experiences are often unforgettable, life-transformative moments in our lives that put us in touch with the divine. Many influential persons from all types of professions, as well as the secret teachers of the Western esoteric tradition, have built their lives around at least one peak experience. These moments are sudden, powerfully felt glimpses into that reality Jim felt we've been kept from knowing. They are deep and rich with vision, beauty, mystery, and knowledge, and will often leave a person breathless with awe, wonder, and hope. Maslow noted that a heightened awareness of reality is often felt in these moments.[7] Twentieth-century British author Colin Wilson created an entire philosophy around peak experiences and how we can have more of them in his 1983 work *The New Existentialism*.

Twentieth-century American Beat novelist and poet Jack Kerouac, whose work and life deeply influenced Jim Morrison, possessed what twentieth-century Irish author James Joyce called "the necessary madness" to express peak experiences with originality, a madness Jim Morrison shared. Kerouac wanted to feel these peak experiences as much as he could, writing in his journals:

> I want uninterrupted rapture. I believe this has been made manifest to me in dreams, and in music, and in the pages of Dostoevsky, in the lines of Shakespeare, in sexual joy, in drunkenness, and in being high on tea. Why should I compromise with anything else or with the "Bourgeois" calm of the backyard lawn . . . On tea I have seen the light. In my youth I was the light. In my childhood I bathed in the hints of light: I hankered, eager. I want a blaze of light to flame in me forever in a timeless, dear love of everything. And why should I pretend to want anything else? After all, I'm no cabbage, no carrot, no stem! A burning eye! A mind of fire! A broken goldenrod! A man! A woman! A SOUL! Fuck the rest, I say, and PROCEED![8]

As the secret teacher's intelligence, sensitivity, talents, and calling are exceptional among us, so was Jim Morrison. These type of people often feel an intense calling to communicate their experience of the infinite to the rest of the world and for all time to affect a change in our consciousness. Like Jack Kerouac and Jim Morrison after him, out of this maddening drive to have and express their peak experiences, a secret teacher will fashion their own identity off the beaten path. Many secret teachers become what Wilson describes as an "outsider" in his 1956 book of the same name (which Jim Morrison read while in high school.) Reflecting on how he came to write *The Outsider*, Wilson said:

> It was while I was writing this novel (*Ritual in the Dark*) that I decided to break off and try to express some of its basic ideas in a volume of philosophy. Inevitably, this book was about "Outsiders," people who felt a longing for a more purposeful form of existence, and who felt trapped and suffocated in the triviality of everyday life. It was a book about "moments of vision," and about the periods of boredom, frustration, and misery in which these moments are lost. It was about men like Nietzsche, Dostoevsky, Van Gogh, T. E. Lawrence, and William Blake, who have clear glimpses of a more powerful and meaningful way of living, yet who find themselves on the brink of suicide or insanity because of the frustration of their everyday lives.[9]

The outsider's need to "rival the real," as Jim Morrison put it, is felt as a strong, overwhelming demand to create space for themselves away from society so they can have solitude to be who they are, to read, study, journal, travel, have more peak experiences, and to bring their unique creations to life out of these "moments of vision." Since their common life purpose is to make us aware of a reality beyond the reach of the five senses and the rational mind, many secret teachers become, like Jim Morrison, outsiders as poets, artists, philosophers, authors, filmmakers, and musicians.

In his 2016 biography of Colin Wilson, *Beyond the Robot*, Gary Lachman writes:

> Civilization is in decline. The Outsider is a product of this. He celebrates freedom, will and the imagination over the intellect, logic and reason. The Outsider is evolution's attempt to create "a higher type of man" and "new unity of purpose;" if this fails, then civiliza-

tion will slide into the gulf, just as all the previous civilizations that failed the test did.[10]

Jim Morrison felt that such a "slide into the gulf" would also be the result of our lack of self-awareness.

> *Twentieth-century culture's disease is the inability to feel their reality. People cluster to TV, soap operas, movies, theaters, pop idols and they have wild emotions over symbols. But in the reality of their own lives, they're emotionally dead.*[11]

In turn, confrontational statements like the one above can render secret teachers vulnerable to harsh criticism, censorship, ridicule, and condemnation, sometimes leading to ostracization by their families, their peers, and their communities. Persecution begins for the secret teacher when the many fall into a collective defensiveness in response to statements of "emotional death." Their attitude is *who are you* to show me, *me?* Attacks upon a secret teacher can therefore be long, ruthless, sustained ordeals of persecution carried out by insecure persons, many of whom have occupied and continue to occupy positions of power. They feel threatened by the secret teacher's mysterious, eccentric persona, strange creations, wild behavior, "moments of vision," and poignant criticisms, and go out of their way to make sure the secret teacher is viewed by society as fake, useless, insane, seditious, criminal, satanic, or all of the above.

Jim Morrison's intention was not to insult us but to wake us up to how we waste precious time by not living and engaging with a full emotional palette and awakened mind. But because of our fear and the ego's arrogance—the walls that we build up to shield us from pain, the distractions in society that dumb down, numb, and blind us to our true selves, and our obsessive pursuit of material things, attention, and money—most of us don't want to hear this sad truth. Tragically, there are many emotionally dead people with no ability to feel their reality. They've become the mere "triviality of everyday life" zombies that many secret teachers throughout history have wanted, like Jim Morrison, to run like hell from.

It wasn't easy for Jim Morrison. The secret teachers of the past often led private, guarded lives, keeping their experience and knowledge of the infinite to themselves largely to avoid persecution. Hence the terms *secret teacher* and *secret society*. The secret teacher's conception of the infinite is referred to in Lachman's *The Secret Teachers of the Western World* as "the rejected knowledge," often seen as a primary source of heresy, blasphemy, and spiritual rebellion by church authorities going back to the time of Hellenistic Alexandria.

Since then, secret teachers who've expressed themselves openly in the past have been subject to harsh persecution. Such was the case with sixteenth-century Italian Renaissance mathematician and Hermetic occultist Giordano Bruno, one of our great secret teachers whom Jim Morrison had an affinity with. Bruno was jailed for seven years in Rome before being sentenced to burn at the stake in 1600 CE by the Roman Catholic Church's Pope Clement VIII after refusing to recant his beliefs. Much the same happened to the twentieth-century French poet, essayist, and playwright Antonin Artaud, another secret teacher artist that inspired Jim Morrison. After being committed by the French authorities, Artaud spent the last years of his life being drugged and put through horrific electric shock treatments.

> *People are terrified to be set free—they hold on to their chains. They fight anyone who tries to break those chains. It's their security . . . How can they expect me or anyone else to set them free if they don't really want to be free?*[12]

For centuries, the secret teacher's path has no doubt been a dangerous one, and Jim Morrison's life was no different. His false criminal conviction in October 1970 was initiated by a tough local and national conservative establishment and community backlash following a concert performed by The Doors in Miami on March 1, 1969. Just eight months after his conviction, Jim Morrison died in Paris, France. His death is just one of many instances in the Western esoteric tradition that shows how the viciousness involved in a public campaign of persecution against a secret teacher can push them towards self-destruction.

We can understand Jim Morrison better as a secret teacher by taking a closer look at some of the well-known and lesser known significant moments of his life: his early childhood encounter with a group of dying native workers (whom his mind at the time classified as "Indians") on a New Mexico highway which he sings about on "Peace Frog;" his discovery as a teenager of one of the first written accounts of the Western esoteric tradition, twentieth-century artist Kurt Seligmann's 1948 book *The History of Magic & the Occult*; the release of the film *Lawrence of Arabia*; a supernatural occurrence Jim witnessed in a Florida church with his college sweetheart, Mary Werbelow; his transformation into a rock star warrior-poet; the fateful Doors concert in Miami; an experimental-independent film Jim made and released in October 1969, *HWY: An American Pastoral*; and Jim's false criminal conviction in the fall of 1970.

Another approach we'll take in our search for Jim Morrison the secret teacher is through the character of William Shakespeare's Hamlet. What struck twentieth-century American literary critic and author Harold Bloom the most about Hamlet's character can also be attributed to Jim Morrison:

> I've never come across a literary figure who is able to combine absolute contraries, and real contradictions as Hamlet does . . . at once more given to theatricality, than any other figure, and also given to a kind of terrifying inwardness which keeps growing and growing further and further into the deeps . . . it's an amazing combination . . . how can you be totally theatrical and totally inward?[13]

Bloom's statement brings us to something that's important to understand: we cannot learn anything of real depth about Jim Morrison from TikTok shorts or YouTube videos that attempt to psychoanalyze him. The late Dr. John E. Mack (a former head of the department of psychiatry at Harvard Medical School) in his 1976 biography of T.E. Lawrence, *A Prince of Our Disorder*—a case will be made that Jim Morrison took great inspiration from T.E. Lawrence—writes:

> I must confess that in the beginning I sought to do a psychological study of Lawrence of the sort more familiar to those engaged in

clinical work . . . But as time went on, I found myself diverted by two dilemmas. First, no matter how fully I was able to "understand Lawrence" through the explication of his personal conflicts, the understanding added little to my appreciation of Lawrence's accomplishments as a man. From the psychological standpoint, although his struggles were interesting and compelling, they differed little from those of many other persons of his or our age and could therefore contribute little to the understanding of human psychology. Second, I found myself becoming steadily more interested in Lawrence's achievements than in his problems; or, stated more precisely, I became fascinated with how he was able to adapt his personal psychology to the historical realities that he came upon, or was able to surmount his personal conflicts in the accomplishment of valuable public services.

When I presented "psychological material" about Lawrence at conferences or meetings, my audience would inevitably offer interpretations about his psychopathology which, however accurate they may have been, left me always feeling that they had not seen Lawrence as I knew him to have been.[14]

If Mack, a renowned Harvard psychiatrist, felt Lawrence couldn't be understood even by his fellow colleagues' psychoanalyses of him, then certainly the videos on TikTok and YouTube say next to nothing about Jim Morrison as a person or artist. Wilson felt, "Great writers succeed in leaving their living quality behind; if we turn from Shelley's poetry to biography, we are only *adding* something to the basic truth of the man, which we already possess in his poetry."[15] This book focuses on Jim Morrison's role as a secret teacher through his music and writings. It's my hope that this new vision of Jim Morrison's life will further magnify the beauty and strangeness that's to be discovered in the *living quality* of Jim Morrison's art.

It was quite a surprise to discover that all the attributes of a secret teacher were once alive and kicking within this iconic classic rock singer with the sensitive punk edge, generous heart, and "wrought iron soul." Strange as this may be (as with all things Jim Morrison), his mysterious life story was just as epic and relevant as the lives of some of our greatest secret teachers. But what makes Jim Morrison such a memorable spiritual figure is how much creative fun he had with his shamanic powers while sharing this healing part of himself with the world. So, it's time for us to attempt to understand and appreciate this mysterious and complicated side of Jim Morrison and the Western esoteric tradition from which much of his poetic magic stems. The core of Jim Morrison's legacy rests upon his revelation of our renaissance nature as magical and divine beings, reminding us as Shakespeare did of "What a piece of work is man" and "In apprehension how like a god." Jim Morrison wanted to save us from the hopeless feeling of despair and futility.

This book's aim is to tantalize the seeking nature of those experiencing their higher selves coming to life. Opening the doors of perception, spiritual awakening, and co-creating with the invisible realms are subtle yet powerful sensibilities that have had an enormous impact on art, music, literature, poetry, and film over these past one hundred fifty plus years. The spirit of all of the past artists, poets, authors, and filmmakers who drank deeply from the mystical springs of the invisible, inner reality flowed like a wild, untamed river through Jim Morrison. Today, the living quality of Jim Morrison the secret teacher is vital to understand in these times that are fertile for a new renaissance.

Last, from here on out, we'll respectfully refer to our rock star warrior-poet hero by just his first name, Jim.

> *0 great creator of being*
> *grant us one more hour to*
> *perform our art*
> *& perfect our lives*[16]

I

Into This House, We're Born

1
It's Not a
Ghost Story

The mind is not a vessel to be filled but a fire to be kindled.

—PLUTARCH

In the year of Jim's birth, 1943, two events occurred in the same month halfway around the world from each other that would change both Jim's life and our lives forever. The results of one would become known to the world on August 6, 1945, with the destruction of Hiroshima, Japan. The popular experience of another kind of bomb, one that goes off in the mind, the world would have to wait two more decades to discover.

> LSD was first synthesized in the Sandoz laboratories in Switzerland by Stoll and Hofmann as a drug possibly used for obstetrics and gynecology and in the treatment of migraine headaches. It was subjected to routine laboratory testing in animals and found to be uninteresting, and its study was discontinued. The hallucinogenic properties of LSD were discovered by Albert Hofmann approximately five years earlier, in April 1943.[1]

Also in April 1943, American physicist J. Robert Oppenheimer assembled the inaugural physics conference at the Manhattan Project's top secret headquarters at what used to be the Los Alamos Ranch School for boys in New Mexico.[2] Beat novelist William S. Burroughs, one of Jim's literary heroes (Jim loved Burroughs's 1959 novel *Naked Lunch*) once lived at the Los Alamos Ranch School as a teenager. Author Ted Morgan in his 1988 biography *Literary Outlaw: The Life & Times of William S. Burroughs* writes:

> For Burroughs, however, the true significance of his stay at Los Alamos had to do with the school's destiny. For after Pearl Harbor, when President Roosevelt had approved work on the atom bomb, the Army Corps of Engineers began looking for an isolated site to build the secret laboratory where the bomb would be made. It happened that J. Robert Oppenheimer, head of the Manhattan Project, as it was called, had taken a pack trip to Los Alamos as a teenager in 1922, and had been struck by the beauty of the place, a beauty he was about to destroy.[3]

The following excerpt is from an article in the Atomic Heritage Foundation's website, "Native Americans and the Manhattan Project:"

> The Los Alamos project site was home to the top-secret Project Y, led by J. Robert Oppenheimer. It was the hub of the Manhattan Project and home to numerous high-stakes experiments conducted by a large team of scientists, engineers, and support staff. The Los Alamos area was also home to several Pueblo communities. The Pueblos trace their heritage to the Ancestral Pueblo people, whose civilization began in 1200 [BCE] and eventually extended over much of the Southwest. The San Ildefonso Pueblo was the nearest to the project site. Its community was small and steeped in tradition. Many of its residents were avid potters, a cultural art that had been practiced there for millennia. The arrival of the Manhattan Project in Los Alamos in 1943 was believed to be a temporary "interference" by outsiders into northern New Mexico. Instead, the "lab on the Hill" has become a permanent reality for the region. During the Manhattan Project, Los Alamos had a significant need for maintenance and custodial workers. Its isolation allowed ample space for experimentation, but it also left few options for local employees. As a result, many Native American people were hired from the nearby San Ildefonso Pueblo. Men were generally employed as truck drivers,

construction and maintenance workers, carpenters, and gardeners. Women were recruited as maids and child-care providers.[4]

Los Alamos National Laboratory is a short distance from the site of the traffic accident that Jim came upon one morning while on a road trip with his family at three years old. A local newspaper reported the accident as having occurred on October 17, 1947, on State Road Number 30 which runs right by San Ildefonso Pueblo.[5] Synchronistically, around the same time and on a very different "road," Jack Kerouac was at the end of a hitchhiking trip that would inspire his 1957 novel *On the Road*, a book without which Jim claimed The Doors would not have been possible. Both journeys would be life-altering.

Jim's longtime UCLA film school friend Frank Lisciandro recorded Jim's chilling recollection of the fateful morning of the accident. This would become the most important thing Jim ever said about his life, a rare glimpse into a secret teacher's sense of self. And in Jim's case, it was the source of his call to become a shaman.

It was the first time I discovered death . . . Me and my mother and father . . . and my grandmother and grandfather were driving through the desert at dawn, and a truckload of Indian workers had either hit another car or [something] . . . but there were Indians scattered all over the highway, bleeding to death. So, the car pulls up and stops . . . and it's my first reaction to death . . . I must've been about four . . . A child is like a flower man, his head is just floating in the breeze, man. . . . I was just a kid, so I had to stay in the car while my father and grandfather went back to check it out . . . I didn't see nothing . . . all I saw was funny red paint and people lying around . . . but I knew something was happening, because I could dig the vibrations of the people around me . . . 'cause they're my parents and all. . . . And that they didn't know what was happening any more than I did. That was the first time I tasted fear . . . And like this is a projection from a long way back, but I do think that at that moment, the souls of the ghosts of those dead Indians, maybe one or two of them, were just running around, freaking out, and just leaped into my fucking soul. And I was like, like a sponge, ready to just sit there and absorb it . . . And they're still there. It's not a ghost story, man, it's something that really means something to me. I'm not gonna cry about it, I don't feel like crying. It's a very tender, personal point.[6]

Jim felt his vulnerability in being the unwitting recipient of spiritual forces that would influence the course of his life: "A child is like a flower, his head is just floating in the breeze." Jim resorted to poetry, journaling, and music to express his experiences with the presence of these entities that were within him. As Nietzsche observed in *Twilight of the Idols*, "What is it that the soul of the tragic artist communicates to others? Is it not precisely his fearless attitude towards that which is terrible and questionable?"[7]

Twentieth-century artist Kurt Seligmann's 1948 illustrated work *The History of Magic & the Occult* may have provided Jim the teenager with a meaningful way to understand his early childhood experience:

In the Greek mind, side by side with the Apollonian dwelt the Dionysiac; along with the harmonious, rational world of plastic form and intellectual clarity there dwelt among the Greek people the dark, the eerie and the undisciplined. The Dionysiac conjured up the dead and induced a belief in witches, ghosts and other apparitions.[8]

Jim would later express this experience in a song he wrote with The Doors called "Peace Frog,"

> *Indians scattered on dawn's highway bleeding*
> *Ghosts crowd the young child's fragile eggshell mind.*[9]

In Brad Durham's documentary "Dawn's Highway," New Mexico State Historian Dr. Estevan Rael-Galvez sheds additional light on the impact of these events:

When he saw the accident take place at the age of three, he ended up thinking about the fact that the ghost of those dead Indians, as he wrote about it, jumped into his body, and really influenced not just his perception of himself in this world but his very soul . . . People's perceptions, reality, perceptions are nine-tenths reality. They may have well been Indians, right? Because to him that's what he saw. And it shaped his life.[10]

Assistant New Mexico State Historian Dr. Dennis Trujillo states:

If Jim Morrison felt they were Indians, they were Indians to him, and that's what was important to him, was in him, was part of him, then it's difficult to suggest that's not so, I think.[11]

This last statement has an affinity with one of eighteenth/ nineteenth-century British Romantic poet William Blake's core beliefs, one of Jim's favorite poets who also had a strong connection to the *invisible, inner reality*:

Does a firm persuasion that a thing is so, make it so? . . . All poets believe it does. And in ages of imagination, this firm persuasion removes mountains; but many are not capable of a firm persuasion of anything.[12]

In Shakespeare's *Hamlet*, written around the same time as Giordano Bruno's execution for preaching his beliefs in the existence of many worlds, and first performed in the year of Bruno's death, 1600—audiences in London were being treated to Hamlet's own enthusiastic *firm persuasion* that his experience with the spirit world wasn't just a ghost story, either. Hamlet was determined to understand this mystery no matter what the dangers may be:

> *Be thou a spirit or goblin damn'd,*
> *Bring with thee airs from heaven or blasts from hell,*
> *Be thy intents wicked or charitable,*
> *Thou comest in such a questionable shape,*
> *That I will speak to thee . . .*

Horatio tries to warn Hamlet of what could happen if he pursues his greatly aroused curiosity:

What if it tempt you toward the flood, my lord,
Or to the dreadful summit of the cliff,
That beetles o'er his base into the sea,
And there assume some other horrible form,
Which might deprive your sovereignty of reason,
And draw you into madness?

Before pursuing the Ghost, Hamlet asks for heavenly protection: "Angels and ministers of grace, defend us."[13] But after meeting the Ghost, Hamlet is gripped by wonder and excitement, and it shocks him out of his grief. From thereon, Hamlet will welcome this mysterious Ghost's appearance and its fateful revelation, providing Hamlet with what Wilson states in *The Occult* is a sense of "purpose and vitality" from engaging "the meaning universe."[14]

The biggest question of Jim's life will always remain unanswered: was one of these dying Indians a shaman? And what would this mean? Bloom writes that "The prince, in the Ghost's view, is to be a sword of vengeance: no more nor less."[15] Was this also the case for Jim? Did Jim unwittingly become "a sword of vengeance" as a modern shaman

Figure 1.1. William S. Burroughs, Mexico City.

Figure 1.2. Jack Kerouac, Merchant Marine photo.

at the behest of those dying Indians or by some other unseen force—
"a nameless one among the Elohim, a stranger god who is his own
Angel of Death"[16]—to avenge in the name of all past Native Americans
their "most foul and unnatural murder" during America's era of
Manifest Destiny? For America's having taken the land they'd held
sacred for hundreds of years around Los Alamos, New Mexico, to build
the world's first weapon of mass destruction? "Where they couldn't
wait," as William S. Burroughs felt, "to make the atom bomb and drop
it on the Yellow Peril."[17]

Jim possessed the fearless spirit of Tecumseh, a great Native
American leader and Shawnee Chief of the Ohio River Valley who per-
ished in the Battle of the Thames while fighting against the Americans
during the War of 1812. Jim's uncompromising attitude in restoring
our connection to the primitive had, in spirit, Tecumseh's fierceness.
Tecumseh dreamed of a vast Indian confederacy to defend the Ohio
River as a borderland between Native Americans and American settlers. In 1808, many Native American warriors came together under
Tecumseh's leadership. During this time, Tecumseh, along with his
brother, Tenskwatawa, also known as *The Prophet*, founded Prophet's
Town near present-day Lafayette, Indiana, at the junction of the
Wabash and Tippecanoe Rivers. Prophet's Town is where a confederacy of midwestern and southern tribes was assembled to make a stand
against American settlers migrating into Native American lands. To
this day, Tecumseh's uncompromising words stir the hearts and minds
of all Native Americans, and demonstrate the respect afforded him by
both friends and enemies:

> William Henry Harrison, Governor of the Indian Territory, was
> given the task of confronting Tecumseh and his confederacy of war-
> riors. Harrison was well aware of Tecumseh's power. In a letter to
> the War Department, he wrote:
>
> The implicit obedience and respect which the followers of
> Tecumseh pay to him, is really astonishing, and more than any
> other circumstance bespeaks him one of those uncommon geniuses
> which spring up occasionally to produce revolutions and overturn
> the established order of things.

Ultimately, Tecumseh's dream of a confederacy was short-lived, but his leadership and words affected many generations.

TECUMSEH: Will we let ourselves be destroyed in our turn without a struggle, to give up our homes, our country bequeathed to us by the Great Spirit, the graves of our dead and everything dear and sacred to us? I know you will cry with me, "Never! Never!"[18]

The Great Spirit is a life force, a Supreme Being, or god, known to the Lakota as Wakan Tanka among other names. Russell Means, a Lakota activist, believes a more accurate translation of Wakan Tanka would be *the Great Mystery*. Jim was the gifted eldest son of one of America's youngest and most brilliant, high-ranking military officers, quite a recruitment for the Great Mystery. This future Adonis-like avenging angel with the warrior-poet's soul had his Venus in Scorpio, one of the most fierce of all astrological placements.

Jim's openly rebellious behavior around the cops who lined the stage at Doors concerts was, in one sense, like Hamlet's taunting question to his father's murderer, Claudius: "How like you this play?" This was Jim as Hamlet, standing "poised, sword in hand . . ." as Bloom writes, "above the kneeling and praying Claudius." "We are so mastered by Shakespeare [and Jim] that we rarely stop to reflect upon how bizarre Hamlet's [and Jim's] story has become."[19] The American Establishment—local law enforcement agencies and the FBI—would respond to Jim as Claudius does to Hamlet: "Madness in great ones must not unwatched go."[20] Jim's provocative antics onstage would in some instances initiate riots. It wasn't long into The Doors' career before the FBI would create a file on Jim.

As Jim grew up and reflected on that early morning in New Mexico, he felt the same wonder and excitement Hamlet had when he exclaims: "There are more things in heaven and earth, Horatio, / than are dreamt of in your philosophy."[21] Strangely, it was at dawn when Hamlet spoke these lines, as just moments earlier, the Ghost anxiously told Hamlet, "But, soft! methinks I scent the morning air."[22]

The dawn is a common image found in some of Western esotericism's most notable titles. Some examples are:

- Jacob Boehme's 1612 work, *Aurora: Dawning of the Day in the East*, written a decade after Shakespeare's *Hamlet*
- The world's most historic occult-based secret society founded in 1887, The Hermetic Order of the Golden Dawn, a name that invokes the sun's rays to shine again upon Blake's "ages of imagination."
- The bestselling 1960 occult work *The Morning of the Magicians* by Louis Pauwels and Jacques Bergier.
- "This is the dawning of the age of Aquarius"—a popular lyric in the 1969 hit song "Aquarius/Let the Sun Shine In," performed by the American pop rock band The 5th Dimension.

Jim, whose rising sign was also in Aquarius, would, like many other spiritual seekers of his time, follow his curiosity about all things occult, esoteric, magical, and spiritual in his search for truth. His decision to view what happened that morning on "Dawn's Highway" as not just a ghost story, but also a meaningful spiritual experience, was Jim's way of welcoming the mysteries of the unknown.

On the cover of The Doors' 1968 album *Waiting for the Sun* we see Jim with his bandmates, Ray, Robby, and John, somewhere in the mountains above Los Angeles waiting for the sun's rays to shine again upon a new age of imagination—and a new album of great songs. Jim wanted us to come along with him in spirit by inviting the unknown, to "give it welcome" as Hamlet did, to wake up to the infinite, and feel alive again by opening the doors of our perception. So we can be like Christ who asked us to consider the lilies in the field, as did British Romantic poet William Blake in his 1863 poem "Auguries of Innocence," perhaps Western literature's greatest expression of cosmic consciousness:

> *To see a World in a Grain of Sand*
> *And a Heaven in a wildflower*
> *Hold Infinity in the palm of your hand*
> *And Eternity in an hour*

Also in October 1947, Jack Kerouac, once encouraged by William S. Burroughs to become a writer, was at the end of a hitchhiking trip

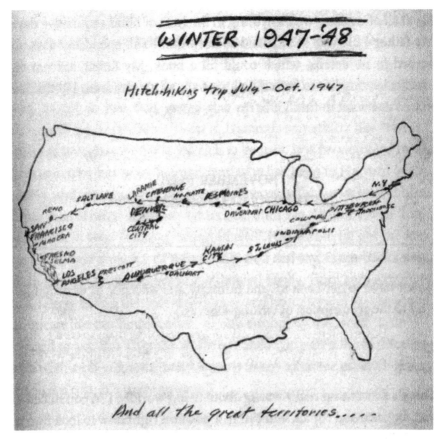

Figure 1.3. Jack Kerouac's hand-drawn map of his travels in 1947.

that would inspire his 1957 novel *On The Road*. Ray Manzarek said The Doors would not have been possible if Kerouac had never written *On The Road*.[23]

We live, we die, and death not ends it.[24]

2
Faculty X

Follow your inner moonlight; Don't hide the madness.
—ALLEN GINSBERG

If there's one author Jim has a close association with in sheer philosophical spirit, it's Colin Wilson. Strangely, Wilson began researching and writing *The Occult* at the same time Jim was performing with The Doors. Lachman in *Beyond the Robot* writes of Wilson's strong affection for America, where he felt at ease and able to do his best work:

> While in America [Wilson] had noticed the growing occult revival. At airport bookshops he bought paperbacks about ghosts, flying saucers, reincarnation, and Atlantis to read on the flight. He had seen some of the effects of the new occult craze in San Francisco, in the Haight and also at the pub where he spent time with poets and occultists.[1]

The Occult was published in the same year Jim passed away, 1971, and contains a central idea in Wilson's philosophy that Jim made poetic use of, an occult power Wilson called *Faculty X*:

> Blake had spoken of the "five windows that light the caverned man," the five senses, but added that there is one through which "he can pass out what time he will." Saint-Martin wrote: "The soul leaves the body only at death, but during life, the faculties may extend beyond it, and communicate with their exterior correspondents without ceasing to be united to their center." He (Saint-Martin) is speaking about Faculty X. At every moment, man is freer than he realizes.[2]

Figure 2.1 Colin Wilson.

Faculty X is not a "sixth sense," but an ordinary potentiality of consciousness . . . a latent power that human beings possess *to reach beyond the present* . . . a sense of reality, the reality of other places and other times, and it is the possession of it—fragmentary and uncertain though it is—that distinguishes man from other animals.[3]

Wilson further explains the connection between Faculty X and poetry:

The poet is a person in whom Faculty X is naturally more developed than most people. While most of us are ruthlessly "cutting out" whole areas of perception, thus impoverishing our mental lives, the poet retains the faculty to be suddenly delighted by the sheer *reality* of the world "out there."[4]

Faculty X is evident in Jim's beautiful and terrifying poem "Horse Latitudes," written while he was in high school, and later turned into a haunting song by The Doors. Sailors of the Spanish galleons on their way to and from the New World sometimes threw their horses overboard when the winds would die in the Sargasso Sea. They did this to conserve drinking water as they didn't know for how long they'd be adrift before the winds resumed. The area of the Sargasso Sea where this occurred came to be known as the Horse Latitudes. Jim had a preoccupation with death throughout his life. For Jim, as "For Hamlet himself," as Bloom notes, "death is not tragic, but an apotheosis."[5] Jim had the feeling of "being there" during the traumatic drowning of these horses (the poem's imagery recalls a nightmarish Goya painting) with that "sense of reality, the reality of other places and other times" that Faculty X imparts through the poet's imagination.

Wilson cites an instance of Faculty X in twentieth-century British historian Arnold Toynbee's visionary experience of an ancient battle scene. Wilson writes in *Beyond the Occult*:

> In the tenth volume of his *A Study of History*, Arnold Toynbee describes several occasions on which he also had these strange glimpses into the reality of the past—not his past, but that of history. On each of these occasions, he actually seemed to see the past, as if he had been transported by a time machine. On one of these occasions, he seemed to see the battle of Pharsalus, which had taken place in 197 [BCE], and saw some horsemen—of whose identity he is ignorant—galloping away from the massacre. It seems clear from his descriptions that he felt this was not "imagination," but some kind of glimpse of the past . . . On a snowy day in 1966, thinking about this curious ability to "make real" other times and other places, I labeled it "Faculty X." But Faculty X should not be regarded as some "paranormal" faculty. It is simply the opposite of that feeling of being "mediocre, accidental, mortal," which all of us feel when we are tired and depressed, and which Sartre calls "contingency." And whenever Faculty X awakens, it tells us that we are not contingent, mediocre, accidental, mortal. Our powers are far greater than we realize.[6]

Aside from this ability to transport us to other times and places, what Blake expresses in *The Marriage of Heaven & Hell*, and as Wilson interprets him, is that the dormant power of Faculty X "removes mountains" created by what Wilson calls *the robot*—this tendency to live our lives on autopilot. Wilson points out that which fascinated Saint-Martin—a French philosopher credited with being the father of Romanticism—is "that man keeps having quite clear flashes of godlike faculties. It is as if some dormant power wakened up in him."[7] Wilson believed, as does Lachman, that our survival depends on developing this Faculty X, stating: "The chief enemy of life is not death, but forgetfulness, stupidity. We lose direction too easily. This is the great penalty that life paid for descending into matter: a kind of partial amnesia."[8]

The way to higher consciousness is grayed out by the partial amnesia created by the robot's *diffusion effect* which is the opposite of concentration.[9] The result is a descent into depression, boredom, forgetfulness, and stupidity.[10] This unconscious succumbing to partial amnesia is a condition of life that Jim dreaded just as much as Wilson did. Jim's warning to us is that at all costs we *cannot* fall into this state that annihilates our greater awareness and begins our slide into the gulf, thereby starving our cerebral existence.

Wake up![11]

Jim knew to be true the invisible forces and energies spoken of by Wilson and other secret teachers, that:

> Primitive man believed the world was full of unseen forces: the *orenda* (spirit force) of the American Indians, the *huaca* of the ancient Peruvians.
>
> [Human beings] need a sense of meaning to release [these] hidden energies . . . [because they] live and evolve by "eating" significance, as a child eats food. The deeper [a human being's] sense of wonder, the wider [their] curiosity, the stronger [their] vitality becomes, and the more powerful [their] grip on [their] own existence.[12]

> [A person] can do things out of love or enthusiasm that would be impossible out of fear. [Their] chief problem at the moment is to escape the narrowness of everyday triviality and grasp the nature of [their] goal; this, in turn, will require the development of what Blake called "imagination," but which it would be more accurate to call Faculty X.[13]

The haunting voice we hear in *An American Prayer* is Jim the secret teacher warrior-poet speaking out of his own desire to engage with invisible energies and powers. His poet's sensitivity is amazed by the sheer *reality* of the world connected with the invisible, inner reality.

All the above form the nucleus of Jim's artistic aims as a secret teacher, warrior-poet: to wake us up into fearlessly validating our own firm persuasions of our mysterious encounters with the unknown. Deep down we know these spiritual confrontations to have real significance for our lives. This was the case for Hamlet, as well as for those who lived long ago in "ages of imagination," when human beings had a stronger awareness of and connection to their occult powers and the invisible realms. Perhaps through a better understanding of Jim's artistic vision, we can open ourselves up to creating a much deeper connection with the divine.

> *I think people resist freedom because they are afraid of the unknown. But it's ironic . . . that unknown was once very well known. It's where our souls belong.*[14]

3
A Spiritual Awakening

The spiritual journey does not consist of arriving at a new destination where a person gains what he did not have or becomes what he is not. It consists in the dissipation of one's own ignorance concerning one's self and life, and the gradual growth of that understanding which begins the spiritual awakening.

—ALDOUS HUXLEY

Throughout Jim's childhood, the Morrisons, a military family, made frequent moves between naval bases. From 1956 until 1958, the Morrisons lived at 1717 Alameda Avenue in Alameda, California, where Jim's father, Captain George Morrison, was stationed at Naval Air Station, Alameda. In the spiritual community, 1717 is considered to be a powerful angel number with several important meanings, one being that when a person begins to experience seeing angel number 1717 repeatedly, such as on license plates or house addresses like Jim's, it's to let them know they're on the cusp of a spiritual awakening.

Jim's high school years began when he was thirteen at Alameda High School, just a few blocks away from his home. Rock music was beginning to make its power known to American youth, and in 1957, Jack Kerouac's *On the Road* was published. In the attic of the Morrison's Victorian home, sometimes in the company of his best friend, Fud Ford, Jim discovered Beat literature and listened to Beat poetry albums such as that of twentieth-century American poet Kenneth Rexroth. Alameda was an important time in Jim's childhood, as he lived near one of Western literary history's greatest renaissances.

Jim and Fud had tons of fun exploring San Francisco across the bay from Alameda when the city's Beat Renaissance was in full swing. They explored famous hangouts like Lawrence Ferlinghetti's City Lights Bookstore where Jim had an unexpected encounter with Ferlinghetti himself. In American artist Frank Lisciandro's 1990 book *Friends Gathered Together,* Ford recalls:

> [Jim] read everything from *Mad Magazine* to the beat poets and novelists of the time. . . . Instead of listening to rock 'n' roll records he'd read Kenneth Rexroth and stuff like that . . . when he'd listen to rock 'n' roll, chances are it would be Elvis. He really liked Elvis . . . [but] more often than not, [we would listen to] comedy or spoken word records. . . . Ferlinghetti and Rexroth both had albums at the locally based *Fantasy Records.*[1]

Ford remembers Jim had strong upper body strength as he could perform the butterfly with ease, the hardest of all swim strokes; that Jim made friends easy and fast; and that Jim was a compassionate person who would show up from time to time to comfort Richard Slaymaker, "the boy" living next door to Jim who was dying. Most of all, Ford remembers Jim as the funniest person he'd ever met, that whenever he saw Jim grinning, he knew somebody somewhere had just slipped on a banana peel. Ford missed Jim greatly when he moved away.[2]

In 1959, the Morrison family moved east across the United States to their new home at 310 Woodland Terrace in Alexandria, Virginia, where Jim would graduate from George Washington High School in June 1961. This is when Jim also met his first girlfriend, Tandy Martin. In *No One Here Gets Out Alive,* we learn that while living in Alexandria, Jim's demeanor became more inward, eccentric, mysterious, and at times bizarre. If his high school girlfriend Tandy Martin's testimony is correct, his behavior would even sometimes become dark and threatening. This was possibly due in part to the effect on Jim's psyche from his deep dive into fifteenth-and sixteenth-century texts on demonology.

All the signs were there of Jim's spiritual awakening. Stories of Jim excusing himself from class by telling the teacher he's having a brain tumor removed (just so he can spend the rest of the day reading) or turning down an invitation to join his high school's most popular fraternity indicate that Jim was *elsewhere*; he could just care less about the ordinary world. This is not typical teenage behavior, a time in life when the need to belong is felt the strongest. Jim was not only following his great intellectual curiosity but was also hot on the trail of learning about the invisible, inner reality, the spirit world, and its influence upon and expression through all of the authors, poets, musicians, and artists whom he loved. Jim may have lived in close physical proximity to his family, friends, and everyone at the high schools, and later, colleges that he attended, but the reality is no one around Jim could possibly fathom the enormous extent to which his consciousness was changing.

There isn't anything easy about going through a spiritual awakening, but Jim managed it pretty well. The need to be alone and the ego-shattering realizations that occur can bring a person to feel they're living in a new reality. The term *spirituality* is defined by Christina and Stanislav Grof in *The Stormy Search for the Self* as:

> . . . situations that involve personal experiences of certain dimensions of reality that give one's life and existence, in general, a numinous quality. C. G. Jung used the word *numinous* to describe an experience that feels sacred, holy, or out of the ordinary. Spirituality is something that characterizes the relationship of an individual to the universe and does not necessarily require a formal structure, collective ritual, or mediation by a priest. . . . The modern term for the direct experience of spiritual realities is *transpersonal*, meaning transcending the usual way of perceiving and interpreting the world from the position of a separate individual or body-ego.[3]

Jim was beginning to take a step back and awake to his life. We have to remember that in the late 1950s, there was no local Barnes & Noble bookstore with an extensive selection of books on self-transformation, the occult, esoterica, or lost knowledge for Jim to go searching through. There wasn't an internet with instant access to all the websites and videos available on spiritual awakening, and there didn't exist the network of transpersonal psychologists that can be found today around Alexandria and Washington, D.C. to reach out to. Jim was on his own and became a spiritual trailblazer in response to his awakening. In addition, teenage life in Jim's time was quite different from today. Jim would later recollect: "When I was in high school and college, the kind of protest that's going on now is totally unheard of. To be a teenager, to be young, was, um, was really nothing, it was kind of a limbo state."[4] While 1950s American youth lived in limbo, Jim was becoming aware of his nature as a secret teacher. What Jim managed to discover through his reading and journaling, both about himself and how the world views those like him, is best described in *The Stormy Search for the Self*:

> Throughout history, people in intense spiritual crises were acknowledged by many cultures as blessed; Respected members of their communities who had been through their own emergencies, could recognize and understand a similar process in others, and, as a result, were able to honor the expression of the creative, mystical impulse.
>
> With the advent of modern science and the industrial age, this tolerant and even nurturing attitude changed drastically. The notion of acceptable reality was narrowed to include only those aspects of existence that are material, tangible, and measurable. Western cultures adopted a restricted and rigid interpretation of what is "normal" in human experience and behavior and rarely accepted those who sought to go beyond those limits.[5]

Jim's spiritual crisis became difficult for him to contain. With no one else in his family or in society to turn to, Jim told Tandy he had a problem he wouldn't discuss with his parents, but he wouldn't describe it to her either. Frustrated and sensing Jim's issue might be spiritual in nature, Tandy had Jim talk to a Presbyterian minister.

If Jim's issue was indeed spiritual—what Jim and this person discussed remains a mystery—then keeping it to himself was probably a smart move. Jim didn't know how his family or Tandy would react, and might've felt he'd frighten them if he revealed what he was going through. In Christina and Stanislav Grof's professional experience, many of their clients going through spiritual awakenings told them:

. . . tragic stories of families and professionals who misunderstood them, of hospital commitments, unnecessary tranquilizers, and stigmatizing psychiatric labels. Often, a process that had originally begun as healing and transformative had been interrupted and even complicated by psychiatric intervention.[6]

In Jim's solitary quest to understand his secret teacher's nature free of outside complications, he found guidance in Friedrich Nietzsche, a problem thinker who saw his life as "a crisis like no other." Nietzsche's philosophy contained novel ideas such as his attempt at creating a new morality for free spirits like Jim who chose to live life on the edge. This would be Jim's destiny, to become a secret teacher/rock star/warrior-poet, a magus, and a shaman while leading an outsider's life on the edge.

Jim's fascination and love for Nietzsche's writings can be attributed in part to Jim's archetype, the ancient Greek god Dionysus. It's a challenging paradigm for a person to have, but the Dionysian archetype is marvelous too, as its mystical, erotic, and ecstatic traits magnify the secret teacher's spiritual nature. In Jean Shinoda Bolen MD's 1989 book *Gods in Everyman: A New Psychology of Men's Lives & Loves*—she explains these dynamics:

Archetypes are preexistent, or latent, internally determined patterns of being and behaving, of perceiving and responding.[7]

Dionysus as god, archetype, and man was close to nature and to women. The mystical realm and the feminine world were familiar to him. He was often an unwelcome and disturbing element, a cause of conflict and madness in mythology, just as Dionysus can be in a man's psyche.

The Dionysus archetype has powerful positive and negative potentialities, stirring up the most ethereal and the basest of feelings, creating conflicts within the psyche and with society. It is an archetype that is present in some men who are mystics, and in others who are murderers. In between, it is the archetype in men (and women) who experience ecstatic moments and intensely contradictory impulses.[8]

It's no wonder Jim was drawn to Nietzsche. Wilson writes in *The Occult* that:

> The profound significance of all this was recognized by the philosopher Nietzsche, who declared himself a disciple of the god Dionysus. He spoke of the "blissful ecstasy that rises from the inner most depths of man," dissolving his sense of personality: in short, the sexual or magical ecstasy. He saw Dionysus as a fundamental principle to human existence; man's need to throw off his personality, to burst the dream bubble that surrounds him and to experience total, ecstatic affirmation of everything. In this sense, Dionysus is fundamentally the god, or patron saint, of magic. The spirit of Dionysus pervades all magic, especially the black magic of the later witch cults, with their orgiastic witch's sabbaths so like the orgies of Dionysus's female worshippers, even to the use of goats, the animal sacred to Dionysus.[9]

Jim's preferred activities related to *shadow work* and the processing of spiritual awakenings. Shadow work involves exploring the unconscious mind to uncover those parts of us that we repress and hide even from ourselves. Jim spent much of his time alone reading and journaling (he was inspired by twentieth-century Bohemian novelist Franz Kafka's journal keeping) and engaging in creative, artistic pursuits such as writing poetry and painting. Grof described that:

> Drawing, painting, and sculpting allow you to channel strong physical and emotional energies, and as you do so, you may well discover some new aspects of yourself . . .
>
> [For example] Spanish artist Francisco Goya felt a sense of increased mastery over his dramatic inner life that came from putting the images within him on canvas.[10]

Jim also journaled to help deal with his pain and loneliness. Mack writes in *A Prince of Our Disorder*:

> It is usual for persons who have undergone severe psychic traumata or who suffer from various forms of emotional distress to try to

understand themselves through introspection: self-understanding is a time-honored path to relief of emotional pain. . . The struggle to deal with the continuing effects of a traumatic experience goes on long after its occurrence, sometimes for the rest of a person's life.[11]

This can certainly be said about Jim in light of his witnessing the gruesome deaths of the native workers when he was three years old. Jim felt that this accident and all of the ensuing trauma, pain, and confusion he felt had occurred in a kind of divine timing, awakening him to not only discover his life purpose but a mystery to continually express through poetry, music, and film. By closely examining his thoughts and feelings with the aid of the poets and writers he read, it seems Jim came to a stunning conclusion about himself early on in life: that he was destined to deliver an important, life-altering message to the world. It's not hard to understand then why Jim preferred solitude. He truly needed the time and space necessary to grapple with the magnitude of everything that was going on with his exploding internal world.

Jim must've spent a lot of time wondering about just who those native workers were, what their roles were in the community, and what the construction of Los Alamos National Laboratory on their land meant, in the spiritual sense, at that point in human history. But one thing is certain: the trauma and the personal revelation that it produced put Jim on what seems to have been a fast-moving path of spiritual awakening. The young, sensitive poet with the secret teacher's openness to the invisible, inner reality was beginning to feel the initial birth pangs of his shaman's life.

Personal, private, solitary pain is more terrifying than what anyone else can inflict.[12]

4

The Secret of Mind-Change Reality

*We think of the magus as the possessor of occult secrets, a
master of esoteric wisdom, who makes use of this knowledge
for his own good as well as for that of his fellow men. He
is a "white" magician, less fond of prodigies than of the
contemplation of nature, in which he discovers marvelous
active forces where others only see familiar things. For
him the power of God is not concentrated in this One, but
permeates every being of the universe.*

—KURT SELIGMANN

Jim possessed a marvelous mind. "Throughout his years at GW
Jim maintained an 88.32 grade average with only minimal effort,
twice being named to the honor roll. His IQ was 149." In Jim's base-
ment bedroom were over a thousand books as his reading habits
intensified after his family moved to Alexandria. "He read the great
French Symbolist poet Arthur Rimbaud, whose style would influence
the form of Jim's short prose poems. He read everything Kerouac,
Ginsberg, Ferlinghetti, Kenneth Patchen, Michael McClure, Gregory
Corso, and all the other Beat writers published. Norman O. Brown's
Life Against Death sat on his bookshelf next to James T. Farrell's
Studs Lonigan, which abutted Colin Wilson's *The Outsider* and next
to it, *Ulysses* (his English teacher in his senior year felt that Jim was
the only one in the class who'd read it and understood it). Balzac,
Cocteau, and Molière were familiars, along with most of the French

existentialist philosophers. Jim seemed to understand intuitively what these challenging minds offered.[1]

A thousand books. All of us would be hard-pressed to know someone so young who was this literate:

> Jim was capable of stunts of intellectual virtuosity. When friends visited his room (in college) he challenged them:
> "Go ahead, pick a book, any book."
> His voice was boastful, but he toed the carpet of his bedroom: the shy magician.
> "Pick any book, open it to the beginning of any chapter, and start reading. I'll keep my eyes closed and I'll tell you what book you're reading and who the author is."
> Jim swept one arm around the room at the hundreds and hundreds of books on top of the furniture and stacked everywhere against the walls."
> He never missed![2]

This tells us something utterly amazing: *Jim read all those books and retained a working knowledge of everything they contained.*

One particular passage in Wilson's *The Occult* partly explains why Jim was so attracted to poetry and music:

> Whenever I am deeply moved by poetry or music or scenery, I realize I'm living in a *meaning universe* that deserves better of me than the small-minded sloth in which I habitually live. And I suddenly realize the deadliness of this lukewarm commitment that looks as harmless as ivy on a tree. It is systematically robbing me of life, embezzling my purpose and vitality. I must clearly focus on this immense meaning that surrounds me and refuse to forget it; contemptuously reject all smaller meanings that try to persuade me to focus on *them* instead."[3]

Jim was learning that his rich imagination and powerful intellect could make him into a true magus. Through his disciplined reading, journaling, writing poetry, drawing, and painting, Jim gained, to borrow Wilson's words from *Beyond the Occult*, "a magical kingdom," giving Jim "an almost drunken sensation of the sheer immensity of the world of ideas."[4] As Conway writes in *Magic: An Occult Primer*:

> If the universe is man on a gigantic scale, the mysterious forces that move it may be equated with those that move man. Through them is woven the fabric of all visible things and it is the magician's task to discover their true nature. To this end he need only cultivate the forces already latent in himself, for they are, of course, the same as those that regulate our world and propel the furthermost star. "Know thyself" was the good advice given at Delphi.[5]

To give more attention to his intellectual interests Jim learned to protect his mind and "reject all smaller meanings." For the spiritually awakening person, it's common to start rejecting anything that feels inauthentic or could be manipulative, and to see the major forces in culture that shape the mind. Jim was no different, as he observed we're "ruled by T.V."[6] on his poetry album *An American Prayer* (it would be most interesting to hear what Jim would have to say about the array of modern technology and gaming devices if he were alive today). Jim would later state during an interview that:

> To me, there's something incredibly sad about a bunch of human beings sitting down watching something take place. The spectacle of millions and millions of people sitting in movie theaters and in front of television sets every night watching a second or third-hand reproduction of reality going on when the real world is right there in their living room or right outside in the street or down the block somewhere. I think it's a kind of tool to somnambulize or hypnotize people into a kind of waking sleep.[7]

Jim learned from writers such as twentieth-century Canadian philosopher Marshall McLuhan—famous for coining the phrase "the medium is the message"—how our minds can be hijacked by outside influences, technology in particular. As Jim would later observe, "Whoever controls the media controls the mind." Jim would've also agreed with American author Daniel Pinchbeck's statement in his 2002 book *Breaking Open the Head: A Psychedelic Journey Into the Heart of Contemporary Shamanism*:

> Is it possible that our society has built up a vast edifice of technology and propaganda to avoid that inner confrontation? Enveloped by media and technology, we have come to prefer secondhand images to inner experience—what Jung called "the adventure of the spirit." The self-knowledge achieved through personal discovery and visionary states seems alien, even repellent, compared to the voyeuristic gaze, virtual entertainment and hypnotic distractions of contemporary culture. Perhaps we are due—even overdue—for a change.[8]

Jim was telling us we're going to "slide into the gulf" by zoning out on television, or for that matter, spending hours surfing the web, scrolling through social media, or allowing ourselves to be overtaken by desires for material things.

Senses become heightened during spiritual awakenings as one becomes more in touch with *the invisible, inner reality* of the present moment. A reevaluation of beliefs and the discovery of new ones is also common.

Who needs
temples & couches & T.V.?
We can do it on a sunny
floor w/friends & make
any sound or movement
that comes. Roll on our
backs screaming w/mirth
glad in the guilt of our
madness. Better to be
cool in our worship &
gain the respect of the
ancient & wise weaving
those robes. They know
the secret of mind-change
reality.[9]

Jim once recalled "I had a book on lizards and snakes and reptiles and the first sentence of it struck me acutely—'reptiles are the interesting descendants of magnificent ancestors'."[10]

Another book Jim had, one he checked out from the local Alexandria library and never returned, was Kurt Seligmann's illustrated work *The History of Magic & the Occult*—first named *The Mirror of Magic: The History of Magic in the Western World* upon its publication in 1948. This book was an important discovery for Jim, and he never returned it, keeping it for years before giving it away to a friend. *The History of Magic & the Occult* is a wealth of occult ideas and philosophies on magic spanning the Western esoteric tradition going back to Mesopotamia, containing valuable information on what Jim would call "the secret of mind-change reality." It is not uncommon for men with their Venus in Scorpio (such as Jim's was) to be interested in the occult and magic.

Seligmann, a Swiss-American, was a surrealist painter in the early twentieth century. Seligmann made a name for himself in the art world with his paintings of medieval troubadours and knights in macabre rituals, provocative art that was right up Jim's alley. Daniel Mack of the Seligmann Center of the Arts explained that: "Surrealism is really another form of alchemy, bringing together a brave encounter with the unconscious and a series of technical skills you had to perfect."[11]

After his emigration to New York City in 1939 from Paris to escape Nazi persecution, Seligmann began including elements of magic, myth, and the occult in his artwork. Seligmann was an astute occultist, once calling out twentieth-century French surrealist poet André Breton for

Figure 4.1 Kurt Seligmann, passport photo.

his lack of knowledge regarding the tarot. If it wasn't for Seligmann's talent and connections, he would've found himself an outsider among outsiders in New York City's art scene for his having so publicly corrected the great André Breton.[12]

Perhaps the quote from Albert Einstein that Seligmann chose to open *The History of Magic & The Occult* with—"The fairest thing we can experience is the mysterious"—also struck Jim's imagination just as "acutely" as the opening statement to the book he possessed on reptiles. With The Doors, Jim would appropriate to great effect his natural gift for mysteriousness and erotism through song, performance, and rock photographs. This is why Jim continues to draw new fans into his "magical kingdom." No other rock star before or since has been able to project such a timeless and magically numinous presence.

Bloom writes, "The Dionysian is a very old kind of man: an ecstatic."[13] Jim's very old soul resonated with Seligmann's magnificent descriptions of the ancient world in *The History of Magic & The Occult*. Jim belonged there, in a time when a secret teacher like himself would've been greatly valued. Jim's timeless appeal partly lay in his capacity to put us in touch with very distant times, very old places, and the intense longing to go back and connect with its primitive magic, for among all primitive and ancient peoples there existed an ever-present reverence for the Great Mystery. Jim's ability to do this with The Doors made him a kind of "magical trigger" for what we can say is the collective Faculty X. Through the "living quality" of Jim's art we can "reach beyond the present" to that "sense of reality, the reality of other places and times." "The *invisible, inner reality*" that Jim felt has been kept from us deliberately these past four centuries. Cosmic consciousness was once a known and accepted part of ancient life.

In the introduction to *The History of Magic & the Occult*, Seligmann writes:

As an artist, I was concerned with the aesthetic value of magic and its influence upon man's creative imagination. The relics of ancient peoples indicate that religio-magical beliefs have given a great impulse to artistic activities, a stimulus which outlasted paganism and produced belated flowers in the era of Christianity.[14]

The best minds of the West were influenced by a higher type of magic. The investigators of nature followed for centuries the path trodden before them by the ancient philosophers and magi. They believed that in magical wisdom lay the secret of the world's harmony.[15]

Seligmann covers familiar occult topics such as witchcraft, astrology, the tarot, vampires, Rosicrucianism, and alchemy—"the youngest magical wisdom . . . [that] flourished in the fourth century, amidst the merciless fight which Christianity was waging against paganism."[16] Alchemy is also called "the *Royal Art*" "because it is at its core a creative process that leads to the perfection, or masterpiece, of human consciousness."

Jim wrote in his journals that "Alchemy offers man an original heroism"[17] and that "Alchemy is an erotic science, involved in buried aspects of reality, aimed at purifying and transforming all being and matter."[18] Jim wrote extensively on this complicated occult subject in his poem *The Lords: Notes on Vision*, found in his only book of poems, *The Lords & the New Creatures*, published in 1969. Jim filled *The Lords: Notes on Vision* with keen insights into cinema's relationship to alchemy, his "thesis on film aesthetics."[19] It's a revealing glimpse into Jim's secret teacher's mind, showing the results of Jim's being a prolific reader. Jim was not satisfied by the superficial meanings found in literature, but would search for deeper truths and revelations.[20]

Seligmann's understanding of magic is similar to Blake's view of the creative, mystical impulse, and through alchemy's principal aim of reconciling opposites, Jim discovered how to achieve wholeness. Seligmann suggests that:

The history of magic, and the occult in the West, from 5,000 [BCE] through the eighteenth century and beyond is largely the history of mankind's efforts to reconcile the opposing forces of Good & Evil within ourselves.[21]

Blake meanwhile sees hell and evil as a creative force. He characterizes seventeenth-century British poet John Milton's creative, mystical impulse as "being of the Devil's party without knowing it,"[22] when considering Milton's imaginative description of Satan in *Paradise Lost.*

Overall, what Blake is telling us in *The Marriage of Heaven & Hell* is that this clash of opposites produces energy, a tension that's critical for all creativity to occur:

> Without contraries is no progression. Attraction and Repulsion, Reason and Energy, Love and Hate are necessary to human existence. From these contraries spring what the religious call Good and Evil. Good is the passive that obeys Reason. Evil is the active springing from Energy. Good is Heaven. Evil is Hell.[23]

Kerouac wrote in his journals:

> I detect a strong dualism—between loneliness, morality, humility, sternness, critical Christianity—and charm, open-mindedness, humorousness, Faustian power and lust for experience. These two sets of impulses will never cease to work in me.[24]

Nietzsche states in *The Birth of Tragedy*: "In all truly productive men instinct is the strong, affirmative force and reason the dissuader and critic."[25] Heaven or good is reason's passive instrument. Wilson also points out this in *The Occult*:

> Rational consciousness is a kind of valve that cuts us off from the full power of the life current inside us. Magic is a recognition of this power, an attempt to devise means of tapping it. Ordinary consciousness could be compared to a picture gallery full of magnificent paintings but lit by dim electric bulbs. The moments of intensity are like a sudden burst of bright sunlight that makes a spectator realize just how dazzling the colors are. *Lower states of consciousness do not understand the higher.*[26]

Magic, therefore, is a means of turning up the illuminating power of our occult abilities and the numinosity of our divine spark within. Magic increases the energy of our wonder, curiosity, purpose, vitality, and aura, deepens our humility and depth as human beings, and provides what Wilson states is a firmer grip on our reality.

Conway writes in *Magic: An Occult Primer* that, "The real rewards of magical study are not temporal benefits but a spiritual understanding of the universe in which we live."[27] Life-saving transformation is the alchemist's goal, unifying the mind, body, and soul and allowing us to access the concealed reality. The source and reason for this concealment we'll get into later, but through our examination of nature, we can discover "marvelous active forces where others only see familiar things."[28]

> **In his retort the alchemist repeats the work of Nature.**[29]

Jim saw experimental filmmaking as a powerful medium that could express his secret teacher's consciousness through its avant-garde capacity to reveal the magic in the mundane aspects of life.

> Strange, fertile correspondences the alchemists sensed in unlikely orders of being. Between men and planets, plants and gestures, words and weather. These disturbing connections: an infant's cry and the stroke of silk; the whorl of an ear and an appearance of dogs in a yard; a woman's head lowered in sleep and the morning dance of cannibals; these are conjunctions which transcend the sterile signal of any "willed" montage. These juxtapositions of objects, sounds, actions, colors, weapons, wounds, and odors shine in an unheard-of way, impossible ways.[30]

Jim's alchemical views of cinema in *Lords: Notes on Vision* also reveal similar artistic aims with Renaissance secret teacher Giordano Bruno's *magical memory*. Jim and Bruno both possessed an uncompromising belief in the power of mind-changing reality to create a new world based on cosmic consciousness.

Lachman writes in *The Secret Teachers of the Western World* that:

> Like Pico [della Mirandola], Bruno made it his mission to reawaken men to their true position in the cosmos, and in perhaps his most controversial work, *The Expulsion of the Triumphant Beast*, he celebrates the return of the Egyptian gods and portrays himself as their avatar.

Bruno is remembered today as a martyr to free thought and a victim of the church's tyranny. But his real importance is as a magician and visionary, and it is in his ideas about "magical memory" that this is most clear. Bruno took seriously the Hermetic injunction that to understand God, one must make oneself equal to Him. His means of doing this was through his "magical memory." Bruno devised a method of impressing on his consciousness divine images of the celestial archetypes, what he called "the seal of the stars," much in the same way that Ficino has used talismans to attract beneficial astral energies. For Bruno, these images were "shadows" or reflections of the Platonic Forms—the title of his book *The Shadow of Ideas* says as much. Taking the images from the Hermetic books, Bruno made talismans and then fixed these symbols in his memory, furnishing his mind in the same way that the ancient rhetoricians furnished their "memory palaces."

As with Ficino, these Hermetic images had great power, and it was through them that Bruno believed he performed magic and impressed his will upon the world. Ficino would never be as bold as to say it, but Bruno had no hesitation in declaring that in this way he became a co-creator with God. His images, ranging through the Great Chain of Being from minerals to man, constituted an inner universe, the center of which was the magician, just as the sun was at the center of the new Copernican cosmos. In this way Bruno stood outside space and time and achieved the "cosmic consciousness" that was the goal of the ancient Hermetists. From humbly using the "natural" energies of the Anima Mundi, the Renaissance magician had now become something much more like God Himself.[31]

Jim's secret teacher sense was much like Bruno's. He saw the power to perform magic with cinematic images in much the same way Bruno viewed Hermetic images as a method for the magician "to impress his will upon the world." There's no mention of Giordano Bruno in *The History of Magic & the Occult*, so it isn't known from what source Jim may have learned about Bruno. However, we can safely assume that our incredibly well read secret teacher warrior-poet knew of Bruno, his Hermetic beliefs, and his tragic fate.

Like Bruno, Jim had no interest in religious doctrine. Alchemy appealed to Jim's chosen life path, the spiritual adventure which Jim would later describe as "the path of the sun." As Nietzsche writes: "If you want to achieve peace of mind and happiness, have faith. If you want to be a disciple of truth, then search."[32] Jim learned from Seligmann that the alchemist held a similar uncompromising attitude in their search for truth:

> The soul of the alchemist could find no peace in the teachings of the established dogma. For the truly pious, *faith* was blessedness; but the alchemist wanted to *understand* God through knowing the marvelous force that God had given to matter. With his intellect he wished to grasp the supreme, and through study and contemplation to ascend gradually to the divine light.[33]

Perhaps it was this statement that kindled Jim's divine spark within and inspired him to sharpen his mind through reading and journaling even more. Creating a mystical experience with his natural gifts for mysteriousness and erotism, in conjunction with his shamanic powers, was a major part of Jim's artistic achievements through his poetry, songs, performance, and experimental filmmaking. As Jim had learned, "The fairest thing we can experience is the mysterious."

The History of Magic & the Occult taught Jim that part of the magician's role in ancient cultures was to put their people in touch with the divine light by becoming a divine light themselves. Bringing back the natural magic of the ancients was the form Jim's adventure of the spirit would take in modern life. To continue with Seligmann:

> If we trace our way further back into the eras of primitive mankind, here too we have reason to believe that magic was no vain observance. The early wizard was a benefactor of his tribesmen, promising assistance against the fearful unknown.[34]

Cinema derives not from painting, literature, sculpture, theater, but from ancient popular wizardry. It is the contemporary manifestation of an evolving history of shadows, a delight in

> *pictures that move, a belief in magic. Its lineage is entwined from the earliest beginning with Priests and sorcery, a summoning of phantoms. With, at first, only slight aid of the mirror and fire, men called up dark and secret visits from regions in the buried mind. In these seances, shades are spirits which ward off evil.*[35]
>
> *Cinema, heir of alchemy, last of an erotic science.*[36]

Sex for Jim was the ultimate experience of the divine—as it should be for all of us—another trait of his Dionysian archetype and central to the alchemist's understanding of nature. Aside from Jim's mysteriousness, his erotism was also a strong factor in drawing us into his *magical kingdom* to experience the divine light. For Jim, sex was the transpersonal experience par excellence. Bolen writes in *Gods in Everyman* that the Dionysus archetype male:

> . . . may put as much of his considerable psychic energy into the sexual realm, as another man might put into his career. He can have ecstatic sexual experiences, sometimes further enhanced by music or intoxicants without being in a deep personal relationship. A sensitive partner may be aware that he is so much into making love, moving into an altered state of consciousness himself, that there is something impersonal about his lovemaking. At that moment, he may be having an archetypal Dionysian experience, not a personal communion. He can be truly drawn repeatedly to a variety of women, or to repeated experience with the same woman if she, too, can love in the moment, as he does. Conquest is not a motivation; the experience itself is.[37]

Christina and Stanislav Grof write in *The Stormy Search for the Self*:

Occasionally, a psychospiritual transformation can begin during intense and emotionally overwhelming lovemaking. Sex also has important transpersonal dimensions: on the one hand, it is a vehicle for transcending the biological mortality of the individual by leading to new birth; on the other it has deep connections with death. The French actually call sexual orgasm "small death" (*petit mort*). Sexual union that occurs in the context of a powerful emotional bond can take the form of a profound mystical experience. All individual boundaries seem to dissolve and the partners feel reconnected to their divine source. Besides being a biological union of two humans, such a situation might be experienced as a spiritual union of the feminine and the masculine principles and appear to have divine dimensions. The deep liaison between between sexuality and spirituality is acknowledged and cultivated in the Tantric spiritual traditions.[38]

Jim once quoted Blake in an interview: "that the body was the soul's prison unless the five senses are fully developed and open. [Blake] considered the senses the 'windows of the soul.' When sex involves all the senses intensely, it can be like a mystical experience."[39]

> *The alchemists detected in the sexual activity of man a correspondence with the world's creation, with the growth of plants, and with mineral formations. When they see the union of rain and earth, they see it in an erotic sense, as copulation. And this extends to all natural realms of matter. For they can picture love affairs of chemicals and stars, a romance of stones, or the fertility of fire.*[40]

Jim wrote *The Lords: Notes on Vision* after his entrance into UCLA's film department. Everything Jim learned in *The History of Magic & the Occult* about the Royal Art of alchemy had remained for him since high school an occult topic of great personal interest.

It's not hard to see why Jim the budding secret teacher never returned *The History of Magic & the Occult*. It's a fascinating and fun read that breaks the circuit of that partial amnesia by putting the reader in touch with the *meaning universe* that the ancient world embraced. How did Jim find this book? Was it mentioned in something he'd read and then set out to find? Or did Jim pull it off the shelf while hanging out at the library one day after school, a book upon first sight that Jim decided to peruse? While strange and perhaps one of those meant-to-be occurrences, the fact is that Jim did find *The History of Magic & the Occult,* an artistic and elegantly written historic account of magic's influence in the West. It helped Jim to become aware of his nature as a secret teacher and influenced his learning about the Western esoteric tradition. It spurred on Jim's welcoming excitement, enthusiasm, and curiosity about magic, the occult, the invisible realms, and the unknown, further sparking his creative, mystical impulse. Seligmann's book also showed Jim that the pursuit of the rejected knowledge has been an ongoing rebellious activity in near-constant war with the modern "notion of acceptable reality."

Most of all, *The History of Magic & the Occult* allowed Jim perspective and context for his intense and ever-unfolding spiritual awakening.

Years later in 1963, while attending Florida State University, Jim gave Seligmann's book to his friend and roommate, Ed Martin, for Christmas. On the back side of the front cover is the Alexandria Library imprint noting its establishment in 1794. On the opposite page, Jim signed it *"Christmas '63 from Jim Morrison."* Martin met Jim when they

Figure 4.2 Jim's "liberated" copy of *The History of Magic & the Occult.*

Figure 4.3 "Christmas '63 from Jim Morrison."

were both living in the same rooming house. Neither of them owned a car so they used to walk to school together. Martin said Jim used to listen to a transistor radio while falling asleep. Some nights, the music woke Martin, and he'd have to get up to turn off the radio while seeing Jim passed out next to it. It's clear that while living with Jim, Martin saw that Jim was a special person. He thoughtfully recalled that: "For his age, I'd say he was probably the most . . . intellectually deep person and well-read I've ever met."[41]

Give us an hour for magic.[42]

5
This is the Land Where the Pharaoh Died

Alexandria is the hymn of age and the beloved of history.
I don't know if I'm the one living in it or if it's living deep
inside my soul.

—ALEXANDER THE GREAT

The body of knowledge contained in *The History of Magic & the Occult* is referred to in Lachman's *The Secret Teachers of the Western World* as "the rejected knowledge"—rejected because it's knowledge that's not "material, tangible and measurable"—and comprises the basis of the Western esoteric tradition.

> The Western esoteric tradition has its source in several mystical and occult teachings of the past: Hermeticism, Gnosticism, Kabbalah, and the Neoplatonism that arose in Alexandria (Egypt) in the early centuries of our era.[1]

> The rejected knowledge posits there is another kind of knowledge that lies beyond what is quantifiable . . . it is not one of physical facts, nor can it be quantified and measured. It is a knowledge of our inner world, not the outer one, a knowledge of what we used to call the spirit or the soul, that invisible, intangible something that animates us and leads us to ask questions about who we are and what our place in this mysterious world can be.[2]

For different people in different ways there is a nagging, insistent sense that something is missing . . . There is the feeling that somewhere, in the background, there is that something that would help us make sense of it all, but that we can't quite put our finger on it. The knowledge offered by the esoteric tradition may be rejected, but the feeling that without it we are somehow incomplete is something that simply won't go away. Whether we like it or not, we seem to be stuck with it.[3]

Jim and his generation would seek the completion the rejected knowledge offers. Lachman writes:

Good or bad, it seemed the collective imagination was hungry for something new, alien and *other* . . . After the dark days of Hitler, World War II, and the shadow of the mushroom cloud, the mid-twentieth century mind seemed to be reaching out for the otherworldly and unearthly. This, of course, could have been nothing more than escapism, a desire to obscure a dreary and dangerous reality with dreams and fantasies, and no doubt many, perhaps most, of the UFO sightings were along these lines. But there seems to have been something in the postwar appetite for the unusual that suggests something more . . . World War II had put a damper on much esoteric work, and most of the secret teachers earlier years were dead. But the taste for *something else* remained.[4]

Wilson attributes another reason for the post-World War II generation's growing fascination with all that's "new, alien and *other*" to their boredom. It's worth mentioning that Wilson once stated he began writing his first book, *The Outsider*, out of his own boredom. Wilson further ponders the nature of boredom in *The Occult*:

Boredom is lack of the capacity for registering subtle variations. And the definition of a living organism is being capable of responding to energy vibrations. These vibrations constitute "meaning."[5]

It is a kind of discouragement, a *slacking of the will* due to a feeling that "it's just not worth it" . . . A little boredom causes total demoralization.[6]

*We're perched headlong
on the edge of boredom[7]*

*The aim of the happening is to cure boredom, wash the eyes,
make childlike reconnections with the stream of life. Its lowest,
wildest aim is for purgation of perception. The happening
attempts to engage all the senses, the total organism, and
achieve total response in the face of traditional arts which
focus on narrower inlets of sensation.[8]*

The cure for this boredom goes back to Wilson's point, that we all have an innate need for this Faustian "longing for the 'occult' . . . the instinctive desire to believe in the unseen forces, the wider significance, that can break the circuit."[9] Persecuted and repressed for the past four centuries, this great hunger to explore the rejected knowledge would emerge with volcanic force within the young people The Doors attracted. Twentieth-century journalist and occultist Nat Freedland noted in his 1972 book *The Occult Explosion*:

The occult explosion is largely a youth phenomenon, with the new breed of student-age psychic explorers superseding the former stereotype of occultism as a concern only to uneducated, lonely oldsters desperate for evidence of an afterlife. Tryout college courses on occult topics have been wildly successful, often attracting several hundred registrants.[10]

Jim said he saw the arc of his life as one in strange synchronicity with the birth of rock and roll and the youth rebellion sweeping across the West. To borrow Mack's words:

[Jim] was able to adapt his personal psychology to the historical realities that he came upon:
"Ya see," he [Jim] said, "the birth of rock and roll coincided with

my adolescence, my coming into awareness. It was a real turn-on, although at the time I could never allow myself to rationally fantasize about ever doing it myself. I guess all that time I was unconsciously accumulating inclination and nerve. My subconscious had prepared the whole thing. I didn't think about it. It was just thought about. I heard a whole concert situation, with a band and singing and an audience, a large audience. Those first five or six songs I wrote, I was just taking notes at a fantastic rock concert that was going on inside my head."[11]

In the 1960s, rock music fast became an exciting way for Western youth to smash through their boredom. The young girl in The Velvet Underground's song "Rock and Roll" complains "There's nothing happening at all" in her life until the day she dials into a New York City radio station and hears rock music for the first time. She goes mad over this new sound, and, well, "You know her life was saved by rock and roll."[12]

> **Rock and roll is the sound of angels telling me truth.**[13]

Strangely, Jim's late teenage home city is named Alexandria. The rejected knowledge contained in *The History of Magic & the Occult* that Jim checked out from his hometown's local library has its roots in the ancient Egyptian city of Alexandria, the Hellenistic cosmopolis credited with being the birthplace of the Western esoteric tradition.

In 331 BCE, Alexander the Great founded Egypt's first Mediterranean port city. The ancient Egyptians built their cities along the banks of the Nile River, so the construction of Alexandria was a novel undertaking. Alexandria would be a new city on an ancient land. No place in the ancient world was more suitable for the kind of city Alexander envisioned than Egypt. The ancient Greek historian Herodotus saw the Egyptians as "scrupulous beyond all measure in the matter of religion . . . and their knowledge of the mysteries of life, death and the beyond had been renowned through the centuries."[14]

Figure 5.1 Artist's vision of Ancient Alexandria's library.

Alexander the Great's vision for Alexandria included building what would become one of world history's greatest and most far-reaching influential achievements, a library where the brightest philosophical, artistic, literary, and spiritual persons from all corners of the ancient world could meet and exchange their ideas. Jim the secret teacher would've felt very much right at home in such a place, a scene that perhaps Jim had once made as part of one of his past, strange lives.

The Nile River was a critical part of ancient Egyptian spiritual life, considered to be a causeway from life to death and the afterlife. The East was thought of as a place of birth and growth, and the West was considered the place of death, as the god Ra, the sun, underwent birth, death, and resurrection each day as he crossed the sky. All the tombs and pyramids are found west of the Nile River as the ancient Egyptians believed that to enter the afterlife, they had to be buried on the side that symbolized death. In *The History of Magic & the Occult*, Seligmann writes:

In the west, the Egyptians believed, lies the world of the dead, where the sun-god disappears every evening; they spoke of the departed as "westerners." The belief in a world of the dead often mingled with the notion of an underworld. It is through this subterranean world that the ship of the sun sails during the night: the dead await it impatiently and rejoice when its divine radiance appears. Then the dead souls, filled with delight, seize a rope from the ship and tow it through the depths. It was also believed that the dead, disguised as birds, soar into the sky where in his heavenly barge Ra, the sun-god, awaits them and transforms them into stars to travel with him through the vault of the heavens. Or again, a lentil field lies high in the northeast, where the grain grows taller than it does on the banks of the Nile, and where the dead live on in peace and abundance. However, this blessed land is waterlocked, and none but the just and righteous may persuade the obdurate ferryman to row them across.[15]

Bolen notes in *Gods in Everyman*: "Hades was associated with the distant West. Odysseus sailed west to Persephone's grove, a wild sunless coast at the edge of the world to find the entrance to Hades."[16]

Let's continue with Seligmann's magical vision of Ancient Egypt, as the mysteriousness of this ancient desert world—Lachman writes "indeed the word 'alchemy' is thought by some to stem from the Arabic *al-kemi*, 'out of Egypt'[17]—was one of "the fairest things" that Jim learned about in his vast reading, making a deep impression upon his great imagination:

In his book *Isis and Osiris* Plutarch says that the Sphinx symbolizes the secret of occult wisdom. Elsewhere he describes it as a magnificent creature having wings of ever-changing hue. When turned towards the sun, they glitter like gold; when towards the clouds, they shine with the reflection of rainbow colors. But even Plutarch, that assiduous investigator, failed to penetrate the mystery. For countless ages, the Sphinx remained the guardian of Egyptian magic.

This colossus, half hewn, half sculpted, had defied millennia. Never in the history of mankind has a statue so lastingly caught the imagination of peoples. The thoughts of countless generations dwell in it:

numberless conjurations and rites have built up in it a mighty protective spirit, a soul that still inhabits this time-scarred giant.

In the Nile lands, images had from ancient times been treated as living, active beings. Since the beginning Egypt had been the home of magical statues whose occult powers could affect the physical world. Thus the awesome figures of the guardian Sphinxes before the temples did more than frighten away the profane. They could reward and punish, as could the king himself whose image they originally represented. The Sphinxes opened their stone mouths and revealed the will of the gods. The fathers of the Christian church distinctly vouch for the phenomenon that statues could speak. The king and the assembled people were often present at the oracle, and scribes wrote down their words on the papyri. In the Siwa oasis stood the image of Ammon, to which Alexander the Great once made a pilgrimage. Ammon promised something dazzling to the Macedonian: mastery over the earth.[18]

Ancient Alexandria's open-minded spirit welcomed many different worldviews. Lachman writes in *The Secret Teachers of the Western World* that:

Alexandria was home to a dizzying assortment of faiths, beliefs, philosophies, and religions. It was, as the novelist Lawrence Durrell, author of *The Alexandria Quartet*, called it, "a city of sects and gospels." Greeks, Romans, Egyptians, Jews, Babylonians, Persians, Phoenicians, Indians, and other peoples filled its maze of streets and squares and temples. Platonists, Pythagoreans, Zoroastrians, Buddhists, Christians, Stoics, and many other followers of man other beliefs met, argued, and learned from each other. As in our time, the Alexandrian Age provided a spiritual marketplace, a bevy of competing teachings, some fraudulent, others profound, meeting a variety of intellectual, emotional, and religious needs.[19]

The great minds of Ancient Greece made it a point to visit Egypt, the homeland of all things esoteric with its mystery schools, as Seligmann points out, "Plutarch assures us that, in their desire to converse with its priests, many Greek thinkers—Solon, Thales, Pythagoras, Eudoxus, even Lycurgus himself—undertook the arduous journey to Egypt,"[20] So it's no wonder Ancient Alexandria became a major influencer of secret teachers and Western esoteric tradition. Among Ancient Alexandria's secret teachers were the Hermetists, whom Lachman notes were:

> perhaps the most secret teachers of them all. We do know whom they worshipped and what they believed, as far as we can tell from their writings. They were disciples of Hermes Trismegistus, the "thrice great one," master of magic, philosophy, and all learning.[21]

We're going to return for a moment to Seligmann's *The History of Magic & the Occult* to learn a bit more about this mysterious figure, Hermes Trismegistus:

Everything relating to alchemy, however, leads us back constantly to Egypt. Zosimus dedicated his book on alchemy to Imhotep, the wise poet and councillor, who lived not much later than 3000 B.C. In Imhotep's beautiful verses we recognize that at an early date the Egyptians already knew the mundane pleasures which the sons of god had taught to the daughters of men:

> Follow thy desire while thou livest,
> Lay myrrh upon thy head,
> Clothe thee in fine linen
> Imbued with luxurious perfumes,
> The genuine things of the gods . . .

Stephanus, who wrote in the seventh century of our era, says that sulphur and lead are synonymous with Osiris. This god, Isis, and the evil Typhon are mentioned often in alchemical writings, and most of them name Hermes Trismegistus as the master of alchemical philosophy. Hermes is the Greek god who conducts the souls to the dark kingdom of Hades, the underworld. "He opens the doors of birth and death." He controls exchange, commerce and learning: he is the gods' messenger, the mediator, the reconciler.

Trismegistus means "three times the greatest," an epithet that reveals in what high esteem he was held. He is not a Greek god but a divinity of the Greek colonists in Egypt. These Greco-Egyptians admired the ancient religious doctrines of the Nile land, which did not appear to have changed since the remote times of the pharaohs, but which in reality had decayed, so that when the Greeks began to study them, not even their symbols were understood by the Egyptian priests.

To continue where we left off with Lachman:

[These] most secret teachers of them all believed that mankind had a divine mission: to journey back through the planets to their invisible divine source and awaken their consciousness to an awareness and grasp of the cosmos. The means of doing this was through *gnosis*—"instant knowledge of spiritual mysteries"—which we can see as a form of "cosmic consciousness."

> *Reaching your head with the cold,*
> *sudden fury of a divine messenger*[22]

Early twentieth-century Canadian psychiatrist and author R. M. Bucke, in his seminal 1901 book *Cosmic Consciousness: A Study in the Evolution of the Human Mind*, defines cosmic consciousness as an evolved mind capable of showing:

. . . the cosmos to consist not of dead matter governed by unconscious, rigid, unintending law; it shows it on the contrary as entirely immaterial, entirely spiritual and entirely alive; it shows that death is an absurdity, that everyone and everything has eternal life; it shows that the universe is God and that God is the universe, and that no evil ever did or ever will enter into it.[23]

Wilson writes that:

Religion, mysticism and magic all spring from the same basic "feeling" about the universe: a sudden feeling of meaning, which human beings sometimes "pick up" accidentally, as your radio might pick up some unknown station. Poets feel that we are cut off from meaning by a thick, lead wall, and that sometimes for no reason we can understand the wall seems to vanish and we are suddenly overwhelmed with a sense of the infinite *interestingness* of things.[24]

Ancient Alexandria's syncretic spirit would reach the Los Angeles, California, of our time, a city located at the farthest edge of the Western world. In Professor John Arthur Maynard's 1990 book *Venice West: The Beat Generation in Southern California,* he writes:

Los Angeles itself had a long tradition of congeniality to the odd and unconventional. Vedanta, Theosophy, Rosicrucianism, spiritualism, New Thought, and the Self-Realization Fellowship had all found homes there, right along with Krishna murti, Paramhansa, Yogananda, Ernest Holmes, and Aimee Semple MacPherson. Nudism, bodybuilding, ethical vegetarianism, Theocracy, and homeopathy all coexisted more or less amiably with circus-tent revivalism, militant atheism, the Nation of Islam, and the Church of Wicca. The city's older, pre-Forest Lawn-era cemeteries were studded with crypts bearing the sun disk, wings, and cobras of Ancient Egypt.[25]

I love the friends I have
gathered together
On this thin raft
we have constructed pyramids
in honor of our escaping
This is the land where
The pharaoh died[26]

II

Thoughts in Time &
Out of Season

6

There's Danger on the Edge of Town

Thanks for the latest and greatest betrayal
Of the last and greatest of human dreams
—WILLIAM S. BURROUGHS

Some of the Western esoteric tradition's greatest secret teachers, as mentioned in the introduction, were intensely persecuted. In 1969 and 1970, Jim would also encounter serious persecution in Miami, Florida.

A secret teacher's safety often depends on the attitudes the authorities of the day have toward the rejected knowledge and its adherents. To put this into perspective, we must go back to ancient times. In *The Occult*, Wilson mentions poet Robert Graves's observation that:

> The most important single fact in the early history of Western religion and sociology was undoubtedly the gradual suppression of the Lunar Mother-goddess's inspiratory cult, and its suppression . . . by the busy, rational solar cult of the Solar God Apollo, who rejected the Orphic tree-alphabet in favor of the commercial Phoenician alphabet—the familiar ABC—and initiated European literature and science. The moon goddess was the goddess of magic, of the subconscious, of poetic inspiration. Human mythology has been "solarized" and then, in the West, Christianized, and the masculine god of reason has usurped an increasingly important place, armed with the irresistible that you can see a thing more clearly by sun-

light than by moonlight. But this is untrue. On the contrary, certain things become invisible in a strong light. Highly conscious, rational modes of thought are like a wide net through which all the smaller fish escape.[1]

Such is the challenging wisdom the secret teacher poses to the powers that champion the rational mind.

In the time of Renaissance Europe, if a person such as Queen Elizabeth I in England were in power, then a secret teacher was in luck. This was the case with one of Western esoteric tradition's greatest secret teachers, sixteenth-century mathematician, scientist, and astrologer John Dee. Dee was famous for coining the phrase "the British Empire," and enjoyed favor and protection under Queen Elizabeth I. Wilson writes in *The Occult*:

Like all true poets and magicians, he was driven by a vision of reality quite different from the commonplace world in which we live out our lives . . . Dee studied magic because he was a poet, for whom it seemed to offer a key to another form of existence; there was nothing of the charlatan about this.[2]

Figure 6.1 John Dee.
Courtesy of Wellcome Images.

But Dee would experience a dangerous and challenging time under Queen Mary's rule, Elizabeth's sister:

Dee was arrested and accused of attempting to kill Queen Mary with sorcery. He was imprisoned in Hampton Court in 1553. The reason behind his imprisonment may have been a horoscope that he cast for Elizabeth, Mary's sister and heiress to the throne. The horoscope was to ascertain when Mary would die. He was finally released in 1555 after being set free and re-arrested on charges of heresy.[3]

Lachman writes that perhaps the most tragic instance of a secret teacher's persecution happened in 415 CE when Ancient Alexandria witnessed the gruesome murder of its last Neoplatonic philosopher, Hypatia, a brilliant mathematician, dialectician, and astronomer. This terrible act was in many ways the lowest point of the Western esoteric tradition and certainly one of its most dangerous time periods. Hypatia drew the suspicion of Cyril, the city's leading Christian patriarch who hated Hypatia, creating the situation that allowed a local mob to attack Hypatia on her way home:

The *parabalani*, "the reckless ones," considered Christian fanatics, who were feared for their exuberant faith and penchant for violence . . . attacked Hypatia on her way home from the academy. Pulling her from her chariot, they dragged her into the Caesarean Church where they stripped her, beat her to death, and then scraped the flesh from her bones with oyster shells (some say roof tiles). They then took her remains to a place called Cindron and burned them. Thus Hypatia became "the greatest of the pagan martyrs" as well as one of our secret teachers.

For the Neoplatonists who remained in Alexandria, it was a sign that they should leave the city, which was no longer a safe haven for philosophy. And so began what we might call an "esoteric exodus." Increasingly, the stream of ideas and teachings emanating from Greek thought—and rooted, perhaps, in the Egyptian Mysteries— would have to act secretly, would, that is, have to go "underground," a survival tactic not uncommon in the history of the Western

Figure 6.2 Hypatia of Alexandria.

esoteric tradition . . . Like a subterranean undercurrent, esoteric ideas moved below the surface, occasionally bubbling up to ground level, but more times than not remaining like a hidden spring at which a few daring souls took refreshment.[4]

By the early seventeenth century, knowledge and practice of all things both occult and esoteric made being a secret teacher criminal. In England, scientist Sir Isaac Newton kept his alchemical experiments a secret with good reason. In Italy, Giordano Bruno, a kind of proto-Jim (as he was a rambunctious person who created problems for himself much as Jim did, and also slept around a lot) held a secret teacher's firm persuasion regarding the invisible, inner reality and was, as mentioned earlier, burned at the stake after being found of guilty of "blasphemy, heresy, magic, and preaching the belief in many worlds."[5]

*A man searching
for lost Paradise
can seem a fool
to those who never
sought the other world*[6]

Figure 6.3. Giordano Bruno.

Twenty-three years after Bruno's execution, hostility towards the rejected knowledge became the norm. Lachman notes in *The Secret Teachers of the Western World* French polymath Marin Mersenne's *Quaestiones celeberrimae in Genesim* was a total rejection of cosmic consciousness:

> Marin Mersenne's attack on the esoteric tradition as a whole . . . took place in 1623. Any vision of the world that saw it as a living intelligent whole, infused with spirit, interconnected by subtle correspondences and invisible forces with which the mind of man could participate, and linked to a higher non-manifest reality, was henceforth seen as not only incorrect, or heretical, but increasingly as pathological, as, indeed, insane. At best it was the product of an ignorant, superstitious sensibility, a debilitating atavism that should be swiftly eradicated.[7]

Not until the late nineteenth century would attitudes towards "the rejected knowledge" and their secret teachers begin to change. Still, secret teachers such as the late nineteenth/early twentieth-century magician and occultist Aleister Crowley continued to endure persecution, as Crowley was called out in his time by one British tabloid as being "the wickedest man in the world."[8]

The 1960s Establishment was out to stop The Doors from waking up America's youth to cosmic consciousness. Jim's secret teacher's mission was to smash the concealment of this reality during a time when it could be done before millions of people. By 1968, The FBI had created a whopping 80-page file on Jim, and the Christian right made it plain to America that Jim was a satanic threat. During a Doors tour stop, Jim spoke to Evangelical & Reformed Church minister Pastor Fred L. Stagmeyer (Jim was impressed with Stagmeyer's reference to himself as a "minister at large"):

JIM: [The Doors] try to provoke a religious experience . . . in the sense of a lot of people communicating.

PASTOR STAGMEYER: (*warning Jim*). This strikes me as a tremendous mystique about what you're involved in here. Most of the quote-unquote "Establishment . . ." they're really concerned about what the hell you're pulling off, it's suspect . . .

JIM: This kind of thing has been going on for a long time now, you know. It's kind of like secular religion.

PASTOR STAGMEYER: (*nervously*) Just don't report me to my bishop![9]

Figure 6.4. "It's fifty percent physical, the records are like only half of it."
Jim Morrison talking with Minister-at-Large Pastor Fred L. Stagmeyer.

Pastor Stagmeyer's warning to Jim was, considering the deep animosity held towards secret teachers like Jim over the past four hundred years, an understatement. Jim's fame rendered him a not-so-secret secret teacher and painted a target on his back that the Establishment and the Christian right would take aim at.

In *The History of Magic & the Occult*, Seligmann takes us to the root of why the Christian right viewed Jim as satanic and reveals why the reality of cosmic consciousness has been, as Jim wrote, kept from us for so long:

> Zosimus of Panopolis, a writer of that epoch, appointed himself the apologist of the alchemical art. His allegories and comments are cited by medieval experts as the most profound and venerable documents of the arcana. Zosimus declared that the knowledge of metals, precious stones and scents dated back to the epoch mentioned furtively in the Genesis: "The sons of God saw daughters of men, that they were fair." The mysterious sons of God were believed to be fallen angels who had mated with the women of antediluvian times. In gratitude, the angels taught these women various arts, obviously with the intention that their companions make jewels, colourful garments and perfumes with which to adorn their beauty. Thus the wise men of ancient times decided that the fallen angels must have been evil, perverters of morals and manners. Tertullian confirms these early beliefs, saying that the sons of God bequeathed their wisdom to the mortals with the evil intention of seducing them to "mundane pleasures."[10]

> Together with *magi* and other illicit arts, alchemy was revealed to mankind by the cursed angels, betrayers of God's secrets. They had been punished for this indiscretion; a curse lay upon the forbidden knowledge which enabled man to rival his creator. Investigation of the hidden works of nature was sacrilegious. St. Augustine shares this conception when he censures "the vain and curious desire of investigation, known as knowledge and science." The rivalry between knowledge and faith had likewise been perceived by Roman writers. In his book *On the Nature of Things*, Lucretius (*ca.* 98–53 B.C.)

exclaims triumphantly: "Thus is religion trod down, by a just reverse; victory makes us akin to the gods."

Throughout the first centuries of our era, the tree of knowledge of the Genesis remained the symbol of such sinful investigation. With the eating of the forbidden fruit, man had become like God, knowing good and evil. No doubt the alchemist accepted such views, yet they proceeded with their investigations just the same. Isis's boast of how she acquired knowledge sounds like a challenge to the passage of Genesis. Gnostic teachings created this entirely new attitude, for many Gnostic sects were indifferent to the problem of good and evil upon earth. The Ophites in like manner worshipped the serpent of the Bible as a beneficent being, since it had rightly directed man to knowledge, the weapon used by him against his creator Iadalbaoth. The tree of knowledge and the serpent were thus to become the most cherished emblems of alchemy.[11]

After the infamous Doors concert in Miami, Florida in March 1969, where it was alleged Jim exposed himself, Jim was put on trial from August to October 1970 and convicted on false charges of indecent exposure and profanity and sentenced to six months of hard labor. Looking cool, calm, and collected, Jim stated during an interview that he found the court proceedings "very interesting."

But the forces arrayed against Jim outside the courtroom were very serious. To apply Seligmann's words, the Christian right saw Jim as being influenced by "cursed angels, betrayers of God's secrets," and that Jim must be "punished for this indiscretion" since the Christian right felt a "curse lay upon the forbidden knowledge which enabled man to rival his creator." Prosecuting Jim was about much, much more than his provocative behavior during the Miami show. Jim's popularity by 1970 was approaching messiah status, an antinomian presence in American youth culture the Christian right wanted to completely destroy. It's not far-fetched at all to believe the Christian right wanted Jim dead. If given the chance to execute him they probably would have. If Jim was the reincarnation of Alexander the Great coming back as an inward-looking secret teacher rock star warrior-poet, then the Christian right was a combination of the *parabalani* of Ancient Alexandria and the Catholic Inquisition in Rome ready to put Jim to death as they did to Hypatia and Giordano Bruno. Robby Krieger remembers in *Set the Night on Fire* that:

> Anita Bryant (who would later become one of the nation's biggest anti-gay crusaders) and Jackie Gleason (who was even a worse drunk than Jim) headlined a Catholic-backed and Nixon-endorsed Rally for Decency in Miami to publicly decry the lewd acts on TV pretending to be outraged by The Doors. It was all so fake. Even if Jim had exposed himself, none of them were at the show to see it. They were just using us to push a fundamentalist agenda, and they didn't care who they hurt in the process.[12]

> *Cold, grinding grizzly bear jaws*
> *Hot on your heels*[13]

Jim's alleged exposure of himself gave the Establishment and the Christian right the opportunity they needed to try to imprison Jim. The desire to do this extended to the highest echelons of American law enforcement. On March 4th, 1969, four days after the Miami show, a report from the FBI's Miami field office was sent to the then director of the FBI—the cruel, humorless, and self-hating J. Edgar Hoover, once blackmailed by the mob. When Hoover realized this power of coercion, he started using blackmail himself. The report to Hoover contained the FBI agents' account of The Doors show that night:

> He pulled out all stops in an effort to provoke chaos among a huge crowd of young people. Morrison's program lasted one hour, during which time he sang one song and for the remainder he grunted, groaned, gyrated and gestured along with inflammatory remarks. He screamed obscenities and exposed himself.[14]

Interestingly, also on March 4th, warrants were issued for Jim's arrest.

After a string of cancellations following the Miami concert, The Doors recovered to perform many more tour dates. But Jim knew he was faced with a difficult situation that had repeated itself throughout history. If Jim lost on appeal, once inside, anything could happen to him. Robby Krieger also remembers in *Set the Night on Fire* that:

> Between court dates, Jim put on a brave face and talked about how he was striking a blow for First Amendment rights. But underneath he was afraid. He was facing several years behind bars, and even if he ended up with a shorter sentence, they'd be sending him to Raiford Prison—the facility that would later house Ted Bundy. Jim had grown up in Florida; he knew Raiford's reputation. No matter how solid his case was, he knew things could still go very wrong for him.[15]

In a partial transcript from the trial, Jim told the prosecutor the custom-made leather pants he wore that night didn't have any pockets.

> Since the pants don't have pockets, sometimes I put my hand in, you know, with the thumb hanging out in lieu of pockets. It was kind of unusual, really [that he wore boxer shorts that evening], because I don't usually wear undergarments. I got out of the habit four years ago.[16]

Doors drummer John Densmore told *The Hollywood Reporter*: "He didn't do it! I was there; if Jim had revealed the golden shaft, I would have known. There were hundreds of photographs taken and tons of cops and no evidence."[17]

Journalist Ann Woolner of the *Albany Times-Union* wrote: "Morrison's case bore all the signs of a political prosecution, a rebuke from the cultural right to punish a symbol of Dionysian rebellion."[18]

According to Bolen in *Gods in Everyman*, this was to be expected:

> The motif of severe persecution and flight is part of the mythology of Dionysus and his women followers. For example, due to the hostility of King Lycurgus, Dionysus was beaten and forced to leap into the sea, while the women who worshipped him were beaten unmercifully in their horror-stricken flight.

By "old boy" standards, the Dionysus man is likely to be either too feminine, too mystic, too counterculture, too threatening, or too attractive and too fascinating, for them to be comfortable with him.[19]

The reaction of others to him is often equally inconsistent. People react negatively and positively to him, hardly ever just neutrally . . . Moreover, a moralistic and puritanical society directs stronger negative messages at Dionysus than perhaps any other archetype.[20]

HOWARD SMITH: But why The Doors?

JIM: I told you, we're the band you love to hate.[21]

7

Lessons of the Ancient War

The ruins of time build mansions in eternity.
—WILLIAM BLAKE

The clearest spiritual connection between Jim and the city name of his late teenage stomping grounds is to history's greatest military leader, ancient Greece's Alexander the Great, whom Jim became enamored with while in high school. It's strange just how much Jim looked like Alexander during his time with The Doors. The combination of Jim's physical appearance, his secret teacher's nature and sharp mind, his rich inner world and imagination, his talents, mysteriousness, and erotism, all helped to make Jim a truly remarkable individual in a time that was welcoming in all things "new, alien, and *other*."

Jim adopted some of Alexander's look from the famous statue made by the sculptor Lyssipos, "the inclination of his head a little on one side towards his left shoulder."[1] For Jim, Alexander was the ideal embodiment of leadership, erudition, action, daring, adventure, and excess. Alexander was tutored as a boy by none other than the great ancient Greek philosopher Aristotle and was also the son of one of Ancient Greece's most capable military leaders, the principled Philip II. Alexander became a greater military genius than his father, achieving more power than any man before or since. Alexander accomplished most of his great military campaigns when only in his twenties. In a strange parallel to Alexander's life, Jim would also accomplish artistic greatness in his twenties with The Doors.

The ancient Greek historian Plutarch wrote in his *Lives of the Noble Greeks & Romans*—also called *Parallel Lives* or *Plutarch's Lives*—that Alexander desired not pleasure or wealth but only excellence and glory. Though toward the end of his life, Alexander was corrupted by his impulsiveness and decadent living. Alexander won every military battle he ever fought in from 338 BCE to 325 BCE, first as a prince alongside his father at the Battle of Chaeronea in 338 BCE and then as the fearless leader of the Greeks through the Balkan, Persian, and Indian campaigns. At first, Plutarch characterized Alexander as possessing great self-control and a distaste for luxury. However, his account of Alexander's life becomes more disapproving, such as with the murder of Cleitus the Black at a banquet Alexander held to celebrate a feast day for Dionysus.[2] Alexander and most present at this banquet were drunk, and Alexander later regretted killing the man who saved his life at the Battle of the Granicus in 334 BCE. In comparison to Alexander's alcoholism, Jim's excessive drinking sometimes brought out "Jimbo," a name Doors keyboardist Ray Manzarek gave to Jim's explosiveness when he drank.

Jim's parents hoped their son would carry on the Morrison family tradition of military service. So, they gave Jim the middle name

Figure 7.1. Hellenistic Marble Head of Alexander the Great circa 323 BCE to 31 BCE.

"Douglas" after the popular World War II military commander of the Pacific Theater, General Douglas MacArthur, a distinguished name in American history to carry within one's own. Jim's father also led an impressive military career. All one needs to do is watch the *Top Gun* films to get a sense of the high-achieving naval aviator life of the late Rear Admiral Morrison. A graduate of the U.S. Naval Academy in 1938, George Morrison witnessed the attack on Pearl Harbor, flew Grumman F6F Hellcat carrier-based fighters in Pacific Theater missions (a fighter that was designed to counter the Japanese Mitsubishi A6M Zero), was an instructor in nuclear weapons programs after the end of the war, and was awarded the Bronze Star with "V" for valor for his service at the joint operation center in Seoul during the Korean War.[3] In 1963, Jim's father took command of the Essex-class aircraft carrier USS *Bonhomme Richard* and commanded the U.S. naval forces where the Gulf of Tonkin incident took place in August 1964 which began the Vietnam War. In 1967, the year The Doors released their debut album, Jim's father was promoted to the rank of Rear Admiral, becoming the youngest admiral in the United States Navy.[4]

"The Commander" was a title Jim often used when speaking about his father to his childhood friends.[5] The Commander was often away from home with his naval duties while Jim was growing up. Jim's childhood was as lonely as Hamlet's. Bloom observes:

> The spirit does not speak of any love *for* his son, who would appear to have been a rather neglected child. . . . The graveyard scene (V.i) allows us to infer that the prince found father and mother in Yorick, the royal jester: "He hath bore me on his back a thousand times, and now—how abhorred in my imagination it is—my gorge rises at it. Here hung those lips that I have kissed I know not how oft.[6]

Bolen's description of a "Sky Father" in *Gods in Everyman* is a window into the kind of relationship Jim may have had with The Commander. A "Sky Father" is:

> a patriarchal god or authoritarian male who lives in the heavens, on mountaintops, or in the sky; thus they rule from above and from a

distance. They expect to be obeyed, and have the right to do what they please as long as they are chief gods.[7]

Often a son has a distant Sky Father who is not abusive, merely emotionally absent and physically not around much . . . As long as a son hopes his father will truly notice him and claim him as his own, the predominant feelings seem to be yearning and sadness. Anger towards the father comes later, after the son gives up his hopes and expectations of being fathered by his father . . . The relationship between emotionally distant Sky Fathers and their adolescent and grown sons often takes on a perfunctory, often ritualized quality. When father and son get together, they have a predictable conversation, a series of questions and answers in which neither gives away anything truly personal, perhaps beginning with "how's it going?" Seen psychologically, such a relationship between a Sky Father and his son takes the form of an apparently comfortable estrangement. Disappointment may lie just below the surface, however.[8]

Bolen further observes that:

Successful men are often absent fathers, emotionally and often physically missing from their children's lives. They sacrifice the possibility of closeness to their children to their jobs, their roles. And they also sacrifice their own "inner child," the playful, spontaneous, trusting, emotionally expressive part of themselves."[9]

As men are forced into a patriarchal setting to sacrifice their own inner child, there in turn "comes the need for the son to live up to his father's expectations—rather than coming into the world with particular gifts and talents, emotional needs, handicaps and personality traits, and possibly even a personal purpose of his own to fulfill."

Jim once said "When others demand that we become the people they want us to be, they force us to destroy the person we really are. It's a subtle kind of murder . . . the most loving parents and relatives commit this murder with smiles on their faces."[10]

Father?
Yes, son?
I want to kill you[11]

The Commander recalled Jim had no interest in the military while growing up, stating in an interview, "He went his own way." In a fitting tribute to a son whose creative work he did not understand, The Commander consulted his Greek teacher and had "True To His Own Spirit" etched in Greek onto Jim's gravestone.[12]

Jim's ambitions had always been intellectual, artistic, and spiritual, something Alexander the Great might've wished he'd followed within himself. In *The Secret Teachers of the Western World*, Lachman tells of the "apocryphal" legend of Alexander, that at age thirty-three he began to cry because he had no place left to conquer as he had become master of:

> all that there was to rule. [This is a] distortion of Plutarch's remark that, at being told there were infinite worlds, Alexander wept because he had not yet conquered this one. . . . The moral seems to be that had Alexander paid more attention to Aristotle, the lure of battle and command might not have gained such mastery over him, and he might have dedicated his life to something more durable than the temporal success of the conquest.[13]

Jim chose to dedicate his life to "something more durable," and once declared:

> *Nothing can survive a holocaust, but poetry and songs.*
> *No one can remember an entire novel. No one can describe*
> *a film, a piece of sculpture, or a painting. But so long as there*
> *are human beings, songs and poetry can continue.*[14]

Christina and Stanislav Grof in *The Stormy Search for the Self* write:

> Humanity has stored the treasures of the emotions, visions, and insights involved in the process of awakenings in paintings, poetry, novels, and music, and in descriptions provided by mystics and

prophets. Some of the most beautiful and valued contributions to the world of art and architecture celebrate the mystical realms.[15]

> *Have you forgotten the lessons of the ancient war?*[16]

Jim told his younger sister Anne that when he recited his poetry during Doors concerts, the audience didn't want to listen. For Jim, this was a big disappointment. Jim's greatest desire was to be known and remembered as a poet.

> *I'll always be a word man*
> *Better than a bird man*[17]

Jim wanted his poetry to endure, not his sex symbol image. Jim once exclaimed in frustration:

> Can you imagine doing that? Posing for a picture? Looking at a camera and posing? It's insane! I must have been out of my mind. If I had the whole thing over to do again, I wouldn't do it. I wouldn't . . . I thought I knew what I was doing. The horrible thing about a photograph is once it's done, you can't destroy it. It's there forever. Can you imagine I'm 80 years old and having to look at myself posing for these pictures? It's too late.[18]

But Jim was fortunate enough to become friends with the late San Francisco Beat Renaissance poet Michael McClure. While Jim was starting high school across the bay in Alameda, McClure was making a name for himself as a poet in the San Francisco Beat Renaissance. Later, Kerouac would base the character Pat McLear on McClure in his 1962 novel *Big Sur*. McClure also has the high distinction of reading his poems at what was perhaps world literary history's most influential poetry reading, held at the Six Gallery in San Francisco on October 7, 1955. Beat poet Allen Ginsberg read his poem "Howl" in public for the first time that night as Jack Kerouac egged him on from the back while drunk.

If Doors keyboardist Ray Manzarek was the first to believe in Jim's lyrical and performance talent, then it was McClure who recognized Jim's originality as a poet while in London staying with Pam and Jim.

> Well, I woke up first the next morning, pretty hung over, and started poking around the apartment looking for something to read, and I found Jim's poetry manuscript. I sat down and read it and thought, holy smoke, this is fantastic, and I was just sort of like ragingly delighted to find such a beautiful first book of poetry.[19]

McClure was instrumental in getting Jim's poetry published. On April 7th, 1970, Jim received the initial copies of his first book of poems, *The Lords & the New Creatures*. McClure recalled:

> Later, when the book had been published and the first copies arrived by mail in L.A., I found Jim in his room, crying. He was sitting there, holding the book, crying, and he said, "This is the first time I haven't been fucked." He said that a couple of times, and I guess he felt that that was the first time he'd come through as himself.[20]

If my poetry aims to achieve anything, it's to deliver people from the limited ways in which they see and feel.[21]

8
Right Back
Where I Came

Come from forever, and you will go everywhere.
—ARTHUR RIMBAUD

Perhaps the most memorable and passionate lines in Jim's poetry that express his desire for us to wake up to cosmic consciousness are to be found in his poem "An American Prayer:"

> *Let's reinvent all the gods*
> *All the myths of the ages*
> *Celebrate symbols from deep elder forests*[1]

Wilson writes in *The Occult* that twentieth-century Irish poet William Butler Yeats believed there to be:

A racial memory, which works in terms of symbols. This racial memory can be reached by "hushing the unquiet mind," by reaching a certain depth of inner stillness where it becomes accessible to the limited individual memory. [Yeats said] "I cannot now think symbols less than the greatest of all powers, whether they are used consciously by the masses of magic, or half-consciously by their successors, the poet, the musician and the artist."[2]

Twentieth-century German philosopher Jean Gebser's stages of consciousness from his 1949 book *The Ever-Present Origin* can help us to gain perspective on Jim's appeal to us to "Wake up!" Gebser detected a shift in consciousness after reading twentieth-century German poet Rainer Maria Rilke's poetry. Jim may have also picked up on this transition through his own extensive reading.

Gebser determined that humanity is moving out of an era he described as "the deficient mode of the mental-rational stage of consciousness." This mental-rational stage humanity has been living in now for some time is now "overripe"[3] and dying out into the "integral structure" of consciousness. This integral stage brings together the four previous stages/structures of consciousness: the *archaic*, the *magical*, the *mythical*, and the *mental-rational*.[4] We contain these four different types of consciousness within ourselves, hence the title of Gebser's book, *The Ever-Present Origin*. Though most interesting and pivotal, this work is also quite a complicated read. Below is a brief and concise breakdown of what these four past stages of consciousness contain as presented by American alchemical acupuncturist and author Jessie Shaw, in her lecture "Gebser's States of Consciousness: An Overview."

THE ARCHAIC

The word "archaic" comes from the Greek word *arkhé*, which means beginning or origin. It's the basis or root of all things. From a Chinese perspective, we can think of it as *the 10,000 things*. It's a place of active nothingness where rests the seeds of possibility. It's a womb-like place [or] nurturing void. In the archaic, human consciousness has not yet begun to surface. It is as yet undifferentiated from the cosmos. From a five-element standpoint, we might associate the archaic state with water.

THE MAGICAL

The word "magic" in magical consciousness goes back to the ancient Persian word *magus* or its plural *magi*. It was the word used to describe a tribe of priests from Medes whose history goes back to the 2nd century [BCE]. They were the religious leaders who also interpreted dreams and gave signs and omens. In the Bible, the three wise men who visited Jesus bearing gifts were from their sect. The word was later adopted by the Greeks and the Romans where it became associated with the magical arts. From a five-element standpoint, [the magical] is akin to the wood element.

Magic's earliest known reference goes back to 522 [BCE] during the time of Darius the Great of Persia. The word magi is found on the Behistun Inscription, a large rock relief on a cliff in Western Iran that was written by Darius the Great. The trilingual inscription was crucial to the decipherment of cuneiform script just as the Rosetta Stone enabled us to decipher Egyptian hieroglyphics. Magical consciousness is tribal with the consciousness of the entire tribe connected to the tribal chief. The tribe is wordlessly connected to his consciousness and intuitively moves and responds just as a school of fish effortlessly move together. In magical consciousness, there is no sense of time, only the present state of now exists. There is no sense of past or future. It's a highly physical state of being with the somatic intelligence of the body taking the lead. Sound and smell dominate and are the critical senses used to take in the surrounding world. Its geometric symbol is the dot, a kind of one dimensionality since human consciousness is just beginning to form in a dot of cohesion. This dot is also like the tip of a magic wand . . . which is considered to be an extension of the shaman herself as she holds it.

In magical consciousness, everyone is interrelated; there are no coincidences and there is no separation of spirit and matter. Rain dancing brings rain, divining reveals the truth, and drawing a slain bison on a cave wall means that it's already as good as dead even as the men gather their arrows to go hunt it. Clinically, we find the presence of the magical through the palpation of the tendons and muscles. We listen for it in the sounds beneath people's words and the words they leave unspoken.

Here's how you might experience me from a magical perspective: you happen to notice me as I'm sitting by a stream playing a ceremonial *icara* on a flute. Imagine you've never heard my voice or actually met me. Your impressions of me are formed solely through my physical being and the sounds emanating from the flute.

THE MYTHICAL

The word "mythical" in mythical consciousness originated in ancient Greece. The word *mythos* appeared quite early in the works of Homer written in the late 8th or 7th century [BCE]. It means speech, narrative or what was used to describe the plot of a play. Other words related to it are *mouth, Muse, myth* or *mysticism*. All are relevant to mythical consciousness. Elementally, mythical consciousness is fire, like when you sit around a fire and tell stories or share your dreams.

Mythical [consciousness] encompasses stories of beginnings like Mua, the mother goddess in Chinese mythology [. . . who repaired] the pillar of heaven to rescue the world from disruption, or [like] the pattern on the back of a tortoise [which] provided the blueprint for the I Ching hexagrams. In mythical consciousness the imagination is keenly alive, dreams are potent, and symbols are abundant. Similar to magical consciousness, everything has meaning, there are no accidents. It's a consciousness of soul awakening and poetic utterances, the language of the heart and soul. As mythical consciousness came into being, people began to have a felt sense of their own personal consciousness and emotions and were no longer acting solely as an extension of the tribal leader. They started to explore their own inner landscapes. In mythical consciousness, the concept of time comes into being with the recognition of the cycles of nature. There's still no conception of past and future, only the turning of the seasons, the rise and fall of the sun, and the planting, growth, and harvesting of the fields.

The symbol of mythical consciousness is the circle, which is in keeping with the cyclical aspects of time and the seasons. The *Tai Chi* symbol represents the undulating spectrum of *yin* and *yang* and their many gradient variations. Analytical, rational, and binary this-versus-that thinking has not yet come into being. Rather, all lies upon a spectrum. Clinically, we see mythical consciousness through the sounds and emotions of the five elements, the symbols and stories of the acupuncture points, and through our patient's dreams.

[Mythical consciousness can be symbolized by] the *ouroboros,* an ancient alchemical symbol of a snake eating its tail. The earliest known depiction of an *ouroboros* is found in a shrine enclosing the sarcophagus of Tutankhamun [that] dates from the fourteenth century [BCE]. . . . Cosmic ouroboros [is about] taking things that are ancient and old and giving them new life by talking about them and discussing what gifts they offer us.

THE MENTAL-RATIONAL

The word "mental" in mental consciousness [has Latin origins]— *mens,* or *mentalis*—it's the first word used in *The Iliad* and means "mind," "wrath," "courage" and "power." It heralds the formation of the ego, the separation of the individual from the multitude, and the separation of humankind from nature. It marks the beginning of directive or discursive thought. Elementally, it's metal. A crucial feature of its emergence is the shift in perspective [that shows up in art]. There's a move from two-dimensional orientation into three [dimensions]. . . . There's now awareness of space and the idea of people being separate from their surroundings. There is now foreground and background. The observer is separate from that being observed. There's a sense of detachment and objectivity. The patriarch takes power and codes of law are enacted. Right and wrong are clearly delineated. The world becomes more black and white and there's a focus on details [with] a tendency to obscure the bigger picture. In Greece, where mental consciousness first made its appearance in the 5th century [BCE], Herodotus, an Ancient Greek historian, wrote about being shocked by the differing roles of Egyptian and Athenian women. In Egypt, they were tradespeople, sat on tribunals, bought and sold real estate, inherited property, got loans, and witnessed legal documents. Not Athenian women. In his writings, Aristotle portrayed women as morally, intellectually, and physically inferior to men. He saw women as men's property and their role purely to serve them.

As regards time, the 7th century Pope Sabinian ordered the ringing of the bells to note the passing hours. [The] first public clock tower was erected in 1283 at the Palace of Westminster, Big Ben's precursor.

Clinically, mental consciousness presents itself to us as we listen to the words and content of people's signs and symptoms. We reason out the potential causes of their ailments from a *TCM* (Traditional Chinese Medicine) standpoint. And perhaps we notice how many do not have conscious awareness of their bodies but are locked up in their eyes. If I were to introduce myself to you from a mental consciousness standpoint, I'd hand you a copy of my resume. You would assess me by looking at my work experience, my academic degrees, and where I went to school.[5]

Now, with all of the above fresh in mind, we will take a closer look at some of the lyrics from "An American Prayer." If we place these stages of consciousness alongside Jim's appeal to us to discover "the ever-present origin" that's within us, we can see that Jim had an enthusiastic secret teacher's appeal to awaken us into the cosmic consciousness that's part of the integral consciousness:

Let's reinvent all the gods

(the "archaic" and the "magical")

All the myths of the ages

(the "mythical")

Celebrate symbols from deep elder forests

(the development of Symbolism in art during the deficient mode of the mental-rational stage of consciousness is meant to signify back to us the invisible realms through poetry.)

However, this shift humanity is going through, from the deficient mode into the integral stage of consciousness, is proving to be quite an unstable one. If we could measure this shift in consciousness on the Richter scale, it would be no exaggeration to say it would register as a 50.0 to a 150.0 quake in consciousness, and this is in all likelihood a conservative estimate. The world has been immersed now for many centuries in the mental-rational stage of consciousness in its deficient mode, the province of the left brain. The explosion of right-brain-based activity has provoked major culture wars across the West that have been steadily escalating ever since the social upheavals of the 1960s. Today, this shift in consciousness is becoming much more intense. This final hour of the deficient mode of the mental-rational stage we're in is indeed Dionysian, "The end of everything that stands," as Jim sings in "The End." Lachman writes:

> According to Gebser, who died in 1973, we are living through the last stages of the deficient mode of the mental-rational structure, and he believed that within a few decades, a "global catastrophe" was, if not imminent, certainly very likely.[6]

The world on fire[7]

Lachman concludes *The Secret Teachers of the Western World* with some sobering thoughts from Gebser which call to mind our current global state:

> For Gebser, the breakdown of one consciousness structure is necessary in order to clear ground for the emergence of a new one. Gebser argues that the unraveling of the western rational mindset that has been taking place throughout the last century and into our own is the prelude and necessary precondition for the appearance of what, as mentioned, Gebser called "the integral structure of consciousness." This is a structure that integrates and transcends the previous structures, a mutation as shattering as the ones that came before. The shift of one consciousness structure to another is no picnic; in a very real sense, whole worlds change in the process. Alfred North Whitehead once remarked that "the major advances in civilization are processes which all but wreck the societies in which they occur." Gebser would agree and would add that out of that wreckage something new and necessary can—must—emerge.[8]

The world since Jim's time has been heading faster and faster into this integral structure of consciousness, an unknown that with each passing day is revealing itself to humanity as a time that will be filled with more of the "new, alien, and *other.*"

The ordinary consciousness associated with the conservative influences in Western society is *not at all* interested in making this change into the integral stage. The kind of freedom and possibilities this new integral consciousness brings to humanity is a real threat to their power. Out of their ignorant fear of losing power, they continue to label persons like Jim as insane and satanic. However, more and more spiritual persons are waking up to the inevitability of this new integral consciousness becoming more the norm and less the fringe province of the outsider, an indication of the rise of Wilson's "new existentialism" that's fast revolutionizing the Western mind. The fear of being persecuted for cultivating an integral mindset—as Jim had done for himself—as a normal, vibrant, and fulfilling aspect of life, such as reviving the occult powers of Faculty X, gnosis, and ascending into cosmic consciousness, is being met head-on by more spiritually emergent persons with each passing day.

> *When you make your peace with authority,*
> *you become authority.*[9]

Twenty-three centuries after Alexander the Great laid down the plans for Ancient Alexandria, and before the mental-rational stage of consciousness would enter its deficient mode, Jim's spiritual awakening would begin to gain significant momentum with his writing poetry, journaling, and studying of books such as *The History of Magic & the Occult* while a high school student in Alexandria, Virginia at the dawning of the integral stage of consciousness. In a few short years, Jim would begin to communicate the cosmic consciousness of the Universal Mind on a scale that Ancient Alexandria's secret teachers and all of the Western esoteric tradition's secret teachers combined could only dare to dream.

Aristotle taught a young Alexander that "All human beings, by nature, desire to know."[10] This desire to experience the unknown, to engage the rejected knowledge through reading, writing, study, creativity, sex, drugs, meditation, magic, mysticism, music, art, travel, poetry, being in nature, yoga, prayer, and so on, comes through Jim's ancient statuesque presence. To be with Jim is, among many things, "to reach beyond the present," to as Jim writes, "All the myths of the ages,"—and to "give it welcome."

Through Jim, we feel the exciting return of Hermes Trismegistus (the thrice great one)—the *via positiva*—as existed during Ancient Alexandria, coming alive again during the Italian Renaissance, the decadent, Meister Eckhart-like musical light and color of the Symbolist palette—the *via negativa*—of fin-de-siècle Paris, and the gritty 1950s Beat San Francisco Renaissance, when the modern sunset West opened itself up to the calming spirit of the ancient Oriental mind. Jim was dynamite being thrown at the four centuries-long campaign of oppression waged against the desire to know this other reality. With Jim, the veil drops, and the flow of our inner mystical rivers and their springs that refresh our purpose and vitality come back to life.

In rock photographs that show Jim tilting his head "a little left on one side towards his shoulder," dripping with sweat from his shamanic paroxysms and poetic outbursts, through this embattled, Alexander the Great-like secret teacher rock star warrior-poet shaman looking and feeling "new, alien and *other*," we come into mysterious, life-transformative contact with that something else we long to know.

> *The only time I really open up is onstage.*
> *I feel spiritual up there.*[11]

III

Specialize in Having Fun

9
Testing the Bounds of Reality

I know that pain is the one nobility
Upon which Hell itself cannot encroach;
That if I am to weave my mystic crown
I must braid into it all time, all space

—CHARLES BAUDELAIRE

In 1962, the British rock band The Rolling Stones was formed. Jim once said he regarded lead vocalist Mick Jagger, born in the same year as Jim, as a "prince among men."[1] Also that same year, the world discovered another kind of prince in British film director David Lean's seven Academy Award-winning British historical epic drama *Lawrence of Arabia*, a film from which Jim might've taken great inspiration. With his strong desire to lead a life that's an "adventure of the spirit," *Lawrence of Arabia* showed Jim how he could achieve success in his secret teacher's mission to awaken the world to cosmic consciousness.

Jim turned nineteen years old when *Lawrence of Arabia* was released in December 1962, one year before Jim would give *The History of Magic & the Occult* to his friend Ed Martin. Set amidst the desolate grandeur of the early twentieth-century Arabian desert in the last half of World War I, with its handsome and elegant lead actor's sparkling blue eyes, the late Irishman from Connemara, Peter O'Toole, *Lawrence of Arabia* has influenced many to both dare the unknown and to become filmmakers. Over sixty years later, *Lawrence of Arabia* continues to dazzle audiences with its adventurous trek into the "new, alien and *other*," breaking the circuit of boredom like no other film since. Jim observed, "I think in art, but especially in films, people are trying to confirm their own existences."[2] This may have certainly been true for Jim with *Lawrence of Arabia*.

We're locked in an image, an act.[3]

One of Jim's close UCLA film school friends (they've asked not to be identified) remembers *Lawrence of Arabia* being shown during a film school course that both Jim and his friend were enrolled in. Even though Jim's friend can't recall for certain if Jim was present the day *Lawrence of Arabia* was shown, he believes "Jim for sure saw this film." As mentioned in Part I, Jim read Wilson's *The Outsider* in high school, in which Wilson discusses T.E. Lawrence's outsider traits and Lawrence's 1926 memoir *The Seven Pillars of Wisdom* about his time leading the Arab Revolt, a book Jim may have also read. And in light of *Lawrence of Arabia's* vast influence over so many important filmmakers from Jim's generation, such as Steven Spielberg, Martin Scorsese, and Francis Ford Coppola, it's more than worth considering that *Lawrence of Arabia* and the real-life T.E. Lawrence may have exerted much influence on Jim.

Wilson declared in *The Outsider* that, "Until an exhaustive, unprejudiced biography is published [on Lawrence], we have nothing but the bare facts of his life, and the evidence of his own writing to go on."[4] These are the "bare facts" of Lawrence's time leading the Arab Revolt, which occurred between 1916 and 1918, the period in which *Lawrence of Arabia* takes place, as retold by Wilson in *The Outsider*:

> At the outbreak of war, Lawrence was posted to Egypt as a Staff Captain in the Maps Branch of the Intelligence service. He found it boring, and when an opportunity came to take a part in the rebellion fomented by King Hussein of Mecca against the Turkish government of Arabia, Lawrence sailed for Arabia without bothering to tell his Intelligence chiefs what he intended to do. He quickly made himself indispensable in the revolt; as the advisor of Fiesal, King Hussein's son, he steered it to success in a period of less than two years. His book *The Seven Pillars of Wisdom* is a record of those two years.[5]

So it's hard to believe that Jim the adventurous freedom lover and aspiring filmmaker missed out on seeing this film about T.E. Lawrence and his quest "to make a new nation, to restore to the world a lost influence."[6] It's conceivable Jim would've been curious to see how David Lean and screenwriter Robert Bolt would bring to life on the big screen this historic chapter in Lawrence's saga. There's no doubt Jim would've been impressed with Lawrence's stubborn determination, his great love for the fierce, Bedouin tribesmen—"the pure and natural simplicity of the Arab unspoiled by Western influences"[7]—and Lawrence's fearless enthusiasm for a dangerous assignment that he insists "is going to be fun."[8]

Perhaps most of all, Jim would've been moved by the passionate appeal Lawrence makes to Prince Fiesal, that he must lead the Arab tribes to their former greatness of nine centuries past: "Yes, you were great. Time to be great again, my lord."[9] In spirit, this feels like the appeal Jim made to us with The Doors, to become great again as awakened persons during those ancient ages of imagination when cosmic consciousness was seen as both an integral and beneficial part of life.

Lawrence of Arabia would've struck Jim as the outsider's path to glory and stardom. If the real-life Lawrence was perhaps the twentieth century's first international rock star, then Peter O'Toole's Lawrence became *the* cinematic rock star of the 1960s. Here was Lawrence as a rebellious misfit in military uniform, an outsider both like the fun-loving, adventurous Jim and the curious, intellectual Jim. Happily, Lawrence flees modern civilization on horseback without any military training whatsoever to live among primitive peoples in a strange desert land. After proving himself, he ends up leading them to victory, becoming somebody else entirely. This is the perfect model for an outsider like Jim to follow in becoming a rock star. Lawrence would give welcome to this unknown, primitive world of the Bedouin tribesmen. Lawrence's dangerous assignment and the excitement his adventure generated gave him heaps of purpose and vitality and a sense of amor fati (the love of one's fate). The real-life Lawrence felt ever since his childhood that he was born to lead a people to freedom. Watching Lawrence dance on the rooftops of train cars in his white outfit and *keffiyeh* while getting his picture taken by an American journalist, winning battle after battle against the Turks, winning the hearts and minds of the wild Bedouin tribes he unites under his leadership may have been for Jim a flashing, prophetic glimpse into his future, showing Jim what was possible. This unforgettable cinematic experience might've given Jim pause to think about what he could later become.

In Dr. John Mack's 1976 book *A Prince of Our Disorder*—Wilson's dream of "an exhaustive, unprejudiced biography" of Lawrence come to life—we learn that the real-life Lawrence possessed "a sense of fun, a joy in life, which, though childlike—or perhaps because it was childlike—his companions found infectious."[10] Lawrence wrote in *The Seven Pillars of Wisdom* that one of the motivations for his involvement in the Arab conflict was "Intellectual curiosity:"

> I wanted to feel what it was like to be the mainspring of a national movement, and to have some millions of people expressing themselves through me: and being a half-poet, I don't value material things much. Sensation and mind seem to me much greater, and the ideal, such a thing as the impulse that took us into Damascus, the only thing worth doing.[11]

Let's just say I was testing the bounds of reality.
I was curious to see what would happen. That's all it was:
just curiosity.[12]

10
A Funny Sense of Fun

Do you think I'm just anybody, Ali? Do you?
—T. E. LAWRENCE IN *LAWRENCE OF ARABIA*

After Jim's high school graduation, The Commander and Mrs. Morrison decided to enroll Jim in St. Petersburg Community College in Florida where he would go to live with his grandparents. Jim the nonconformist then decided to skip his graduation ceremony, thereby angering The Commander, and gave his girlfriend Tandy Martin just one day's notice that he was leaving Alexandria, upsetting her as well.

According to his younger sister Anne, Jim wanted the complete works of Friedrich Nietzsche as a graduation present:

> He devoured Friedrich Nietzsche, the poetic German philosopher whose views on aesthetics, morality, and the Apollinian-Dionysian duality would appear again and again in Jim's conversation, poetry, songs, and life.[1]

Nietzsche continued to inspire Jim. Nietzsche's existential/ aesthetics-based philosophy is centered around summoning the will to overcome and celebrate life through poetry and music. In the autumn of 1865, one of the great turning points in Nietzsche's life occurred in a used bookshop in Leipzig, Germany, where Nietzsche discovered German philosopher Arthur Schopenhauer's 1818 book *The World as Will & Representation*. Schopenhauer felt "that all nature, including man, is the expression of an insatiable will to life; that the truest understanding of the world comes through art and the only lasting good through ascetic renunciation."[2] Nietzsche would spend the last several years of his life expanding upon Schopenhauer's words—minus the "ascetic renunciation" and pessimism—to create his philosophy of the *ubermensch,* the "overman." Nietzsche was able to realize his philosophical visions due to his worsening health issues that forced Nietzsche to give up his teaching position at the University of Basel with a small pension. At the time, Nietzsche was the youngest tenured professor in German academic history, having attained this position without his ever having earned a doctorate or even a teaching certificate.[3]

Nietzsche advocated for a positive view of one's life, what he called amor fati. This enthusiastic embracing of everything that can happen to a person, both the good and the bad, in which one would willingly live their life all over again just as it was, stems from Nietzsche's core idea of "the eternal recurrence of the same:"

> What, if some day or night a demon were to steal after you into your loneliest loneliness and say to you: "This life as you now live it and have lived it, you will have to live once more and innumerable times more" . . . Would you not throw yourself down and gnash your teeth and curse the demon who spoke thus? Or have you once experienced a tremendous moment when you would have answered him: "You are a god and never have I heard anything more divine."[4]

Holding fast to amor fati was how Nietzsche was able to cope with the losses, failures, and health challenges that bedeviled him throughout his life. Through working out what would become the twentieth century's most influential philosophy, Nietzsche wrote in his 1888 book *Twilight of the Idols* one of his most powerful statements: "If we possess our why of life we can put up with almost any how."[5] Nietzsche felt his personal "why" was to restore "purpose and vitality" to philosophy and to modern humankind by teaching amor fati. In section 276 of *The Joyous Science*, Nietzsche writes:

> I want to learn more and more to see as beautiful what is necessary in things; then I shall be one of those who makes things beautiful.

Figure 10.1. Friedrich Nietzsche, Basel. Photographer: Hartmann.

Amor fati: let that be my love henceforth! I do not want to wage war against what is ugly. I do not want to accuse; I do not even want to accuse those who accuse. Looking away shall be my only negation. And all in all and on the whole: some day I wish to be only a Yes-sayer.[6]

Nietzsche's profound declaration of radical self-acceptance in his 1878 book *Human, All Too Human: A Book for Free Spirits* may have been lifesaving, inspiring words for Jim—the secret teacher outsider—at the beginning of his adult life:

And so, onwards . . . along a path of wisdom, with a hearty tread, a hearty confidence . . . however you may be, be your own source of experience. Throw off your discontent about your nature. Forgive yourself your own self. You have it in your power to merge everything you have lived through—false starts, errors, delusions, passions, your loves and your hopes—into your goal, with nothing left over.[7]

After transferring to Florida State University, Jim continued to amaze and entertain his educators and classmates with virtuoso displays of intellectual power and his weird brand of deadpan, black humor. Jim continued his wide reading and journaling, his fast-maturing secret teacher's mind becoming sharper and more aware. Jim wound up living in "a book-littered trailer" behind a girl's boarding house after being kicked out by his roommates for consuming all their food and beer. Jim also got himself arrested, the first of a bunch of clinks to come, on September 28, 1963, when he was hauled in on multiple charges stemming from his actions while intoxicated. At a Saturday night football game, drunk from what was described as "a fair amount of wine," Jim proceeded to make fun of the football players and the people in the crowd at Doak Campbell Stadium. Before Jim was cuffed, he stole an umbrella and a police officer's helmet from a squad car, and was charged with petty larceny, disturbing the peace by being drunk, and resisting.[8]

Before transferring to FSU, Jim met the first adult love of his life, Mary Werbelow. While at a party, Jim told her he wanted to direct movies, confiding in Mary his plans "to realize his lifelong dream of enrolling in the school of cinematography at UCLA" so he could "learn to translate his ideas and fantasies into film."[9] Jim held an interesting view of filmmaking that had the avant-garde, experimental filmmaker's sense of artistic freedom:

> The good thing about film is that there aren't any experts. There's no authority on film. Any one person can assimilate and contain the whole history of film in himself, which you can't do in other arts. There are no experts, so, theoretically, any student knows almost as much as the professor.[10]

Jim's relationship with Mary would last three years. While attending FSU, Jim made numerous trips to be with Mary.

> I lived in Florida at a very formative period in my life. I always loved the landscape most of all. I used to hitchhike from Tallahassee to Clearwater almost every weekend. I had some friends who lived near there. I got to know the landscape pretty well. To me, it was a strange, exotic, exciting place.[11]

Lawrence felt the same way about Syria during his visits while in college, writing to his father that "This is a glorious country for wandering in."[12] Perhaps *Lawrence of Arabia's* spectacular desert landscapes, the same ones Alexander the Great had crossed and recrossed during his military campaigns in the Middle East, might've made Jim even more eager to become a filmmaker in Southern California's desert atmosphere.

Interesting similarities can be found between Jim and both the movie character and the real-life Lawrence. The description of Lawrence made by the character of American journalist Jackson Bentley at the beginning of *Lawrence of Arabia*—"He was a poet, a scholar, and a mighty warrior. He was also the most shameless exhibitionist since Barnum & Bailey"[13]—is strangely similar to Jim's view of himself:

> *A natural leader, a poet,*
> *a Shaman, w/the*
> *soul of a clown*[14]

Cross-correlation can also be made between Lawrence, Jim, and Hamlet, as Bloom felt Hamlet was "a dramatist, a poet, and an intellectual."[15] Just as strange, Jim and Lawrence were both avid readers (Lawrence's preferences were for medieval literature and history), shared masochistic tendencies, were daredevils who liked to risk walking on high ledges, and were classic outsiders who became icons of rebellion. Even more strange is that *Lawrence of Arabia's* plot seems to foretell Jim's arc with The Doors. Just as Lawrence meets Sherif Ali alone at a well and helped Lawrence to lead the Arab Revolt, Doors keyboardist Ray Manzarek met up with Jim alone on a beach and would help guide Jim into becoming the voice of his generation's spiritual rebellion. Strangest of all is Lawrence's military success in the field despite his having no combat training or experience whatsoever. Jim similarly achieved musical success with The Doors despite never having received any music lessons nor even engaging in musical activity.

Both Jim and Lawrence have since been etched into our collective imagination by the outfits they wore: the white outfit and keffiyeh of

Lawrence and the white Mexican wedding shirt, tight black leather pants, and boots Jim wore to create the Lizard King image. Lawrence would look back on his two years leading the Arab Revolt in *The Seven Pillars of Wisdom,* a memoir that contains some of literature's most haunting observations, one of which may have inspired Jim:

> All men dream: but not equally. Those who dream by night in the dusty recesses of their minds wake up in the day to find it was vanity, but the dreamers of the day are dangerous men, for they may act their dreams with open eyes, to make it possible.[16]

In yet another strange parallel, Jim also reflected upon his tumultuous rock star life in his poetry album *An American Prayer,* released in 1978, in which he wondered what part of him would find its way into eternity.

> End w/ fond good-bye
> & plans for future
> —Not an actor
> Writer—filmmaker
> Which one of my cellves
> Will be remember'd
> Good-bye America
> I love you[17]

❃

What makes *Lawrence of Arabia* important to Jim's story has to do with the feeling of pain. T.E. Lawrence is a good example of someone living out Nietzsche's understanding of life, that "He who has a why to live for can bear almost any how." The transformation Jim would undergo in Venice in the summer of 1965 and during his first year with The Doors had its own particular set of trials just as difficult in its way as Lawrence's transformation into a war hero. Lawrence's ability to not mind pain while accomplishing the impossible, such as crossing the Nefud Desert, rescuing Gasim from certain death, and taking the city of Aqaba after uniting two warring Arab tribes, had gained the respect of the Bedouins. What Wilson says about Lawrence's attitude toward pain in *The Outsider* can also be attributed to Jim:

> This capacity of Lawrence's to bear physical pain is of central importance in understanding him. His clear-sighted intellect could not conceive of moral freedom without physical freedom too; pain was an invaluable instrument in experiments to determine the extent of his moral freedom.[18]

In an example of this fortitude, Lawrence entered a town held by the Turks during the Arab Revolt and received a severe beating before the Turks let him go.

As in Lawrence's case, Jim may have put himself in dangerous situations on purpose, such as getting himself beat up by members of the Hell's Angels in Blythe, California, in their way the fierce Bedouins of 1960s California. Besides "testing the bounds of reality" out of his strange curiosity—something akin to what we'll learn is Lawrence's "funny sense of fun"—Jim's provocations seemed to serve him as a rite of passage in becoming a rebellious leader. It would speak to Jim's ability to tolerate pain, and in doing so, to become as tough as the Hell's Angels in his own rock star way, in determining, as Wilson said of Lawrence, "the extent of his moral freedom." And like the real-life Lawrence, there may also have been an element of masochism in Jim's personality. It's best to let Robby Krieger walk us through this side of Jim:

> Jim loved to get into fights, but he would always lose. Most guys who pick fights are doing it to look tough or to prove something. Jim didn't care about dominating people physically. He never threw the first punch; instead, he provoked people with words or acts of destruction until they finally took a swing. He wasn't a weakling— he could've defended himself if he wanted to—but then again, he was usually so wasted that a stiff breeze could have knocked him off his feet. Was it masochism? Manipulation? Pushing emotional limits? Symbolically striking back at his authoritarian father? I used

to chalk it up to drunken stupidity—which it was—but now I recognize it as *calculated* drunken stupidity.

Liquor was always the catalyst. Jim wouldn't even think of saying or doing something to start a fight when he was sober. He was always a perfect gentleman, even to cops. Underneath it all he never wanted to actually hurt anybody. . .

Once Jim and I were eating at a diner when some navy boys came in and started picking on us about our long hair. The standard taunts: calling us girls and so forth I muttered something back under my breath, probably a smart-ass remark about their sailor suits. Whatever I said, Jim repeated it loudly for their benefit and then took the insults to the next level. They grumbled back at us, but things died down and we finished our meal in peace.

As we were leaving, Jim went to make a call from the phone booth outside. The sailors followed us out. They tried to grab me, but I shook them off and ran. I turned to see Jim pinned inside the phone booth, with one of those sailors strangling him and bashing his face against the glass. Jim shouted, "Call the cops!"

The sailors got in a few more licks and left Jim in a bloody pile on the ground. I ran back to help him and offered to take him to the hospital. He shrugged it off and said he okay.

The incident was hardly his fault, but it was yet another example of Jim being a magnet for violence and reveling in it. I'll never really understand the psychology of what drove him to fight, but I'll never forget the look on Jim's face when he was being flattened against the glass of that phone booth."

"He was smiling. Ear to ear."[19]

Nietzsche felt the earliest forms of Greek tragedy "had for its theme only the suffering of Dionysus:" "From the smile of this Dionysus sprang the Olympian gods."[20]

Pain is meant to wake us up. People try to hide their pain.
But they're wrong. Pain is something to carry, like a radio.
You feel your strength in the feeling of pain.[21]

Figure 10.2. "No, Dryden, it's going to be fun."
Peter O'Toole as T.E. Lawrence, *Lawrence of Arabia.*

In an early scene in *Lawrence of Arabia*, Dryden issues a warning to Lawrence, who delivers his famous retort about "fun." In the previous scene, Lawrence revealed what this "funny sense of fun" is by extinguishing a match between his fingertips, stating:

LAWRENCE: The trick . . . is not minding that it hurts . . .

DRYDEN: Only two kinds of creature get fun in the desert, Bedouins and gods, and you're neither . . . for ordinary men it's a burning, fiery furnace

LAWRENCE: No, Dryden, it's going to be fun.

DRYDEN: It is recognized that you have a funny sense of fun.[22]

Lawrence's "funny sense of fun" would've made a lasting impression on Jim, perhaps causing him to feel that he and other spiritually emergent persons had to specialize in this sensibility, as Jim partially advocates in the song "Take It as It Comes." The story goes Jim was inspired to write "Take It as It Comes" after attending one of Maharishi Mahesh Yogi's lectures on how to take life at your own pace, though Krieger thinks Jim's inspiration was more sexual than about spiritual enlightenment.[23] Learning to slow down to recapture a childlike sense of wonder and self-healing awareness is certainly a part of Jim's message. Though Jim may have also meant learning the "trick" of how to not mind the pain involved in a spiritual awakening while, to borrow Lawrence's words, striving "to restore to the world a lost influence." This also may have meant, in Jim's mind, that perhaps he had to receive a beating from time to time to "earn" his position as a spiritual rebel and shock his audiences to wake up.

> *I like people who shake other people up*
> *and make them feel uncomfortable.*[24]

The experience of spiritual awakening itself is complicated and uncomfortable. It's joyful, exhilarating, and exciting—as Hamlet experiences after his meeting with the Ghost—but it's also, as we learned earlier, chaotic, frightening, and painful, and is usually preceded by what is known as "the dark night of the soul." Lawrence's "funny sense of fun" is the attitude you need to get through a spiritual awakening while learning to co-create a new life and world with the invisible realms. In *The Occult Explosion*, Freedland notes: "Bucke argued that an ability to function in an altered state of consciousness as well as in a normal waking state was necessary for humanity's evolution to a higher level."[25]

This is part of the "trial," so to speak, of learning how to co-create with the invisible realms, what Christina Grof felt during her spiritual awakening: "Managing to conduct a normal, daily life was difficult since I often felt as though I were straddling two worlds: the world of everyday reality and the complex, colorful demanding world of my unconscious."[26] In *The Stormy Search for the Self*, spiritual awakening is defined as learning how to live in two different worlds: ordinary consciousness and spiritual awareness of the invisible realms.

One world is the ordinary, familiar reality in which you have certain expectations to fulfill, roles to play, and obligations to meet. The other is the domain beneath the everyday layer, the vast pool of the unconscious, which contains unknown possibilities. When the inner realm becomes increasingly available, it intrudes into ordinary awareness, and the separation between the two domains begins to crumble . . . It will not stop until it has run its course. The intense period of awakening may take quite some time, ranging from a few months to a number of years. There may be times in which the transformation process is more troublesome or obvious than others, but generally it is continuous until finished.[27]

The accumulation of psychic happenings of various kinds can be very disturbing. When such episodes are so overwhelming and convincing that it is difficult to dismiss them, the situation becomes very frightening, since the old foundations of security have been shattered and one feels like an entirely naive and uninformed newcomer in an unknown and mysterious world.[28]

Take the highway to the end of the night[29]

The music The Doors made helped their fans to cope with the strangeness and the pain involved in their spiritual awakenings as well as the chaotic events that were unfolding around them in their "new, alien and *other*" America. Jim had become what Seligmann describes in *The History of Magic & the Occult* as the "wizard" who was the "benefactor of his tribesmen, promising assistance against the fearful unknown."[30] Jim's appearance on the world stage was in strange synchronicity with an era that saw the first major shift into the integral stage of consciousness. Keep in mind Gebser's warning of the pain that accompanies a shift in consciousness with the power to change whole worlds. Blake observed in his *Proverbs of Hell* that: "The roaring of lions, the howling of wolves, the raging of the stormy sea, and the destructive sword, are portions of eternity too great for the eye of man."[31] To feel the destructive sword of spiritual awakening upon ordinary consciousness, to share this with so many waking up, was to both participate in and witness nothing less than a spiritual apocalypse. For many, the veil had fallen; the invisible, inner reality was now not so invisible. Many rock music fans were also dropping the same strong LSD that Jim was taking, tripping out on their ascending spiritual lives and a nation in chaos while also feeling "Lost in a Roman wilderness of pain."[32] Both the young and the old alike were witnessing along with Jim such gruesome and traumatic "portions of eternity" as the Vietnam War, the explosion of protests by oppressed races against discrimination, and political assassinations that were being broadcast on TV, sometimes live, for the first time—all shattering what Jim called our "fragile, eggshell mind." No picnic at all. These events caused an entire generation to begin looking inward while finding their heroes in artists like Jim, a young person who had been looking inward his whole life. With his gift for theatricality, part of Jim's role with The Doors was to give a voice to the pain, rage, confusion, and frustration that the young people of Jim's generation were feeling, a "Sadness falling/Like burned skin" all around them, as Jim wrote in his poem "Newborn Awakening," a reference to the use of napalm by the American military during the Vietnam War.

Could any Hell be more horrible than now, and real?[33]

Lawrence tried to back out of the violent "portions of eternity" he'd helped to create. The real-life Lawrence was haunted for the rest of his life by his actions during the Arab Revolt. The sensitive, well-read Romantic medievalist with no prior war experience had turned into a cold-blooded killer. In the latter half of *Lawrence of Arabia*, Lawrence abandons the Arab Revolt for a short time to find, as he put it, his own "ration of common humanity." General Allenby, sensing Lawrence might leave the field, challenges Lawrence to follow through on his calling to unite and free the Bedouin tribes: "Not many people have a destiny, Lawrence. It'd be a terrible thing for a man to flunk it if he has."[34]

In his 1999 book *Light My Fire: My Life with The Doors*, Ray Manzarek writes about a tense moment one day in the band's office when Jim wanted to quit. Jim felt he was having a nervous breakdown: "I'm tellin' you, Ray. I can't take it."[35] To get a sense of what Jim may have been feeling, let's remember our earlier reading of Christina and Stanislav Grof's words from *The Stormy Search for the Self*:

> The accumulation of psychic happenings of various kinds can be very disturbing. When such episodes are so overwhelming and convincing that it is difficult to dismiss them, the situation becomes very frightening, since the old foundations of security have been shattered and one feels like an entirely naive and uninformed newcomer in an unknown and mysterious world.

Jim realized he was fast becoming a new kind of avatar for an unprecedented mass occult/spiritual awakening. There was no way for Jim to know where it was all going to lead. After all, he was the door between things known and unknown. Jim was down to "live dangerously," as Nietzsche advocated, but perhaps this was a little more than he bargained for. The pressure may have contributed to Jim's drinking as his malevolent alter ego "Jimbo" began to surface more and more. To Ray, Jim's walking out at that point given their success was insane. But in hindsight, Ray writes in *Light My Fire* that he later arrived at a more sensitive understanding of what was going on with Jim:

> That day in the office, Jim knew he was in a battle for his soul. He knew he was up against a formidable opponent. He just didn't know *whom* he was fighting. All he could feel was that he was being torn apart. Ripped in two. And he came to us for help. Jim didn't want "Jimbo" to take over but he was losing the battle on his own. If only I had known then what I know now. I could have helped.[36]

Lawrence was lucky enough to survive the twentieth century's first major war. Lawrence's *Macbeth*-like rise to prominence from lieutenant to major and then to colonel during the Arab Revolt was followed by his enjoying almost two more decades of life as a world-famous war hero. Jim had just a few precious months alone with his girlfriend, Pamela Courson, before his death. There would be no "ration of common humanity" for Jim as an aging rock and roll legend.

It may have been in pieces, but I gave you the best of me.[37]

Part of *Lawrence of Arabia's* timeless appeal lies in its evoking our desire to do something great. While growing up, Jim felt he was born for greatness. Regarding the achievement of great things, Abraham Maslow would ask his students this question: "If not you, then who?"[38]

Towards the middle of the first half of *Lawrence of Arabia*, A British soldier yells out to Lawrence "Who are you?" from a world that

Figure 10.3. "Who are you? Who are you?"
Peter O'Toole as T.E. Lawrence, *Lawrence of Arabia.*

Lawrence, for a time, no longer belongs to.[39] This question "Who are you?" is also directed at the audience. Not asking ourselves who we are is a sure way to fall into that dreaded partial amnesia.

This is a much, much more painful place to live. Bolen in *Gods in Everyman* quotes the regretful words of a powerful editor-in-chief at a national news magazine who suffered from a lack of purpose and vitality:

> Each morning I struggled into my suit, picked up my briefcase, went to my glamorous job, and died a little. I needed something, but I wasn't sure what. I knew I wanted to be tested, mentally and physically. I wanted to succeed, but by standards that were clear and concrete, and not dependent on the opinions of others. I wanted the intensity and camaraderie of a dangerous enterprise.[40]

> *Did you have a good world when you died?*
> *Enough to base a movie on?*[41]

For this great leap into the integral stage of consciousness to happen—
in and of itself "a dangerous enterprise"—Jim is telling us to do what
Lawrence did: leave behind our comfort zone. Jim also took inspiration
for his secret teacher's dangerous assignment from Nietzsche's influential statement on living dangerously in *The Gay Science*:

> For believe me!—the secret for harvesting from existence the great-
> est fruitfulness and the greatest enjoyment is: to live dangerously!
> Build your cities on the slopes of Vesuvius! Send your ships into
> uncharted seas! Live at war with your peers and yourselves! Be
> robbers and conquerors as long as you cannot be rulers and possess-
> ors, you seekers of knowledge! Soon the age will be past when you
> could be content to live in hidden forests like shy deer. At long last
> the search for knowledge will reach out for its due:—it will want to
> rule and possess, and you with it![42]

"Know thyself" is one of the Delphic maxims inscribed on the
pronaos (forecourt) of the Temple of Apollo at Delphi, the first "com-
mandment" of both Western philosophy and the Western esoteric tradition. Wilson writes, "The Outsider's first business is self-knowledge."[43]
This is the core message of *Lawrence of Arabia*. Discovering who you
are by living dangerously is another way to break the circuit of that partial amnesia which in turn revitalizes self-worth with a renewed sense of
purpose and vitality. The answer to the question "Who are you?" is to
be lived out through discovering and acting upon what makes a person
unique, through which they can find their "why." This is Jim's message
on "Shaman's Blues."

> *There will never be*
> *Another one like you*
> *There will never be*
> *Another one*
> *Who can do the things you do*[44]

Lawrence of Arabia would kick off a decade of rebellion, inspiring many
seekers to live dangerously on the path of occult/spiritual exploration,

intrepid spirits who, like Jim, were willing to test themselves and think differently. Achieving what seems impossible to everyone else becomes possible for the person who leaves behind their comfort zone. What Lawrence proved to the world is that he wasn't just your average bureaucrat stuck in a map room—"the drama of the rationalist suffocating in the dusty room of his personal consciousness, caught in the vicious cycle of boredom and futility, which in turn leads to still further boredom and futility"[45] as Wilson notes in *The Occult*—but someone with a destiny he would not back down from. Lawrence convinces an astonished and disbelieving Sherif Ali that "Aqaba is over there. It's only a matter of going," this port city occupied by the Turks that was separated from the rest of Arabia by the forbidding Nefud Desert. This can only be said by a person who has, at the very least, a strong ability to overcome fear and not mind pain. Sherif Ali looks back at Lawrence in total disbelief, telling him "You *are* mad." Sherif Ali makes it clear to Lawrence that "The Nefud is the worst place God created," and that "It cannot be crossed." But Sherif Ali guides Lawrence and the Bedouin tribesmen through the harrowing Nefud despite how insane it is to do so to his rational mind, which ultimately led to a victory at Aqaba. This shows an important leadership quality both Lawrence and Jim possessed, what Mack describes as "the capacity of enabling" that allows "others to make use of abilities they had always possessed but, until their acquaintance with him, had failed to realize."[46]

> *Expose yourself to your deepest fear; after that,*
> *fear has no power, and the fear of freedom shrinks*
> *and vanishes. You are free.*[47]

Jim and Ray had the same attitude about achieving rock music success. If Sherif Ali were present that day on the beach with Jim and Ray, he'd have said "You're *both* mad!" In a strange parallel to add to the growing list, Lawrence and Sherif Ali's recruitment of the Howietat fighters, the earning of British military support, and the encounter with the American journalist, is echoed in Jim and Ray's serendipitous discovery of guitarist Robby Krieger and drummer John Densmore to form The Doors. Jim's enabling capacity would bring out the musical talents of Manzarek, Krieger, and Densmore. Their fans in turn made sure they kept their residency at the Whiskey à Go-Go where they won over music producer Paul Rothchild and Elektra Records president Jac Holzman, who both guided The Doors into greatness and propelled Jim into worldwide fame.

Jim did want to lead the private life of a poet, what President John F. Kennedy once described as "the quiet work of centuries."[48] But like Lawrence, Jim wasn't going to back down from his calling, either. Life was out there in a world ready to wake up to its divinity, hungry to experience the unknown and everything that was "new, alien and *other*," to give full sway to "the instinctive desire to believe in the unseen forces, the wider significance that can break the circuit," to leave the dull 1950s behind, and *dance, dance, dance.*

Through songs like "Take It as It Comes," Jim was telling us that to leap into a new world we must leave our comfort zones behind and embrace that funny sense of fun. And, as Woody Guthrie advised other musicians, to "Take it easy, but take it."[49] After all, the idea is to have a blast along the way—"No, Dryden. It's going to be fun."

> *Go real slow*
> *You'll like it more and more*
> *Take it as it comes*
> *Specialize in having fun*[50]

11

I'll Never Look into Your Eyes Again

Jesus . . . Did you see what God just did to us, man?
—DR. GONZO IN *FEAR & LOATHING IN LAS VEGAS*

There is another little-known supernatural event besides the New Mexico accident that's significant to Jim's life. Bill Cosgrave's 2020 memoir *Love Her Madly: Jim Morrison, Mary & Me* is a riveting account of Cosgrave's friendship with Mary and Jim taking place in Los Angeles several months before and during Jim's earliest days with The Doors. One night at Mary's Westwood apartment, Mary and Jim told Cosgrave about a vision they shared together one night at a church in Florida.

> Jim was searching for truth and meaning elsewhere—in books, in his mind. And then, late one night, while they were in Florida, Mary coaxed Jim.
>
> "Please, Jim, come to church with me right now. There will be no one there. Just you and me. The door is always open."
>
> Jim reluctantly agreed.
>
> They drove to her church, and not a soul was in sight. Heavy wooden doors groaned open as he followed her in. Suffering faces of stained-glass saints were softly illuminated by the muted street light. Their footsteps echoed off the ancient wood floor, bouncing around the cavernous church. Mary led Jim to a pew halfway up. She slid in, motioned for him to sit down. A trace of incense was in the air. It was quiet as a tomb. Jim was gazing around.

"Why are so many candles lit over there?" Jim pointed.

"Shhh!—you have to be quiet, Jim!"

"Why, there's no one here."

"Shhhh. You have to be respectful. People come and light a candle, make an offering, and say a prayer."

"How come there are so many?"

"Lots of people believe, Jim. . . and pray."

Mary reached down and rotated the padded prayer board. Got down on her knees and prayed. Palms together, eyes closed, she beseeched God to let Jim believe.

"Please, God, please help me. Show Jim you exist."

Jim was bored, looking around. *What a lark. All these statues.*

People worshipping marble. Believing what they're told. There was a portrait of Jesus, fair-skinned, blue-eyed. He thought he was a swarthy-skinned Jew. *Man, is this place quiet . . . dark.* There was a dim red light over the exit door. Mary was still praying.

Jim shifted. Looked up. A pinpoint of light. He looked away, looked up again. The ceiling must have been three stories high. The pinpoint became a little brighter. *Was that there before? Must've been*, he thought.

He looked up again. What the hell's happening? He looked at Mary, head bowed eyes squeezed shut. The dot got brighter, slightly larger. Who's fucking with the lights, man? He looked up again. *Where the hell's the extension cord for the light up there?* His eyes scanned left and right. There was no cord. Nothing attached to the light. But it wasn't even a light bulb. It was round and glowing. Suspended in mid-air—growing brighter, more intense. Jim looked up in awe. He took a quick glance at Mary. The thing was so fucking bright he couldn't look directly at it. Mary was now staring up in wide-eyed wonder at the blinding light, transfixed.

Jim was stupefied. What the fuck? He leapt up and headed for the door. Mary followed.

Jim stood on the concrete stairs, heart racing. "What was that? Did you see that! What the hell's going on?" Breathing slower. Calming down. Looking back at the closed door, he moved toward it and cautiously opened it. They looked inside. Dead still. No motion, no light, not a sound or a soul in sight. Bathed in darkness. Flickering candles along the side wall. Up there? Nothing.

The story ends and we move from the kitchen into the tiny living room. Jim and I lounging on her thrift-shop sofa. Across from us, Mary, legs tucked under her in the chair, looks at us. "It was a sign from God," she says calmly.

I look at Jim. "What do you think it was?"

"I, ah, don't know, man." He lights up another joint and hands it to me.

"But it was real."[1]

Mary and Jim experienced "the transcendent divine," "a typical example," as Christina and Stanislav Grof point out in *The Stormy Search for The Self*, "would be a vision of God as a radiant source of light of supernatural beauty."[2] Chapter 3 in *The Stormy Search for The Self*, "Encountering the Divine," begins with a quote from the New Testament:

Suddenly a great light from heaven shown around me . . . Those who were with me indeed saw the light and were afraid . . . So I said, "What shall I do, Lord?" And the Lord said to me, "Arise and go into Damascus, and there you will be told all things which are appointed for you to do." And since I could not see for the glory of that light, being led by the hand of those who were with me, I came into Damascus.

Mary held her own firm persuasion about what she saw, believing that God had revealed Himself to Jim while she prayed. For Jim, who was searching for truth "in books" and "in his mind," what happened that night was confusing, but the vision he shared with Mary may have haunted him for the rest of his life. While contemplating the spiritual implications, Jim wrote in his journals:

Saul of Tarsus on the road to Damascus. Blindness elevated him to St. Paul. Why is blindness holy? . . . The Mani taught that man was created as a helper by the messenger of the Supreme God of Light to assist by his life and efforts in gathering the scattered, thereby

Figure 11.1. Michelangelo Buonarroti (1475–1564),
The Conversion of Saul (circa 1542—1545), fresco, Cappella Paolina,
Vatican Palace, Vatican City.

weakened, atoms of light and lead them upward. For light has shone into the darkness and wasted itself and is in grave danger of being swallowed wholly . . . Man can assist in the salvation of light.[3]

> *Thank you, O Lord*
> *For the White Blind Light*[4]

Bolen describes in *Gods in Everyman* a "dismemberment" common to the Dionysian archetype:

The motif of dismemberment is woven through the myths of Dionysus who shared the same fate as Osiris, an earlier, Egyptian god. Later, the crucified Jesus Christ had the role of the divine son who suffers death and is resurrected. The Dionysian archetype predisposes a man (or woman) to the possibility of psychological dismemberment or crucifixion, caused by his inability to reconcile powerful opposites within. "Being on the cross" between two opposing tendencies is a common affliction of a Dionysian man.[5]

Christina Grof recalled during her spiritual emergency as she described in *The Stormy Search for the Self* that "To my horror, I became identified with an agonized crucified Christ as well as with his murderers."[6] For Jim the secret teacher, this inner struggle would come back to his wrestling with those opposing forces of good and evil inside us, and perhaps in the spirit world as well.

This dismemberment is also found in Delta bluesmen and their music. Josephine Matyas and Craig Jones write in their 2021 book *Chasing the Blues: A Traveler's Guide to America's Music* that:

Early blues performers often moved from town to plantation to city—from juke joint to party house to street corner—sometimes leaving a trail of unfathered "yard" children in their wake. In the ironic juxtaposition of Saturday night/Sunday morning, they sometimes alternated between street corners busking for nickels and Sunday morning fire-and-brimstone sermons preaching the gospel. Blues and gospel are intertwined—the vocal characteristics of gospel songs are a fixture in the blues; the rhythms and twelve-bar structure were imprinted into the gospel sway in Black churches. They share an emotional intensity, although the subject matter is different. Take "Jesus" out of a rollicking gospel song and replace it with "baby," and you've got a blues tune.[7]

Cancel my subscription to the resurrection
Send my credentials to the house of detention[8]

Save us!
Jesus!
Save us![9]

Mary broke up with Jim not long after they told this story to Cosgrave. She felt that all Jim knew was books but not enough about himself.[10] General Murray thought the same of Lawrence before sending him off into the desert: "Who knows. Might even make a man out of him." Now that he'd graduated from UCLA, Jim couldn't pay the rent on his Goshen Avenue apartment in Westwood as his parents cut him off. Mary wouldn't let Jim move into her apartment, either.

> By now, Jim and Mary were drifting apart. She still insisted on including stardom in her destiny—a conviction Jim had humored at first and then tried to discourage. Then she said she might audition as a go-go dancer at the Whiskey à Go-Go, a club that had opened on the Sunset Strip in January. Jim told her he didn't want her in a short fringed skirt in a glass cage, shaking her ass off for middle-aged drunks. They fought again when she got an agent, who told her not to appear in a film Jim wanted to make because it would be damaging to her career to be in a student film. They fought a third time when Mary appeared unexpectedly at Jim's apartment and caught him with another girl. Jim told Mary she had no right to come to his place unless she was invited. Besides the fights, there were polite but annoying reminders that, in her opinion, he was taking too many drugs.[11]

Crushed, broke, and not knowing what else to do or where else to go, Jim began sleeping under the Santa Monica Pier. He hung around Venice during the day, getting stoned and writing in his journals. Cosgrave remembers finding Jim one afternoon sitting cross-legged on the sand looking "utterly alone and vulnerable . . . Rejected by his soulmate, the woman he had adored for three years, he is despondent. His sadness is palpable."[12]

What elaborate plans did Jim have in mind with Mary, his "beautiful friend," his "only friend" during those past three years? There's every indication Mary was in love with Jim—she took him to a church to find God—and that Jim was in love with her. Mary's IQ was greater than Jim's and she was even more well-read than he was as they often had long, stimulating conversations.[13] In the stunningly beautiful and super intelligent Mary Werbelow, Jim enjoyed what Nietzsche had wanted with Lou Andreas-Salomé but couldn't achieve. But the loving, intimate connection, both highly affectionate and intellectual, that Jim had with Mary was now gone.

Many of us have felt the excruciatingly painful experience of losing our first loves. Nineteenth-century Russian novelist Ivan Turgenev captures this agony in the story of sixteen-year-old protagonist Vladimir Petrovich in his 1860 novella, *First Love*:

> I burnt as in a fire in your presence . . . but what did I care to know what the fire was in which I burned and melted. It was enough that it was sweet to burn and melt. . . . She tore herself away, and went out. And I went away. I cannot describe the emotion with which I went away. I should not wish it to ever come again; but I should think myself unfortunate had I never experienced such an emotion.[14]

The intensity of these feelings is passionately felt in a song Jim wrote about Mary, "The Crystal Ship." For this often lonely, tortured soul, viewed by Tandy Martin's mother as someone "unclean, like a leper,"[15] Jim may have wondered with real sadness if anyone was ever going to love him.

Christina and Stanislav Grof write in *The Stormy Search for the Self* that when a significant relationship ends the "dream is shattered, and the emotional stress that ensues may initiate a transformation process for him. Very painfully, he realizes that he does not have the power over the forces of life and death, that he is subject to forces beyond his command."[16]

"I'll never look into your eyes again" is what Jim wrote when he thought of Mary while working out the lyrics to "The End."[17] He smoked joint after joint, learning to forget, and emulated Baudelaire in sublimating his pain into poetry, "That if I am to weave my mystic crown / I must braid into it all time, all space. . . ."

Jim was now on his way to becoming much like "Aurens" in *Lawrence of Arabia*. To borrow American film director Martin

Scorcese's words, "It's a character . . . that's filled with self-destruction . . . and self-loathing . . . he's constantly testing himself . . . pushing himself."[18]

> *Let me tell you about heartache & the loss of God*
> *Wandering, wandering in hopeless night*

IV

The Time to Hesitate Is Through

12
The Path of the Sun

I felt a great, inexplicable joy so powerful that I could not restrain it but had to break into song, a mighty song with room for only one word: joy, joy! . . . and then in the midst of such a fit of mysterious and overwhelming delight, I became a shaman, not knowing myself how it came about. I have gained my enlightenment, the shaman's light of brain and body.

—ESKIMO SHAMAN

Mary's rejection got Jim to think about who the right girl for him would be. Jim confided in Bill Cosgrave that he wanted "to meet a girl who is completely un-hung up about her sexuality. Open, free, no limitations,"[1] a desire right in line with the sexual revolution. Jim met this person during The Doors' residency at the Whiskey à Go-Go in 1966: "And then she walked in the door. Pamela Courson. All freckle-faced and redheaded and creamy white skinned. Fresh out of Orange County. Fresh off the farm of the mind and with a fire in her eyes."

> *Her dark red hair*
> *The soft white skin*
> *Look! She's coming in here*
> *I can't live through each slow century*
> *of her movement.*

She was the dame of this film noir story. The gorgeous, tragic, little wisp of a girl who was destined to become Jim's inamorata . . . and his doomed partner. Juliet had entered Romeo's playground. And death smiled."[2]

Jim fondly referred to Pam as his "cosmic mate." Robby Krieger writes in *Set The Night on Fire*: "The bottom line is she was weird, he was weird, and they were lucky they both found each other to be weird with."[3]

Pam's archetype was that of Persephone, well suited for Jim's Dionysian archetype. Persephone "represents spring, everlasting youth, innocence, and pureness. She often stays receptive to change and was young in spirit all her life."[4] Magick Altman in her 2016 book *Magick Tarot: A Journey of Self-Realization* offers a glimpse into what Pam may have been feeling when she drove up from Orange County into Hollywood with her friends to be a part of the Sunset Boulevard rock music scene:

> When I turned 16 it was 1966 and the San Francisco Bay Area was sizzling with new visions of the Age of Aquarius. Like a young Persephone, I ran off to The City every chance I had to be part of this dance of the dawning of a new era. Along with so many of our sisters, we left our poor Demeters mourning for the loss of their innocent children. As carefree as The Fool, we were dazzled by The Magician and all the muses of that unforgettable time.[5]

Jim would leave behind the pain of losing Mary in the first verse of "The End" to venture off with Pam into their weird, open relationship, "Lost in a Roman wilderness of pain." Whatever kind of future Jim may have once wanted with Mary was now in the rearview mirror. Jim had a new vision of life, one in which he had to keep his eyes on the road and his hands on the wheel: "The world we suggest is a new wild west. A sensuous, evil world. Strange and haunting, the path of the sun."[6]

Jim's "new wild west" calls for the realization of what Seligmann writes in *The History of Magic & the Occult* is the alchemist's goal: "a union of soul and mind with the divine," and as Jim writes in *The Lords: Notes on Vision*, "purifying and transforming all being and matter." The alchemical transformation of uniting the soul, the mind, and "the divine light" is "the path of the sun." Seligmann writes in *The History of Magic & the Occult* that:

> The best that existed below, the adept believed, could only be linked to what was above. The most perfect thing on earth was gold; and above, the only body whose rays reached into the heaven of the angels was the sun. Among the divine things, the sun was the lowest. Thus gold was linked with the sun, which is halfway between the supreme and the earth, the mediator between man and God.[7]

Jim's vision of a "new wild west" means leaving behind your comfort zone for the wilderness—the only place where an alchemical transformation can take place in the existential sense—as both Lawrence and Jim did; you can't "know thyself" until you lose yourself.

> *Can you picture what will be?*
> *So limitless and free*
> *Desperately in need of some*
> *stranger's hand*
> *In a desperate land*[8]

The shock of Jim's new homeless living situation also forced him to consider what direction to take. He thought about moving to New York City to begin an experimental filmmaking career. Jim once told Ray he wanted to find Lithuanian-American avant-garde filmmaker, poet, and artist Jonas Mekas, considered to be "the godfather of American avant-garde cinema," and make movies with him. But Jim had second thoughts about moving to New York City—"Film is a hard medium to break into. It's so much more complex than music; you need so many more people and so much equipment."[9]

Jim wasn't about to enter Hollywood, either. Cosgrave in *Love Her Madly* recalls Jim's utter contempt for Hollywood, calling it "a bunch of bullshit" and that Hollywood films are "syrup for the masses." Jim loved French New Wave avant-garde filmmakers like Françoise Truffaut and Jean-Luc Godard: "The guy's a genius. Go see *Contempt*. Man, the French are so far ahead of Hollywood. *Lola*—what a film!"[10]

Perhaps Jim also decided to stay in Los Angeles as its year-round mild weather and warmer temperatures would allow him a Bedouin-like existence. While writing *The Outsider*, which made Colin Wilson famous overnight throughout England in 1956, Wilson camped out in his sleeping bag on Hampstead Heath in London to avoid paying rent. Nine years later in 1965, Jim found himself living a similar vagabond existence in Venice before becoming famous as an outsider with The Doors.

Strangely, Jim's life from 1959 to 1965 can be seen as mirroring the rejected knowledge's migration from Ancient Egypt to Renaissance Italy. Jim went from his own private ancient Alexandria-type secret teacher formation on the east coast (with his own massive library) to his own private renaissance blossoming in Venice on the west coast. In the seventh century CE, the rejected knowledge was displaced from Ancient Alexandria and then brought into the world of classical Islam—a connection with *Lawrence of Arabia* as T. E. Lawrence's travels during his university days were in close vicinity to the all-important Harran (the city of pagans), in southeastern Turkey. This is where the rejected knowledge found haven during Europe's Dark Ages. The rejected knowledge was then rediscovered during the Italian Renaissance, reaching the mind of Giordano Bruno in the late-latter half of the sixteenth century.

Polish-born, Jewish-American journalist, writer, and poet Lawrence Lipton, Venice's most noted Beat poet in the nineteen-fifties, wrote a poem entitled "Bruno in Venice West," in which Lipton imagines Giordano Bruno coming to 1950s Venice. "Bruno in Venice West" is found in a posthumously published book of Lipton's poetry, *Bruno in Venice West & Other Poems*.

Lipton, through his fifty-three-verse-long poem—only the first five verses are quoted here—seems to foretell Jim's arrival a few years later in Venice, bringing Bruno's secret teacher spirit, mind, sexual openness, and rebellious, rambunctious behavior with him.

> *Velvet and warm sweat under the torches*
> *the Procession entered the city, tall bronze men*
> *on the bronze great horses and the boys*
> *carrying banners, the fat prelates wheezing*
> *under the icons, and the musicians*

✺

Up Main street, pausing to erect
the great crucifix in the Circle
before the U.S. Post Office, turning
into Windward avenue to St. Marks
Hotel, their flags and vestments, clowns

In motley, peddlers hawking live birds
and Turkish sweetmeats, drunks and tarts
lurching along under the colonnades
like any Saturday night, the P.A. horns
blasting rock 'n' roll, sob ballads

At the tavern doors, the winos
wandering in and out of the alleys,
blinking in the neon lights, and you
Giordano Bruno between the halberdiers
and the smoking torches wandering

In the wind off the Pacific, here
in this our Venice by the western sea
as when, hooded, under the marble
colonnades of old Venice once
you walked, curing the Doges, burning[11]

Love cannot save you from your own fate.[12]

13
A Vast, Radiant Beach

Because it's getting to be the blue hour and that's the time when everything is revealed.

—JOHN RECHY

Jim's transformation would take place in a Los Angeles beach neighborhood once called the "Venice of America" with its ornate-Venetian style businesses, also known as "The Coney Island of the Pacific." Jim discovered Venice after transferring to UCLA.

> Weekends Jim went to the Venice beach. Venice had been a Mecca for the Beat generation in the 1950s and the bohemian tradition clung to it. Poets, painters, and students lived cheaply in big rooms in once-elegant Victorian homes or in cabins beside the crumbling canals.[1]

Venice satisfied Jim's earthy side (Jim's moon was in the sign of Taurus) with its panoramic coastline, spectacular sunsets, cool, distant views of the Santa Monica Mountains, and boardwalk, pier, canals, and back streets. Christina and Stanislav Grof write in *The Stormy Search for the Self* that: "There are certain situations in life that are particularly conducive to peak experiences. This often happens in extraordinary natural settings."[2] Venice became this kind of locale for Jim.

> Venice was ideal for Jim. The small artistic community was attracting more and more long-hairs, runaways, and artists every day. Bodies covered the beach; tambourines clanged merrily to the dozens of

transistor radios; dogs chased Frisbees; cross-legged blue-jeaned circles smoked pot; LSD was sold over the counter at the local head-shop. San Francisco had Haight, and Los Angeles had Venice. The time of the hippie was just beginning.[3]

During this time, Jim would make a clean break from his parents, escape the draft, and begin his shamanic initiation. American painter, author, and alchemist Marlene Seven Bremner in her 2022 book *Hermetic Philosophy & Creative Alchemy*, writes that: "Alchemy is something to be experienced, an initiation, on par with a shamanic or Dionysian death, dismemberment, and reintegration."[4]

In twentieth-century Romanian historian and philosopher Mircea Eliade's classic 1964 book *Shamanism: Archaic Techniques of Ecstasy* he explains that shamanism itself means "techniques of ecstasy" which compliments Wilson's definition of Romanticism in *The Occult* as "based on moments of ecstasy." Eliade notes: "like any other religious vocation, the shamanic vocation is manifested by a crisis, a temporary derangement of the future shaman's spiritual equilibrium."[5] This is what Jim was about to put himself through.

Jim may have discovered Eliade's *Shamanism* when the English translation came out in 1964. He had written the majority of *The Lords: Notes on Vision* at this point after entering UCLA's film department in January of 1964. Jim said, "A lot of passages in it, for example, about shamanism turned out to be very prophetic several years later because I had no idea when I was writing that I'd be doing just that."[6]

Jim would also turn up full blast his creative, mystical impulse in response to his rich peak experiences, those "rare, exciting, oceanic, deeply moving, exhilarating, elevating experiences that generate an advanced form of perceiving reality, and are even mystic and magical in their effect upon the experimenter," both sober and while stoned on cannabis, LSD, and other substances, inspiring Jim to write some of rock music's greatest songs.

Christina and Stanislav Grof write in the *The Stormy Search for the Self*:

Whatever specific symbolic form the shamanic journey takes, the common denominator is always the destruction of the old sense of identity and an experience of ecstatic connection with nature, with the cosmic order, and with the creative energy of the universe. In this process of death and rebirth, shamans experience their own divinity and attain profound insights into the nature of reality.[7]

At the same time, Jim would also experience the terrifying trials of shamanic initiation:

During the visionary journey to the underworld, the future shaman experiences attacks by vicious demons and evil spirits who expose them to incredible tortures and cruel ordeals. The malevolent entities scrape the flesh from the bones of their victims, tear out their eyeballs, suck out their blood, or boil them in heated cauldrons. The tortures culminate in the experience of dismemberment and total annihilation. In some cultures, this final destruction is mediated by an initiatory animal who tears the novice apart or devours him. Depending on the ethnic group, this can be a bear, wolf, jaguar, giant snake, or any of a variety of others.[8]

I think the highest and lowest points are the important ones. Anything else is just . . . in between.[9]

The Venice of 1965 was not the super expensive, gentrified neighborhood it is today but a run-down enclave of dilapidated shacks, houses, and buildings all shambled together along its once-dirty canals. In his 1991 book *Venice West: The Beat Generation in Southern California,* Professor John Arthur Maynard describes that Venice has seldom been an entirely respectable place. Founded in 1905 as a genteel retreat for esthetically-minded Los Angeles businessmen, it quickly became the Coney Island of the West—and image-wise, at least, things have been all downhill from there.[10]

Lawrence Lipton's description of late 1950s Venice at the beginning of his 1959 novel *The Holy Barbarians* paints a vivid picture of the beach town Jim now inhabited. It's quite possible Jim read *The Holy Barbarians*, as Maynard writes:

> Lipton's book became the outsider's handy one-volume guide to the beat scene, complete with photographs, capsule biographies, transcribed conversations, a ready-made historical context, and even a glossary of beat jargon in the back. It was a distorted picture but a vivid one, and it has stuck.[11]

In the first chapter of *The Holy Barbarians*, "Slum by The Sea," Lipton writes:

> It is Sunday in Venice. Not the Venice of the Piazza San Marco and memories of the Doges. Venice, California, the Venice of St. Mark's Hotel where the arched colonnades are of plaster, scaling off now and cracked by only a few decades of time, earthquake and decay. This is Venice by the Pacific, dreamed up by a man named Kinney at the turn of the century, a nineteenth-century Man of Vision, a vision as trite as a penny postcard. He went broke in heart and pocket trying to carry his Cook's Tour memories of the historic city on the Adriatic into the twentieth century.
>
> The oil derricks came in and fouled up his canals, the Japanese moved in and set up gambling wheels and fan-tan games on the oceanfront, and the imitation palaces of the Doges became flop joints. The Venice Pier Opera House, where Kinney dreamed of Nellie Melbas warbling arias and Italian tenors singing Neapolitan boat songs, went into history instead as the ballroom where Kid Ory first brought New Orleans jazz to the West Coast. And the night air was filled, not with songs of gondoliers, but with the air-splitting screams from the roller coasters of the Venice Amusement Park.[12]

Jim was now impoverished, living on Venice's ghostly streets. How was he going to respond, to use Wilson's words, to his secret teacher's "longing for a more purposeful form of existence?"[13] In Christina and Stanislav Grof's view, Jim was now in a full-blown:

Spiritual emergency, a crisis in which the changes within are so rapid and the inner states so demanding that, temporarily, these people may find it difficult to operate fully in everyday reality.[14]

The word emergency, suggesting a sudden crisis, comes from the Latin *emergere* ("to rise" or "to come forth") [indicating] a precarious situation [with the] potential for rising to a higher state of being.[15]

Jim withdrew from society to go deeper into his "magical kingdom" before "*emerging*" as a rock star warrior-poet with The Doors.

As the inner world becomes more active, one may feel the need to temporarily withdraw from daily activities, becoming preoccupied with intense thoughts, feelings, and internal processes. Relationships with other people may fade in importance, and the person may even feel disconnected from the familiar sense of who he or she is. As this is happening, one may feel an encompassing sense of separation from oneself, from other people, and from the surrounding world. For those in this state, even familiar human warmth and reassurance are unavailable.[16]

Jim felt that:

> Between childhood boyhood
> adolescence
> & manhood (maturity) there
> should be sharp lines drawn w/
> Tests, deaths, feats, rites
> stories, songs, & judgments[17]

Venice was the destined place for this sharp line to be drawn between Jim's childhood past as the privileged son of The Commander and Jim's manhood as the future rock star warrior-poet of spiritual awakening and cosmic consciousness. Venice already had a history of its bohemian poets, authors, and artists being tough, gritty rebels and visionaries, and Jim would become the most defiant one of them all.

Maynard notes Venice was: "the *third* beat community—third, that is, after North Beach and Greenwich Village, which continue to draw most of the scholarly attention because of the "star system" that necessarily characterizes literary history."[18]

> The gates slammed hard on the Venice beats. It was one thing to harbor strange ideas; it was another, in the language of the theater, to "kid the show." In Southern California, the show was economic growth—and the unquestioning belief in its goodness. From 1953 to 1963, the Los Angeles metropolitan area added 300,000 new residents a year, or not quite one thousand per day . . . By 1960, the "Southland" held seven and a half million people, and there was no reason for most people to think it would ever end. Growth was nature's way, and the best thing about it was that there seemed to be something in it for everybody . . . That makes it particularly ironic that the Venice beats, preaching the virtues of having nothing in a place where everyone expected to have more tomorrow, should be left out of most accounts of the Beat Generation. They were the movement's point men where the attitudes it challenged were strongest, and yet the inference seems to be that they were not "real" beats—just amateurs from the no-class end of California.[19]

Jim could've faded away, living hand-to-mouth and job-to-job provided he ever chose to get one. Jim's sister Anne was afraid "[Jim would just] be a poor beatnik all his life . . . that no one would recognize his talent."[20] After all, there was nothing in American culture to be had career-wise "to honor the expression of the creative, mystical impulse" that once existed in the primitive and ancient world.

Though Jim felt what twentieth-century British philosopher Bertrand Russell felt, that "I *must*, before I die, find *some* way to say the essential thing that is in me, that I have never said yet."[21] Jim's taste for the avant-garde and his desire to lead a life that was an "adventure of the soul" prompted him to find a novel way to express himself. So, Jim began to dream of fronting a rock band, having the gut feeling that's where his poetic, secret teacher's spirit would find release, expression, and fulfillment. The primitive spirit which held the belief that "the world was full of unseen forces: the orenda (spirit force) of the American Indians, the huaca of the ancient Peruvians" that Jim wanted to bring to life has a home in rock, blues, and jazz. Jim also knew he had the looks to front a rock band and that he could write. Although his response to his friend Sam Kilman, when he asked Jim if he could sing, was an emphatic "Fuck no! I can't sing!"[22]

But Jim was hearing melodies and writing down amazing lyrics to them. In his new relaxed, carefree state of being with no more class schedules or the odd job to show up for—Bolen notes in *Gods in Everyman*: "whenever the man is aware of the clock, Dionysus is not present"[23]—Jim decided rock music was the answer. His thinking made sense. Rock music had what Nietzsche was longing for as he writes in his 1872 book *The Birth of Tragedy Out of the Spirit of Music* that in:

> Singing and dancing, man expresses himself as a member of a higher community: he has forgotten how to walk and talk, and is about to fly dancing into the heavens. His gestures express enchantment. Just as the animals now speak, and the earth yields up milk and honey, he now gives voice to supernatural sounds: he feels like a god, he himself now walks about enraptured and elated as he saw the dogs walk in dreams. Man is no longer an artist, he has become a work of art: the artistic power of the whole of nature reveals itself to the supreme gratification of the primal Oneness amidst the paroxysms of intoxication.[24]

Eight years of intense concentration through reading, writing, and journaling that fought off the dreaded partial amnesia had built up a spectacular tension within Jim. Wilson writes about the necessary tension one needs to create, that "you have to sow before you can reap."[25] Jim had cultivated his mind with an extraordinary amount of poetry, literature, and knowledge, and had responded to it in his journals with enough thoughtfulness and insight that gave him the intellectual maturity of a forty-year-old with a Ph.D. This is why Jim was able to deliver so many memorable, timeless observations about life with calm authority at such a young age. Jim was much like Hamlet in this way, as Bloom states Hamlet is: "The only character in all of literature who seems to have an authorial consciousness all his own. You want to quote him on all sorts of matters, the way you would quote Emerson or Montaigne."[26]

Now Jim's time was about to happen in the second half of nineteen-sixties Los Angeles. Bolen writes in *Gods in Everyman*:

> In the 1960s, the hippie movement was an expression of this aspect of the Dionysian archetype, with its use of LSD and marijuana, the wearing of bright colors and sensual materials, being "flower children," having love-ins and celebrating the sexual revolution, dropping out of schools and jobs.[27]

Bloody red sun of fantastic L.A.[28]

14
Who Are Our Friends?

The one who talks about the future is a rascal. The present is the only thing that matters. To invoke one's posterity is to make a speech to maggots.

—LOUIS FERDINAND CÉLINE

Jim's pack in 1965 was a smart and rowdy bunch of "ambitious future auteurs."[1] They spent their time together in much the same way as the late nineteen-forties Ginsberg-Kerouac-Burroughs New York City set. Intense conversations and debates over Jung, alchemy, and Nietzsche occurred as well as experimentation with hallucinogenic drugs. Lachman writes:

> One factor helping the occult's rise to dominance in popular culture was the growing "psychedelic movement." Experimenting with peyote and other mind-altering drugs had been part of the "new age" fin-de-siècle. Crowley, Yeats, and the pre-Freud sexologist Havelock Ellis had done so, as had Thomas De Quincey and Baudelaire with opium before them. But it was Aldous Huxley's experiments with peyote's derivative, mescaline, that made its mind-altering effects widely known.
>
> Leary first experienced "magic mushrooms" in Mexico in 1960, and soon after, at Harvard, he ran a number of psilocybin sessions with some of the "Beat Generation:" Jack Kerouac, Allen Ginsberg and William S. Burroughs.[2]

In Jim's life, there was:

Big John DaBella, a self-described hustler and former longshoreman who often boasted about sexual adventures in a way that delighted his fellow students.

Dennis Jakob, who was described by a fellow student as "the best mind to have remained in the nineteenth-century."

Phillip O'leno, one of Morrison's best friends at UCLA, [felt that] Jim was a very talented and very brilliant person who was a little too young to be wise.[3]

Jim also had two other UCLA film school friends, Frank Lisciandro and Paul Ferrara, both of whom worked with The Doors to make the 1969 documentary *Feast of Friends* and with Jim on his 1969 experimental-independent film project *HWY: An American Pastoral*.

But the one person who saw Jim's potential to become a rock star was organist Raymond Daniel Manzarek. Ray graduated with Jim from UCLA with an MFA in cinematography. When Jim told Ray he was moving to New York City, Ray remembers feeling a bit sad, that he was going to miss his "avant-garde stoner, rebellious psychedelic poet pal."[4] Bloom writes: "What matters is that Horatio loves Hamlet, and desires no existence apart from the prince."[5]

Ray was happy to see Jim in Venice two months later. Jim attracted Ray back into his life while Ray was out wandering the beach, also wondering what direction he should take his life. But in the life of Jim the magician, there are no coincidences; this was not a chance reunion. Seligmann writes in *The History of Magic & the Occult*:

To the magus, there exists no accidental happening; everything obeys the one law, which is not resented as a coercion but rather welcomed as a liberation from the tyranny of chance. The world and its gods submit to this law, which binds together all things and all events. *Certa stant omnia lege:* everything is established solidly by that law which the wise man discerns in happenings that appear accidental to the profane. The curve observed in the flight of birds, the barking of a dog, the shape of a cloud, are occult manifestations of that omnipotent coordinator, the source of unity and harmony.[6]

Ray was impressed with Jim's lyrics to "Moonlight Drive" and wanted to begin rehearsing right away. He was also fast sold on Jim's idea to name their rock band The Doors.

Jim's and Ray's friendship is best understood through Bloom's interpretation of Hamlet's and Horatio's friendship in *Hamlet*:

> Hamlet is the subject and object of his own quest, an intolerable truth that helps him render him into so destructive an angel, so dangerous an aesthetic pleasure that he can survive only as a story able to be told by Horatio, who loves Hamlet precisely as the audience does, because we are Horatio.[7]

According to Robby Krieger in *Set the Night on Fire*, there was also a father/son dynamic to their friendship:

> Ray was paternal toward all of us since he was several years our senior—he was almost seven years older than I was—but when it came to Jim, the father-son dynamic was especially pronounced. Ray, the indulgent father, was patient, protective, and forgiving, even when Jim, the wayward son, rebelled against him.[8]

Ray could see that even though Jim had no formal musical training, Jim had a natural ear for music that complimented his secret teacher's mystical nature. Ray also sensed Jim had the shaman's gift to put us in touch with the invisible realms. Bolen writes in *Gods in Everyman*:

> The Dionysian archetype of eternal youth was personified by the rock star and the rock culture. Jim Morrison of The Doors and Mick Jagger of The Rolling Stones embodied the archetype in the 1960s. ... The realm of the invisible world feels both familiar and fascinating to the Dionysian man and may lead him to profound insights. He may be a "closet mystic" who, while operating effectively in the

world, finds that his Dionysian element provides him with a hidden source of meaning.[9]

Nietzsche's work supports Bolen's observations. He writes in *The Birth of Tragedy* that: "Dionysiac excitement is capable of communicating to a whole crowd of people the artistic gift of seeing itself surrounded by a host of spirits with which it knows itself to be profoundly united."[10] Jim could stir his audiences into a Dionysian frenzy and give them the spine-tingling feeling that something otherwordly was happening onstage that also included them, something that was extraordinarily beautiful yet almost too terrifying to behold. The other side—the spirit world—opened up through Jim, and whether or not the members of the audience understood what was happening, they could feel it. This is not the experience that your typical 1960s American teenager out to rock for the night was expecting. There was Jim the rebellious, angry young man and world-famous rock star sex symbol performer out there fronting his amazing band. And then there was Jim the shaman, the secret teacher warrior poet out to fulfill his life purpose with a vengeance, waking up audiences to what was strange and unknown with his intense, mysterious, and dangerous presence. Jim was able to make a deep, long-lasting impression with his natural dramatic skills, leaving the audience stunned, bewildered, and thoughtful. Very few people in history have been able to shake up so many people—even long after their passing—with such life-altering intensity.

Hence Blake's monumental statement from his poetry book *The Marriage of Heaven & Hell*—"If the doors of perception were cleansed everything would appear to man as it is, Infinite,"[11]—had a strong appeal to Jim the mystic. Twentieth-century British novelist and philosopher Aldous Huxley, a great secret teacher of the modern age, felt there was no better title for his 1954 book on psychedelic experiences with mescaline than Blake's words, naming it *The Doors of Perception*. Jim simplified Huxley's title into something more direct and memorable as the name for his rock band, calling it The Doors.

There are things known and things unknown
and in between are the doors.[12]

Just as much as the opportunity for rock and roll success, Ray could also see that Jim was a special person born to communicate the secret teacher's message of cosmic consciousness at a unique moment in time. The strong winds of Ray's Aquarius air sign and carnival organ sound complemented Jim's Sagittarius fire sign and strange, avant-garde surrealist/Symbolist lyrics. This was completed by Robby Krieger's signature guitar sound and John Densmore's brilliant percussion to whip up a musical bonfire.

Everyone thought Ray was nuts to start a rock band with Jim. But Ray had a strong faith in Jim's ability to write great songs and deliver performances that would make an impression on the audience:

> Were it not for Ray Manzarek's vision it is highly unlikely that Jim Morrison would've become a rock singer. Without Manzarek's encouragement and influence, Morrison was far too undisciplined to have taken the time to work with his voice. Manzarek saw something in Morrison that no one else had seen before, and even more important, he had the discipline and the patience to wait for Morrison to develop.[13]

A true friend is someone who lets you have total freedom to be yourself.[14]

※

In their 1991 biography *Break on Through: The Life & Death of Jim Morrison*, authors James Riordan and Jerry Prochnicky note another person who had an influence upon Jim:

> [A] maverick, rowdy, self-titled philosopher named Felix Venable. . . . It was Felix who taught Jim to do drugs and booze, and it was Felix who continually encouraged him to break on through no matter what was on the other side. . . . Felix was like Dean Moriarty gone to film school. Or worse, he was like a Neal Cassady who had finally decided that he had to do something with his life. And that decision carried just enough real commitment to getting

him to the cinematography department. Once he was there, however, his ambition had waned again, leaving Felix in a sort of permanent cruising state.[15]

If the Venice Beats identified more with Charlie Parker—"Charlie Parker was an electrician. He went around wiring people"[16]—Jim saw himself as *On the Road's* larger-than-life character Dean Moriarty. Based on Kerouac's real-life friend and road pal Neal Cassady, Dean Moriarty was the prototypical awakened, sensitive American madman, "a sideburned hero of the snowy West."[17] Jim, along with Venable, were those *mad ones*, as Kerouac describes Dean Moriarty:

the ones who are mad to live, mad to talk, mad to be saved, desirous of everything at the same time, the ones who never yawn or say a commonplace thing but burn, burn, burn like fabulous yellow Roman candles exploding like spiders across the stars and in the middle you see the blue center light pop and everybody goes "Awww!"[18]

Jim cast himself in this same light:

[I see myself] as a great shooting star, a huge, fiery comet. Everyone stops and gasps and points up and says . . . "Oh look at that!" Then whooosshh! I'm gone. But they'll never see anything like it ever again—and they'll never be able to forget me.[19]

Jim had the fictional Dean Moriarty's charisma and was just as crazy as Moriarity to experiment with nineteenth-century French teenage poet Arthur Rimbaud's radical ideas on how to "attain the unknown."[20]

In professor and literary critic Wallace Fowlie's 1990 book *Poem & Symbol: A Brief History of French Symbolism* (Jim once wrote a letter to Fowlie thanking him for his translation of Rimbaud's poems that Jim carried around with him), Fowlie writes:

Rimbaud laid the basis for a new opening out onto a supernatural and surreal world . . . poetry changed from an art of lyricism to one of inquiry and exasperation, to a search for values and metaphysical assurances . . . the visible world is the image of a secret universe . . . Man has to learn how to work back from the visible to the invisible.[21]

The "temporary derangement of the future shaman's spiritual equilibrium" that Jim experienced in Venice was in part brought on by Jim's having taken to heart what Rimbaud wrote in what is perhaps modern literature's most influential statement:

I say one must be a *seer*, make oneself a *seer*. The Poet makes oneself a *seer* by a long, gigantic and rational *derangement of all the senses*. All forms of love, suffering and madness. He searches himself. He exhausts all poisons in himself and keeps only their quintessences. Unspeakable torture where he needs all his faith, all his superhuman strength, where he becomes among all men the great patient, the great criminal, the one accursed—and the supreme Scholar!— Because he reaches the *unknown*! Since he cultivated his soul, rich already, more than any man! Let him die as he leaps through things unheard of, unnameable: other horrible workers will come; they will begin at the horizons where the other one has collapsed![22]

I believe in a long, prolonged derangement of the senses in order to obtain the unknown.[23]

Figure 14.1.
Arthur Rimbaud,
October 1871.
Photo: Etienne Carjat.

Jim's attraction to Rimbaud's poetry and ideas fit his Dionysian archetype's compulsion to explore the unconscious side of life. The poetic images that arose out of Jim's unconscious that express his deep-diving, secret teacher's mind are indeed reptilian. Bolen notes in *Gods in Everyman* that: "Hades and Dionysus are one and the same,"[24]

Hades' realm is the unconscious, both personal and collective. Therein reside memories, thoughts and feelings that we repressed, everything too painful or too shameful or too acceptable to others to allow to be visible in the upper world, yearnings we never embodied, possibilities that remained dim outlines. In the underworld of the collective unconscious exists everything possible to imagine becoming, everything that has ever been.[25]

I am the Lizard King
I can do anything[26]

15

An Intense Visitation
of Energy

LSD is just a tool to turn us into what we are supposed to be.
—ALBERT HOFFMANN

In the summer of 1965, Jim grew out his hair and lost weight. The clean-cut, chubby college intellectual disappeared. The FSU undergrad who once got up at the crack of dawn as not to miss out on the generous helpings of cafeteria fare had put himself on a crash diet. Jim the lean and mean "electric shaman" came to life. Christina and Stanislav Grof write in *The Stormy Search for the Self*:

> People in a transformation process may also change their appearance. They may cut or grow their hair or be attracted to clothes that reflect a departure from the norm. Examples can be found in the psychedelic culture of the sixties and seventies, when many people had spiritual insights and, instead of expressing them in ways acceptable to the established society, felt moved to convey them by forming a separate or "counter" culture characterized by expressive clothing, jewelry, hairstyles, and even brightly painted cars. . . . For some, these new ways of behaving are temporary stages in spiritual development, while for others they may become a permanent part of a new lifestyle.[1]

Jim's use of hallucinogenics also increased. Jim's UCLA film school friend Phil O'Leno recalls in Frank Lisciandro's 1990 book *Friends*

Gathered Together that Jim wasn't using drugs for fun but for "a true transcendental space to arrive at."[2] Jim decided it was time to explore everything he'd ever read on alternative states of consciousness by writers such as Carlos Castaneda and Aldous Huxley.

Ray Manzarek fiercely states during an interview that:

> Rock and roll was not inspired by drugs . . . it wasn't drugs. Today, it's drugs, cocaine and crack [and] heroin. . . . All people were doing back in the sixties was smoking the herb. It was just hemp. It was just a mild intoxicant that would open the doors of perception . . . All we were doing was just opening the doors of perception. And that's where the music came from. That's where the name The Doors came from. . . . It was a whole different consciousness. It was an expansion of consciousness.[3]

Jim would often smoke a joint first thing in the morning and write. "He's forever writing in a notebook," Cosgrave remembers.[4]

> Jim may be broke, but he seems to have an inexhaustible source of weed. He is also dropping acid. With his film school degree behind him and the endless summer before him, he doesn't seem to be concerned about anything. He doesn't talk about getting a job. He's on summer holidays, sitting on the sand, staring at the sea. All he wants to do is what he's doing: write, dope, acid.[5]

Drugs are a bet w/ your mind[6]

Jim was having a blast tripping on the strong LSD that was legal and available to buy over the counter in 1965. It cannot be overstated how much of an impact LSD had on Jim's life and art. LSD had an enormous healing effect on Jim as it not only opened his unconscious mind even further but also his doors of perception into the invisible realms. Christina and Stanislav Grof write in *The Stormy Search for the Self*:

> Encounters with the divine regions during the process of spiritual emergence are extremely healing. Reaching them, one often feels

positive emotions such as ecstasy, rapture, joy, gratitude, love, and bliss, which can quickly relieve or dissolve negative states such as depression and anger. Feeling oneself to be a part of an all-encompassing cosmic network often gives a person who has problems with self-esteem a fresh, expanded self-image.[7]

Jim would create just such a new image for himself that would soon thrust him into the spotlight of the 1960s "all-encompassing cosmic network." To begin discussing LSD's effect on Jim, Wilson's words on psychedelic drugs from *The Occult* are illuminating:

Psychedelic drugs, which have the effect of immobilizing the "logical mind," and putting the subliminal power in the driving seat of personality, can produce revelations of beauty or horror. The mind that opens itself to "subliminal meanings" has shed its defenses, thrown away its insulation, its "shock absorbers." Daylight consciousness has the refuge of common sense, of "objective reality." But in subliminal states, the dividing line between reality and one's personal fantasies becomes blurred; and without a certain knowledge and discipline, the mind is at the mercy of its own tendency to morbidity. Graves comments correctly that the nightmare is one of the cruelest aspects of the White Goddess.[8]

In Stanislav Grof's 1975 study *LSD: Doorway to the Numinous*, Grof explains how LSD functions as a catalyst to activate the unconscious and hidden layers of the personality to create:

four major levels, or types, of LSD experiences in the corresponding areas of the human unconscious: 1) abstract and aesthetic experiences, 2) psychodynamic experiences, 3) perinatal experiences, and 4) transpersonal experiences.[9]

Each of these four kinds of LSD experiences had an enormous influence on Jim and can be written about at length. But it's the transpersonal aspect of Jim's fun with LSD that further awakened the secret teacher within him. Transpersonal LSD experiences are defined by Grof as:

> experiences involving an expansion or extension of consciousness beyond the usual ego boundaries and beyond the limitations of time and/or space.[10]

> LSD sessions had the form of profound religious and mystical experiences, quite similar to those described in the holy scriptures of the great religions of the world and reported by saints, prophets, and religious teachers of all ages.[11]

Little wonder a person is said to be "peaking" when their LSD "trip" is at its greatest intensity as the experience is similar to Maslow's definition of peak experiences. Jim ingested gigantic amounts of LSD, once telling his bandmates before taking the stage on the night he first sang the famous Oedipal section in "The End" at the Whiskey à Go-Go that he was on 10,000 micrograms of LSD.[12] The average acid dose varies between 100 and 400 micrograms, providing a trip that can last anywhere from eight to eighteen hours.

According to Grof's research, Jim did take enough LSD to "break on through" to experience the supernatural presence of the invisible realms. This must've been for Jim at times a terrifying experience, part of his shaman's initiation.

> Transpersonal experiences occur only rarely in early sessions of psycholytic therapy; they become quite common in advanced sessions after the subject has worked through and integrated the material on the psychodynamic and perinatal levels.

> In yet other cases, the subject experiences a complete loss of his own identity and a complete identification with the consciousness of another being or entity.

> The second broad category of transpersonal experiences would then

involve phenomena that are not part of "objective reality" in the Western sense. This would apply to experiences such as communication with spirits of deceased human beings or with superhuman spiritual entities, encounters or identification with the various deities, archetypal experiences, and so on.[13]

Jim was experiencing a spiritual bolt of lightning. In *The Stormy Search for the Self,* Christina and Stanislav Grof write:

In some forms of spiritual emergency . . . people can feel consumed by strange and at times overpowering bursts of energy. They might feel pulsing electrical charges, uncontrollable tremors, or sensations of some unknown force streaming throughout their systems. Their heart rate may increase and their body temperature rise. Why does this happen? These manifestations are often a natural physiological accompaniment to abrupt changes in consciousness; they may also be specific characteristics of a certain form of spiritual emergency, such as the awakening of Kundalini.[14]

Other experiences involve a revelation of dimensions that one is not aware of in everyday life: they transcend time and space and are inhabited by celestial and mythological beings. These experiences are often accompanied by intense sensations of a potent spiritual force that floods the body. People perceive the mystical realms to be pervaded by a sacred or numinous essence and an unfathomable beauty, and they frequently see visions of precious gold, sparkling jewels, unearthly radiance, luminescence, and brilliant light.[15]

Aside from being "a vision of God as a radiant source of light," "the transcendent divine" can also be experienced as:

Visions of various archetypal beings, such as deities, demons, legendary heroes, and spirit guides . . . Other experiences do not involve merely individual suprahuman entities but entire mythological realms, such as heavens, hells, and purgatories, or various sceneries and landscapes unlike anything known on earth.[16]

In that year there was
an intense visitation
of energy.
I left school & went down to
the beach to live.
I slept on a roof.
At night the moon became
a woman's face.
I met the Spirit of Music.[17]

※

An appearance of the devil
on a Venice canal.
Running, I saw a Satan
or Satyr, moving beside
me, a fleshy shadow
of my secret mind. Running,
Knowing.[18]

16

The Call of the Wild

The shaman's essential role in the defense of the psychic integrity of the community depends above all on this: men are sure that one of them is able to help them in the critical circumstances produced by the inhabitants of the invisible world. It is consoling and comforting to know that a member of the community is able to see what is hidden and invisible to the rest.

—Mircea Eliade

Jim read twentieth-century mythologist and author Joseph Campbell's 1949 book *The Hero with A Thousand Faces* with great attention, wherein Campbell writes: "The two worlds, the divine and the human . . . are actually one . . . The realm of the gods is a forgotten dimension of the world we know"[1]

In Venice, Jim answered what Campbell refers to as "a call":

Like the hero of the monomyth, the person in a spiritual emergency receives a call. The subtle film that separates our everyday lives from the amazing world of our unconscious mind becomes transparent and finally breaks down. The deep contents of the psyche that we are ordinarily unaware of erupt into consciousness in the form of images, powerful emotions, and strange physical feelings. A dramatic visionary odyssey into the depths of the psyche has begun. Like the heroic stories that we know from mythology, it involves dark forces and terrifying monsters, dangers of all kinds, and encounters with supernatural beings as well as magical interventions. . . . In psychological terms, we can think of it as an emergence of elements from the deep unconscious, particularly from its archetypal levels, into everyday consciousness. If the hero responds to the invitation and accepts the challenge, he or she embarks on an adventure that involves visits to strange territories, encounters with fantastic animals and superhuman beings, and numerous ordeals. After the successful completion of the journey, the hero returns home and lives a full and rewarding life as a deified being—worldly leader, healer, seer, or spiritual teacher.[2]

Wilson writes in *The Occult*:

The shaman excites himself into a divine frenzy or ecstasy through drum beating and dancing, until he passes into a trance, when his spirit is supposed to have left his body. In his trance he makes the sounds of various birds and animals—he is supposed to be able to understand their language.[3]

Jim went into shamanic trances and ecstasies onstage, making all kinds of wild animal sounds while drummer John Densmore thrashed away on his drums to aid Jim in summoning the healing magic of the spirit world. Jim had now found his "why to live for," and with his powerful, cultivated mind, his strong sense of self and purpose, and his Olympian-like physical stamina, he was ready to "bear almost any how" in achieving his secret teacher's dangerous assignment.

> *Each generation wants new symbols, new people,*
> *new names. They want to divorce themselves from*
> *their predecessors.*[4]

Jim was taking his first steps along the hero's path. Bolen writes in *Gods in Everyman* that:

If he is to grow psychologically, the Dionysus man must leave behind his identification with the divine child and eternal adolescent and become the hero. Psychologist Erich Neumann in his classic description of the origin and growth of male consciousness writes of the need for the androgynous son-lover to become the hero. To do this, Neumann says that he must deliberately expose himself to the unconscious and the non-ego, which is the darkness, nothingness, the void, the bottomless pit, the underworld, the primordial womb of the Great Mother where the ego can dissolve into the unconscious and be devoured or overcome by irrational fears—the monsters and evils of the unconscious. The hero must endure the perils of the underworld and emerge with his ego intact and strengthened by the encounter.[5]

Bolen's definition is complemented by Eliade's view:

For, of course, the shaman is also a magician and medicine man; he is believed to cure like all doctors, and to perform miracles of the fakir type, like all magicians, whether primitive or modern. But beyond this, he is a psychopomp, and he may also be priest, mystic and poet." A "psychopomp" is a person who conducts spirits or souls to the other world, as Hermes or Charon.[6]

Eliade writes there is no relationship between the cult of Dionysus in Ancient Greece and shamanism. Though Bolen notes in *Gods in Everyman* the role of the shaman is connected to the Dionysian archetype, with it being a *trait* of Jim's Dionysian archetype to seek to intensify experiences with hallucinogens and alcohol. The Dionysian archetype is "drawn to whatever intensifies experience for him. Mood-altering or hallucinogenic drugs attracts him, as does music."[7] Eliade however, makes the point in *Shamanism* that taking drugs before shamanic ceremonies is a recent decadence and argues there is no relationship between the cult of Dionysus in ancient Greece and shamanism.[8]

Bolen further presents the North American shaman's life within the context of Jim's Dionysian archetype:

In the tribal society of the Native American, the shaman is very important as the mediator and intercessor between the invisible world and the physical world. The man who became a shaman was often marked from childhood as different from his boyhood peers. The shamanic psyche is very often that of an androgyne— a male-female, as Dionysus was described as "man-womanish," and called "the womanly one." Apparently psychological androgyne, the inward experience of both masculine and feminine perceptions, is a key to entering this realm. The shamanic vision is of nonordinary reality, the altered state of consciousness which Carlos Castaneda and Lynn Andrews write in their books about their own initiations by shamans or medicine women. In Jungian psychology, which values development of the feminine in men, the invisible world is the world of archetypes, dreams, and active imagination. Dionysus called women out of their ordinary lives to revel in nature and to rediscover an ecstatic element in themselves. Essentially, he initiated them into a shamanic experience. Dionysus the god was an initiate and priest of the Great Goddess.[9]

Add to this Eliade's observation in *Shamanism* that a person is usually "reluctant to become a shaman, and assumes his powers and follows the spirit's bidding only when he is told by other shamans that otherwise death will result."[10] It makes you wonder just what kind of a grip those Indian spirits had on Jim having been exposed to their influence at such a tender age—"A child is like a flower, his head is just floating in the breeze, man. I was just a kid."

> *In the séance, the shaman led. A sensuous panic,*
> *deliberately evoked through drugs, chants, dancing,*
> *hurls the shaman into trance. Changed voice,*
> *convulsive movement.*
> *He acts like a madman. These professional hysterics,*
> *chosen precisely for their psychotic leaning,*
> *were once esteemed.*
> *They mediated between man and spirit world.*
> *Their mental travels formed the religious life*
> *of the tribe.*[11]

✳

The shamanic found expression in Jim's lyrics and poetry in part by way of what is known in the occult world as *correspondences*. Conway writes in *Magic: An Occult Primer*:

> In magic the underlying similarity between things is systematized by identifying correspondences between them. From time immemorial magicians have sought to establish the natural affinity that exists between certain planets, metals, jewels, birds, beasts, herbs, colors, flowers and scents.[12]

Jim was aware of this in *The Lords: Notes on Vision*:

> *Strange, fertile correspondences the alchemists*
> *sensed in unlikely orders of being.*
> *Between men and planets,*
> *plants and gestures,*
> *words and weather.*[13]

Correspondence is associated with another nineteenth-century French Symbolist poet, one of Jim's favorites, Charles Baudelaire. In reference to Baudelaire's famous poem "Correspondences," Lachman writes that *correspondences* are: "the recognition that there are direct links between the heavenly and earthly worlds and that the phenomena of the physical world are a kind of symbol or 'alphabet' of the higher ones."[14]

Speak in secret alphabets[15]

Baudelaire's influence on Jim and modern literature, in general, is profound. Fowlie writes in *Poem & Symbol*:

> It is impossible to estimate how much Baudelaire's so-called morbidity and taste for extracting beauty from unusual experiences developed because of his hatred for the world in which he lived. The wide range of themes in contemporary poetry, extending from the classical theme of Gregory Corso's poem *Uccello* to the lyrics of Bob

Dylan and Jim Morrison, is owed in some degree to Baudelaire's example.[16]

In Baudelaire, Jim found a poet attracted to the strange and macabre just as much as surrealist painter Kurt Seligmann was:

The word associated with Baudelaire in the new aesthetic credo was *bizarre*. In announcing in his salon of 1855 that "le beau est toujours bizarre" ("beauty is always strange"), he indicated that the artist's attraction to the strange is an element of his personality and separates him from most men, who submit easily to the conventional and the traditional, who prefer not to be startled by originality. Those impulses that manifest themselves in the subconscious—fantasies, hallucinations, and sentiments of fear—and which in most men are not allowed to develop represent the sources of experiences in man's moral and physical life. The artist, for Baudelaire, feels a desire to know and explore such fantasies that border on dreams and nightmares.[17]

Figure 16.1.
Charles Baudelaire, 1856.
Photographer: Félix Nadar.

Lachman highlights Baudelaire's poem "Correspondences" as an example of how Swedenborg's *correspondence* is applied:

> to the haunting, elusive resonances that link colors, scents, shapes and sounds. "Nature is a temple," Baudelaire tells us, "through which we pass symbolically." . . . The effect is a sense of "the strange expansion of things infinite," "the question that things are something more than they seem, that some mystery envelopes them, an aura of possibility, the analogical way of seeing the world that we have seen is linked to a right-brain mode of consciousness. Swedenborg believed that in an earlier time the truth of correspondences was common knowledge, but that we have lost it because of our self-obsession, which suggests something like the loss of our more right-brain mode of consciousness.[18]

Bringing "the truth of correspondences" back into "common knowledge" is a big part of the fast-approaching integral stage of consciousness. Perhaps one big reason why Jim loved tripping on LSD is that it heightened his secret teacher's sensitivity to this "strange expansion of things infinite." Twentieth-century American beat poet Allen Ginsberg noted "LSD shows you more of what isn't there."[19]

Lachman writes that correspondences also ignite an excited curiosity with synesthesia:

> the strange condition in which sensory modes blend, in which one hears colors and sees sounds, which suggests a *unity* behind phenomena. Perhaps the best-known example of this is from Arthur Rimbaud's poem "Vowels," which ascribes different colors to the letters: A, black; E, white; I, red; O, blue; and U, green." Such associations harken back to the Kabbalistic notion of an *Adamic language* (Boehme), a primal speech in which the unity between speaker and world is undefiled. The art movement that emerged from this, Symbolism, was responsible for some of the most important works of the late nineteenth century, from the operas of Richard Wagner to the paintings of Gustave Moreau and Odilon Redon—both of whom were occult enthusiasts—and the intensely Hermetic poetry

of Stephane Mallarme. Along with the modernism that followed, Symbolism was saturated in occult, Hermetic and esoteric ideals. It showed that the world was not the mechanical clockwork of the materialist scientist, but a forest of question marks, each suggesting some possible answer to the riddle of life.[20]

This Adamic language is in the same occult neighborhood as the "angelic conversations" out of which secret teacher John Dee with his scrying partner Edward Kelley transcribed the Enochian language "designed to express the primal essence of things." Dee described the language in his diaries as "Angelical," the "Celestial Speech," the "Language of Angels," the "First Language of God-Christ" the "Holy Language" or "Adamical" as it was, according to Dee's Angels, used by Adam in Paradise to name all things, the original spoken language before the Fall. The term "Enochian" is from Dee's assertion that the Biblical Enoch had been the last human being to understand the language. The Enochian language is to be spoken from the abdomen as it is "a barbarous, rich-sounding language."[21]

Jim didn't have formal vocal training, but he understood how to sing from the gut. Lisciandro described Jim's grunts and terrifying screams onstage as "coming from another world"[22] that expressed "the primal essence of things." A big reason why Jim got into rock music in the first place was to make us aware again of what Wilson stated in *The Occult*, that: "Primitive man believed the world was full of unseen forces: the orenda (spirit force) of the American Indians, the huaca of the ancient Peruvians."

The spirit of Madimi commanded Dee and Kelly to swap wives, an unthinkable act for those times, to which in return Madimi would reveal to them the secrets of the universe. (Madimi went silent afterward and the angelic conversations stopped.)[23] Dee and Kelly carried out Madimi's request. The Oedipal section in "The End" was perhaps Jim's spiritual agreement, so to speak, to take as deep a dive as possible into the *meaning universe*. In *The Birth of Tragedy*, Nietzsche writes:

There is an ancient folk belief, particularly prevalent in Persia, that a wise magus can only be born from incest: our immediate interpretation of this, with reference to Oedipus the riddle-solver and suiter of his own mother, is that for clairvoyant and magical powers to have broken the spell of the present and the future, the rigid law of individuation and the true magic of nature itself, the cause must have been a monstrous crime against nature—incest in this case; for how could nature be forced to offer up her secrets if not by being triumphantly resisted—by unnatural acts?[24]

> *Fuck the mother,*
> *kill the father,*
> *fuck the mother,*
> *kill the father,*
> *fuck the mother,*
> *kill the father*[25]

This visceral and even approach to language and communication is referenced in a number of works. Jim pays homage to this Adamic language on The Doors song "The WASP (Texas Radio & The Big Beat)." Twentieth-century French actor, poet, and playwright Antonin Artaud stated in his book *Here Lies*: "All true language is incomprehensible." Twentieth-century author and literary critic Susan Sontag notes in the introduction to her 1988 book *Antonin Artaud: Selected Writings* that: "The unintelligible parts of Artaud's late writings are supposed to remain obscure—to be directly apprehended as sound."[26] Kerouac had a similar approach to this profound expression of the *incomprehensible* in his fiction, stating in his journals: "It's not the words that count but the rush of truth which uses words for its purposes."[27]

> *Comes out of the Virginia swamps*
> *Cool and slow, with plenty of*
> *precision*
> *And a backbeat narrow and hard*
> *to master.*
> *Some call it heavenly in its*
> *brilliance*
> *Others, mean and rueful of the*

Western dream.
. . . Soft driven, slow and mad like some new language.[28]

Jim finds "the unintelligible" in the Texas blues spirit coming over the radio soft, mysterious, and beautiful yet with a reptilian, threatening origin. Jim makes the distinction here between an openness to the eternal beauty of the ancient and primitive compared to those who view it as threatening to the materialist, left-brain-driven Western dream. The struggle for the Western esoteric tradition's secret teachers has always been against the lies of ordinary consciousness and its hostility towards the infinite that is "heavenly in its brilliance."

Jim was quite conscious of his affinity with reptiles. He once recalled reading a book on snakes and lizards that influenced him: "It struck me acutely—reptiles are the interesting descendants of magnificent ancestors."[29] In addition, Jim said:

> There's something deep in human memory that responds strongly to snakes . . . that the lizard and the snake are identified with the unconscious and the forces of evil.[30]

> [Jim saw] "the universe as a mammoth snake, and all the people and objects, landscapes, as little pictures in the facets of their scales. I think peristaltic motion is the basic life movement."[31]

The animal world is present throughout Jim's lyrics and poems as correspondence with the invisible realms. From Jim's asking us to "Ride the snake to the ancient lake" in to his poem "The Celebration of the Lizard," the poetic, LSD-inspired language Jim creates to describe these reptilian "correspondences" evoke like Baudelaire's poem those "haunting, elusive resonances that link colors, scents, shapes and sounds."

Jim's identification with reptiles can also be attributed to the transpersonal nature of his LSD experiences. Grof writes that phylogenetic (evolutionary) experiences involve:

> a complete and quite realistic identification with animals on various levels of phylogenetic development. As in the case of ancestral expe-

riences, it is accompanied by a sense of regression in historical time; the subject has a very vivid and convincing feeling that the animal specimens that he identifies with are part of phylogenetic history and that he is exploring the evolution of the species in nature. The objects of identification are most frequently other mammals, birds, reptiles, amphibians, and various species of fish.[32]

In *The History of Magic & the Occult*, Seligmann writes:

About two thousand years before our era, a reform took place: a caste of priests was founded in whom all occult knowledge was concentrated . . . Trees spoke to them, as did serpents, "wisest of all animals."[33]

Some sects of Gnosticism . . . worshipped the serpent of paradise who had planted in man's heart the yearning for knowledge. This snake, the Ouroboros, became an alchemical emblem. It is found in Cleopatra's book on gold-making, the *Chrysopeia*. The serpent's body, divided between light and dark, signified to the adept that in the material world good and bad, perfection and imperfection, are bound together in matter. For matter is One, are as the alchemists used to say: "One is All." In Cleopatra's book, this axiom is encircled by the Ouroboros. In the three concentric circles in the upper left, a mysterious text elaborates this idea: "One is All, by him is all, and for him is all, and in him is all. The Serpent is one; he has the two symbols (good and bad) . . . The evil serpent of paradise was transformed by the Gnostics into the beneficent Ouroboros."[34]

> The Universe, one line, is a
> long snake, & we each are
> facets on its jeweled skin.
> It moves inexorably, slowly
> winding peristaltic intestinal
> phallic orgasmic ass-wriggling
> slow.[35]

The Lizard King persona Jim created by wearing tight black leather pants both on and offstage is also a preference attributed to his Dionysian archetype. Bolen writes in *Gods in Everyman*:

> To invite Dionysus to be present may require getting out of one's usual environment, out of one's usual clothes, out of one's habitual persona or roles: Dionysus's gift of the vine, music that moves the dancer into a spontaneous sensuality, a Mardi Gras or masked fantasy ball—anything that loosens the hold of the mind and the grip of time helps bring Dionysus closer.[36]

Wilson writes in *The Occult* that: "Serpents symbolize wisdom, also coldness and deadliness."[37]

> *He's old*
> *And his skin is cold*[38]

17
And We're on Our Way

To live is the rarest thing in the world. Most people exist,
that is all.

—OSCAR WILDE

Jim's "magical kingdom," rich from his wide, intense reading and journaling of the preceding eight years began exploding into song and poetry. His poetic talents and dark, voyeuristic imagination, now fusing with his LSD-drenched perceptions in deep connection with the invisible realms collaborated to express what was in Jim that was: "never said yet—a thing that is not love or hate or pity or scorn, but the very breath of life, fierce and coming from far away, bringing into human life the vastness and fearful passionless force of non-human things."[1] The height of Jim's generosity was in allowing us to have a fun time participating in his strangely numinous magical kingdom.

However, The Commander was not at all supportive of Jim's rock music ambitions. In a letter written by George Morrison during Jim's criminal trial, an attempt by Jim's father to disabuse any negative view of Jim, The Commander noted he had not seen Jim since 1965. He writes:

We have had very little contact with him since that time, due partly to physical separation and partly because of some criticisms from me. While in London, I was called by an old friend in California who had been approached by Jim for a loan to finance his first record. Concerned by his appearance, particularly his long hair, the friend called me. I, in turn, wrote Jim a letter severely criticizing his behavior and strongly advising him to give up any idea of singing or any connection with a musical group because of what I considered to be a complete lack of talent in this direction. His reluctance to communicate with me again is to me quite understandable.[2]

Bolen writes that: "Lack of paternal approval is a common experience for a Dionysus boy, who by being himself never seems to please his father."[3]

The intense nature of Jim's rebellion can also be understood in esoteric terms through a bit of astrology. Yes, Jim can be heard on *An American Prayer* telling the audience that astrology is just "a bunch of bullshit." But Jim kept a copy of *The History of Magic & the Occult* for years, so this was strange for Jim to say.

Jim's north node sign was in Leo. Living life from the intention that the north node sign instructs is how a person finds fulfillment, though it's not at all easy. Those with their north node in Leo are called to be out in the spotlight with their individuality and creative expression. Jim's south node was in Aquarius. The south node is considered "the comfort zone," and if a person falls into the trap of their south node, they can lead a more predictable, comfortable life, though not fulfilling. There are many who fall for this safety net, and they may seem successful and content on the outside, but are often angry, critical, bitter, isolated, unhappy, and, of course, ultimately unfulfilled. Jim's Aquarius south node has much to do with being a team player and conformity. It's associated with professions in uniform, such as policemen, firemen, and the military. You can see where this is going. Even though Jim might've enjoyed great success if he'd followed in his father's footsteps, perhaps later even becoming a high ranking politician—quite possible given Jim's great charisma, intelligence, gregariousness, and social status—this would've been, for Jim, the safe, comfortable path.

Jim showed no interest in a military career while growing up, as his father stated, though Jim might've given serious thought to becoming a naval officer. Who wouldn't? There it was all laid out for Jim by his powerful and successful father, as Philip II had done for Alexander the Great. But in doing so, Jim would've had to exert a lot of energy to contain his Dionysian tendencies and traits. Bolen writes in *Gods in Everyman*:

> A Dionysian man is usually out of step with his fellows. He's not at home in the locker room or the board room because male relationships in these settings are so impersonal and goal oriented. He is too much of an individual to be a team player, too little interested in competition, and too unconforming to manage to be "one of the guys."[4]

To Jim's enormous credit, he followed his gut feeling that a naval career wouldn't be right for him, that this would be selling himself out to the sure and safe *Sky Father*'s path. Military life would've been for Jim a living death, spiritual suicide. That partial amnesia Jim wanted to escape would've become total amnesia.

Instead, in the summer of 1965, Jim unwittingly aligned his secret teacher's dangerous assignment with his Leo north node. This is part of what makes Jim a heroic person. Bolen writes in *Gods in Everyman*:

> All men and women in patriarchal cultures face the same temptations: Will they identify with the aggressors and join them? Moments of truth and times of decision continually arise, when the survival of a Luke Skywalker—or his feminine counterpart, Princess Leia—is at stake in us. As long as we live, life is a never-ending story that presents us with these moments of choice.[5]

Jim once accompanied The Commander aboard his first aircraft carrier command, the USS *Bonhomme Richard*.

> On January 8, 1964, shortly before leaving his family in Coronado to begin classes at UCLA, Jim joined his father on maneuvers in the Pacific—his hair freshly cut. Unfortunately, it wasn't cut short enough to please, and when Jim arrived at the "Bonny Dick," as the carrier was called, he was rushed to the ship's barber for another trim, this one exactly like the captain's own: clipper short on the back and sides, just long enough on top to part. Jim was angry, but silent.

The captain was proud but wary. He took Jim to the bridge and introduced him to the officers. Jim shook hands and acknowledged the introductions graciously, without smiling. An official navy photographer took some pictures. Later in the day some humanlike targets were tossed overboard, and Jim was given a machine gun and offered the opportunity to shoot at the objects bobbing in the ocean below.[6]

There's a photograph of Jim in *No One Here Gets Out Alive* standing beside his father on the bridge, and another of Jim aiming the weapon out to sea that he was given to fire. What was Jim thinking while standing beside his father? What were Jim's thoughts while firing that weapon? What was he thinking that night as he lay in bed going over the day's events in his mind?

Ray once asked Jim if The Commander was hard on him. Jim's responded, "Fuck yes, he was."[7] Again, think of the world of the *Top Gun* films; the navy was *not* Jim's world. By the summer of 1965, Jim's need to break away from anything having to do with his parents, authority, and conformity in uniform had become *super powerful*.

> *I'm interested in anything about revolt, disorder, chaos,*
> *especially activity that seems to have no meaning.*
> *It seems to me to be the royal road toward freedom.*[8]

Jim's need to leave the familiar, the comfortable, the conforming, and the stifling—for the sake of his now rapid spiritual awakening—packed the power of those mighty Saturn V rockets used in the late nineteen-sixties by NASA to propel Americans out of the atmosphere, into space, and to the moon.

Perhaps what is strangest of all about Jim's life is that the magnitude of both his rebellion and his intense occult/spiritual awakening were so great they came to mirror the popular occult/spiritual awakening that was breaking loose across the West. Everyone attracted to Jim's "new, alien and *other*" presence, voice, and lyrics felt Jim embodied their rebellious impulses, thoughts, feelings, and spiritually emergent lives.

> *We want the world and we want it,*
> *now*
> *Now? NOW!*[9]

Jim made a clean break with his parents to have total freedom to become himself. It's with good reason Jim repeats the phrase "Learn to forget" four times in "Soul Kitchen," with a self-soothing, healing gentleness. Bolen writes in *Gods in Everyman* that: "For men, life is a series of separations and disidentifications, beginning with mother, whom they must leave and whom they must not be like."[10]

> *Mother?*
> *I want to . . .*[11]

Eliade writes in *Shamanism* that "The shaman begins his new, his true life by a 'separation'—by a spiritual crisis that is not lacking in tragic greatness and in beauty."[12] At last, it was time for Jim the secret teacher poet to both go his way and to go all the way with his creative, mystical impulse.

> *Give me songs*
> *To sing*
> *And emerald dreams*
> *To dream*
> *And I'll give you love*
> *Unfolding*[13]

☀

Jim faced one last challenge in his transition from college student to secret teacher-rock-star-poet-shaman. The immediate threat the draft posed to his freedom. Jim had passed his physical exam with the army and lost his student deferment. The army classified him 1-A.

This terrified Jim. Military conscription is a nightmare scenario for any freedom-loving, creative Sagittarius. Scenes of the sensitive, bookish Lawrence becoming a cold-blooded killer in *Lawrence of Arabia* may have also popped into Jim's mind. Lawrence had confessed to General Allenby that he enjoyed executing Gasim. It's a mindset Jim understood.

> *The sniper's rifle is an extension of his eye*
> *He kills with injurious vision*[14]
>
> *Modern circles of Hell: (?) kills President.*
> *Oswald enters taxi. Oswald stops at rooming house.*
> *Oswald leaves taxi. Oswald kills Officer Tippitt.*
> *Oswald sheds jacket. Oswald is captured.*
> *He escaped into a movie house.*[15]

Becoming an actual killer is not what Jim had in mind for himself. So, Jim lied to the army, declaring he was still enrolled at UCLA. He then went to the registrar's office to enroll himself in courses he never took. Later, John Densmore drove Jim to his physical. Jim had consumed a variety of drugs beforehand. It was July 14th, 1966, Bastille Day in France. Jim told them at the induction center he was a homosexual and that they'd be "the sorriest motherfuckers on earth"[16] if they took him. Jim was rejected.

Jim then did what indie rock singer-songwriter Chan Marshall, better known by her stage name Cat Power, stated in an interview she tells herself when she wants to get out of a pickle: "Well, you take your one foot and you put it in front of your other foot, and then you go forward into your fucking future."

> *The time to hesitate is through*[17]

V

This Ancient &
Insane Theater

18
Paradise Now

*I call for actors burning at the stakes, laughing at the
flames.*

—Antonin Artaud

Jim had been "testing the bounds of reality" with The Doors during their live performances ever since the band's Whiskey à Go-Go
days. But when The Living Theatre came to Los Angeles, Jim found the
inspiration to test the limits even further.

Jim saw The Living Theater's production of *Paradise Now* performed
at USC in February 1969 just days before the Miami concert. He went
to a week's worth of performances and bought front-row seats for himself and his friends. At the time, Jim was feeling the pressure to remain
fresh and creative with The Doors. Jim told composer-in-residence at
the New York Philharmonic, Fred Myrow, that: "If I don't find a new
way to develop creatively within a year, I'll be good for nothing but
nostalgia."[1]

Jim was also figuring out a new approach to performing in arenas.
The Doors were no longer playing smaller venues within America's hip
underground music scene. Most of their audiences were now made up
of American teenagers out to party and get off on Jim's stage antics. Jim
told his sister Anne that he felt he had to put on a show as ticket prices
weren't cheap. Even though Jim gave them their money's worth, the kids
didn't care to listen to Jim's poems when he recited them.

Mick Jagger came to Los Angeles to attend The Doors' July 5th,
1968, debut performance at the Hollywood Bowl. He was looking
for some pointers from Jim on how to entertain a large crowd as The

Rolling Stones were preparing for their first arena tour and wanted to learn whatever he could from Jim.

The audience that night felt let down. Jim's performance, though a good one, was low-key, not what the audience was expecting or wanted. Even though Jagger thought the show was a failure and felt he'd seen everything not to do, he was a gentleman in expressing how he felt, stating "[The Doors] are nice chaps, but they [went on] a bit too long." Krieger told Densmore that Jim took acid before the show. "GODDAMN IT!" Densmore responded as he flung his drumsticks on the floor.[2]

> *I see myself as an intelligent, sensitive human, with the soul of a clown which forces me to blow it at the most important moments.*[3]

The madness that Horatio warns Hamlet may come to him in his pursuit of the Ghost was now beginning to erupt with a fury in Jim's life. But experiencing madness both on and offstage was part of Jim's spiritual awakening and shamanic calling. The Ghost scene in *Hamlet* is an inversion of the crucifixion story in the New Testament; the "Good Thief," Dismas, alive in this world, asks the dying Christ crucified along with him, "Remember me when you come into your kingdom," Dismas's request for mercy. For Hamlet, the Ghost held an intention not to remember him out of pity but to avenge his murder, to show no mercy for his killers. The Ghost knew Hamlet would respond with an insatiable drive for vengeance, one in which Hamlet nearly goes mad. For Jim, the spirits of those dying native workers had jumped into his three-year-old soul *no questions asked.* Jim's increasingly strange behavior from his high school years and into his time with The Doors was a sure sign of the madness that these indwelling spirits were pushing him into without mercy, as Jim said he drank to deal with their demanding voices in his mind.

Christina and Stanislav Grof write in *The Stormy Search for the Self*:

Certain spiritual traditions offer an alternative view of this kind of "madness." "Holy madness" or "divine madness" is known and acknowledged by various spiritual traditions and is distinguished from ordinary insanity; it is seen as a form of intoxication by the Divine that brings extraordinary abilities and spiritual instruction. In traditions such as Sufism and the Native American culture, sacred figures recognized as fools or buffoons are known to embody the state. Revered seers, mystics, and prophets are often described as inspired by madness.

Divine madness is described by the Greek philosopher Plato as a gift from the gods: 'The greatest blessings come by way of madness, indeed of madness that is heaven-sent. It is when they were mad that the prophetess at Delphi and the priestess at Dodona achieved so much for which the states and individuals in Greece are thankful; when sane, they did little or nothing. . . . madness [is] a divine gift, when due to divine dispensation.[4]

Twentieth-century Scottish psychologist R.D. Laing in his 1967 book *The Politics of Experience and The Bird of Paradise* states madness can also be described as altered states of consciousness.

Transcendental experiences *sometimes* break through in psychosis, to those experiences of the divine that are the living fount of all religion.

Madness need not be all breakdown. It may also be break-through.

The person going through ego-loss or transcendental experiences may or may not become in different ways confused. Then he might be legitimately regarded as mad. But to be mad is not necessarily to be ill, notwithstanding that in our culture the two categories have become confused. It is assumed that if a person is mad (whatever that means) then *ipso facto* he is ill (whatever that means). The experience that a person may be absorbed in while to others he appears simply ill-mad, may for him be veritable manna from heaven. The person's whole life may be changed, but it is difficult not to doubt the validity of such a vision. Also not everyone comes back to us again.[5]

Bolen writes in *Gods in Everyman*:

To be a man with a shamanic personality in a culture that emphasizes "getting ahead in the real world," is to be out of step.

The adolescent religious mystic who has an ecstatic vision of the Madonna feels as unacceptable as the taker of hallucinogenic drugs. Both—like Dionysus—also seem to others, to be courting madness.[6]

> *Once I had a little game*
> *I liked to crawl back in my brain*
> *I think you know the game I mean*
> *I mean the game called 'go insane'*[7]

Laing's statement here from *The Politics of Experience* brings us to the heart of who Jim was and what he wanted to do for us as an artist:

Sanity today appears to rest very largely on a capacity to adapt to the external world—the interpersonal world, and the realm of human collectives. As this external world is almost completely and totally estranged from the inner, any personal direct awareness of the inner world have already grave risks. But since society, without knowing it, is starving for the inner, the demands on people to evoke its presence in a "safe" way, in a way that need not be taken seriously, etc. is tremendous—while the ambivalence is equally intense. Small wonder that the list of artists, in say the last 150 years, who have become shipwrecked on these reefs is so long—Hölderlin, John Clare, Rimbaud, Van Gogh, Nietzsche, Antonin Artaud.[8]

> *It takes large murder to turn rocks in the shade*
> *and expose strange worms beneath. The lives of*
> *our discontented madmen are revealed.*[9]

> *Artaud—that brave man's*
> *effort to escape the collective*
> *conscience & drive cannibals*
> *down Main Street. These*
> *heroic madmen, doom'd to*
> *failure & bad teeth*[10]

If Hamlet learned there are more things in heaven and earth than are dreamt of in anyone's philosophy, then Artaud is the one artist who sought to prove Nietzsche correct, that: "There is more wisdom in your body than in your deepest philosophy."[11] It was during Jim's time at FSU while acting in his first play that he discovered Artaud.

> Jim's director, Sam Kilman, introduced him to the writing of Antonin Artaud, who wrote his cry for revolution in the theater from insane asylums during the 1930s and 1940s: "We must recognize that the theater, like the plague, is a delirium and is communicative; that is the secret of its fascination." Jim loved it.
>
> "Jim was interesting to work with," says Keith Carlson, the actor who played opposite him in *The Dumbwaiter*. "Every night waiting for the curtain to go up, I had no idea what he was going to do. He was difficult to key on, because he tended to play the role very differently all the time. He wasn't keying on me, or on the dialogue, or on any of the traditional things. He played scenes and delivered lines with an inflection that seemed totally unmotivated, or at least unexpected. There was a constant undercurrent of apprehension, a feeling that things were on the brink of lost control.
>
> Back in those days [in 1963], everyone was uptight about any obscenity on stage but we had some wonderfully obscene rehearsals. There was no obscenity during any of the performances, but with Jim, we just never knew."[12]

Krieger felt Jim's unpredictability was a great asset to The Doors:

> You didn't know what he was going to do next onstage, just like you didn't know what he was going to do next in real life, and you were always on the edge of your seat waiting to find out. Even if you were in the same band with him. It may have occasionally made him a challenge to deal with, and it may have made the practicalities of planning a career more difficult, but it drew you in. It couldn't have been simpler, and yet it couldn't have been more powerful. And it's why he's still drawing people in to this day.[13]

Jim's vision of "an ancient and insane theater" was inspired by Artaud's theater as:

a rite of transformation—the communal performance of a violent act of spiritual alchemy. Artaud summons the theater to renounce "psychological man with his well-dissected character and feelings . . . and social man, submissive to laws and misshapen by religions and precepts," and to address itself only "to total man"—a thoroughly Gnostic notion. . . .

The mark of Gnostic thinking is that it is enraged by all limits, even those that save.

"All true freedom is dark," Artaud [writes] in *The Theater & Its Double*, "and is infallibly identified with sexual freedom, which is also dark, although we do not know precisely why."

Both the obstacle to and the locus of freedom, for Artaud, lie in the body. His attitude covers the familiar Gnostic thematic range: the affirmation of the body, the revulsion from the body, the wish to transcend the body, the quest for the redeemed body.

"Nothing touches me, nothing interests me," [Artaud] writes, "except what addresses itself directly to my flesh." . . . There is a mind in the flesh, a mind quick as lightning."[14]

Bolen writes in *Gods in Everyman*:

When Dionysus is a strong archetype, that man is embodied—that is, he reacts with his body, which is for him a sensory organ, and he feels emotions in his body. Being totally in his body when he dances or makes love is the positive expression of this embodiment.[15]

Bloom notes:

Richard Lanham, rhetorically more than aware that Shakespeare is "writing a play about the kind of play he is writing," brilliantly echoes Hamlet: "Human flesh is sullied with self-consciousness, with theatricality."[16]

It's fifty percent physical,
the records are like only half of it.[17]

The body tries to tell the truth. But, it's usually too battered
with rules to be heard, and bound with pretenses so it can
hardly move.[18]

Jim found Artaud's erotic sense of freedom in The Living Theater and their most popular play, *Paradise Now.* The Living Theater adopted the artistic aims of Artaud's Theater of Cruelty, a radical departure from the traditional Western theater in which the artist overwhelms the audience's senses. The audience is pushed into the middle of the play and made to engage with the performance on a gut level. The audience was to be "shocked" out of their complacency, an idea which fit in well with Jim's intent to wake us up from that partial amnesia. For Artaud, this was a form of "cruelty" that needed to be inflicted upon the audience.

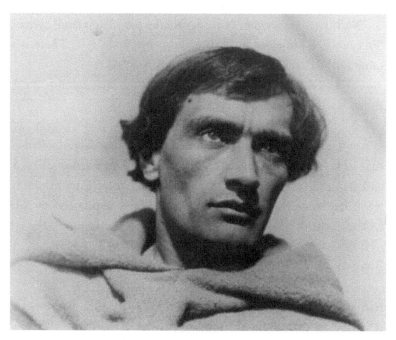

Figure 18.1. Antonin Artaud in *The Passion of Joan of Arc*, 1928.
Director: Carl Dreyer.

Artaud's theater is a strenuous machine for transforming the mind's conceptions into entirely "material" events, among which are the passions themselves. Against the centuries-old priority that the European theater has given to words as the means for conveying emotions and ideas, Artaud wants to show the organic basis of emotions and physicality of ideas—in the bodies of the actors.[19]

The Living Theater took Artaud's artistic vision to a new level with *Paradise Now*. A semi-improvisational piece involving audience participation, *Paradise Now* was notorious for a scene in which the actors recited a list of social taboos that included nudity while disrobing, which led to multiple indecent exposure arrests during performances.

> *I rely on images of violence, which bring the shock of pain, to penetrate the barriers people erect and defend, not simple defenses; the phony facades people leave behind. Blocking their perceptions from coming in, and blocking their feelings from coming out. There are two ways I try to shatter those facades, or at least make a hole where something can get in, to let the trapped feelings out—one way is violence, pain. The other is eroticism.[20]*

Jim once described The Doors as "erotic politicians" campaigning for complete artistic freedom. In a television interview in August 1970 at the Dade County Courthouse in Miami, Jim stated:

JIM: I think, uh, that nudity, [it's] really a cyclical phenomenon. [I think] it comes, it gets very liberal and extreme and it goes back and reacts the other way, and just seems to be a cycle in entertainment.

REPORTER: In other words, you feel the same liberalism performed in the theater—in acting—should be also generated in music?

JIM: Well in the realm of art and theater, I do think that uh that there should be complete freedom for the artist and performer . . . Uh, I'm not personally convinced, uh, nudity is always, you know, always a necessary part of a play or a film but the artist should feel free to use it [if he feels like it].[21]

Jim realized Artaud's theatrical vision into a Bosch-like Adamite scene not ever to be forgotten on March 1, 1969. This night saw Jim as the *Lawrence of Arabia* of rock, "testing the bounds of reality" to their fullest. This was the Jim who walked high ledges, took running jumps off fourth-floor hotel room balconies, and allowed strangers to toss all kinds of unknown pills into his mouth at parties. Perhaps Jim got drunk at the airport in New Orleans to loosen himself up, to push it in a city he knew was ultra-conservative. Just flirting with exposing himself while drunk onstage, (which Jim did) would be dangerous, not just to The Doors' career as a band but to Jim's freedom.

Jim was present when the police showed up at the end of one of the *Paradise Now* shows. He knew what could happen, but well, Jim just wouldn't have been Jim if he didn't push it. So, it became one of those nights that saw Jim's Dionysian archetype unfold in all of its dark glory and insanity.

Dionysus was known as the god who was mad and the god who drove his followers insane. He sent the mind reeling. When he suddenly appeared, his Maenads were transported into ecstasy and rapture, frenzied dancing and raging fury. Something Dionysian happens at rock concerts, especially when the star suddenly appears on stage, and the audience goes mad. There is the frenzy, the drugs, the dancing, and on faces in the audience, expressions of ecstasy and rapture.[22]

Dionysus (known to the Romans as Bacchus) was God of Wine [and] the god of ecstasy and terror, of wildness and the most blessed deliverance.[23]

Jim "the most blessed deliverance" showed up late and drunk after missing a flight to Miami out of New Orleans. Smashed, Jim interrupted songs with screaming fits meant to provoke the audience as The Living Theater did with *Paradise Now*. "I wanna see some action out there!" Jim got many in the audience to strip down to almost nothing. They went nuts when Jim began teasing them that he was going to pull out his cock.

You've come to see a show, a spectacle like you've never seen
before, something to blow your minds, haven't you? Well, I'm
going to show you something. How about if I pull out my cock?
Will that do it for you? Would you like to see me pull out my
dick and shake it around? How about that? [24]

The audience roared their approval back at Jim.

It's not surprising it all came down to Jim's "stable friend" as he refers to his cock in one of his poems in *An American Prayer*, "Lament."

Expression of an innate, intense sexuality is an essential issue for Dionysus. A Dionysian man may be heterosexual, homosexual or bisexual. Whether he is a wildly promiscuous rock musician or a celibate priest, sexuality is a forefront concern. Naturally sensual, his erotic nature is easily evoked. He may put as much of his considerable psychic energy into the sexual realm, as another man might put into his career. [25]

Jim's voyeuristic, Adamite side can be traced back to his early high school days in Alameda.

Many of Jim's afternoons are spent at Fud's, writing dozens of wildly scatological and sexually explicit radio commercials about the problems of "butt-picking and masturbation." . . . [One drawing] showed a man with a Coca-Cola bottle for a penis, a mean looking can opener for testicles, one hand held out and dripping with slime, more of the slime hanging from his anus. [Another] showed a man with an erect penis the size of a baseball bat, a small boy kneeling in front holding on, licking his pointed teeth in anticipation. Jim made hundreds of these drawings. [26]

Lament for my cock
Sore and crucified
I seek to know you
Acquiring soulful wisdom
You can open walls of mystery
Strip show [27]

The scene Jim created that night in Miami can also be understood through what Wilson writes about the black mass depicted in French author J.K. Huysmans's 1891 novel *Là-bas*. It all comes back to Jim's secret teacher's aim to wake us up out of our partial amnesia:

> What comes out so clearly in the description of the black mass is the desire of the participants to *shock themselves* out of their normal state of dullness. One of the most curious features of all such ceremonies—witch's sabbaths and so on—is the emphasis on ordure and dirt. In Huysmans, it becomes clear that the whole thing, far from being horrifying and sinister, is merely an expression of bourgeois frustrations. Parents demand that children keep clean, therefore it gives a sense of wickedness to wallow in dirt. The "blasphemies" sound is completely harmless to anyone who is not a Catholic and who does not accept that disbelief in the divinity of Christ involved eternal damnation. The convulsions are intended to afford the same kind of relief as pornography. I have commented earlier on the element of deliberate nastiness that some pornographers throw in as a final touch of naughtiness; this is also present in Huysmans's mass: "Another [woman], sprawling on her back, undid her skirts, revealing a huge and distended paunch; then her face twisted into a horrible grimace, and her tongue, which she could not control, stuck out, bitten at the edges, harrowed by red teeth, from a bloody mouth." The Devil's realm is supposed to be ugliness. But the reader can sense an element of self-contradiction in Huysmans's account. So much ugliness and unpleasantness can hardly make the mass sound wicked, for who would want to witness anything so nauseating? So, he takes care to mention that there are attractive women present, "Junonian brunettes," even a young girl. And in so doing, he reveals the paradoxical absurdity of Satanism. The element that makes the black mass attractive is perfectly normal, healthy, pagan sex. The driving force behind it is the sexual repression that is inevitable in all civilizations, where leisure gives everyone time to daydream about sex. The ugly crones with bitten tongues are an attempt to disguise this truth. A mere twenty years after *Là Bas*, D.H. Lawrence was undermining the whole foundation of

this kind of infantile diabolism by emphasizing that sex is a liberating activity; the penis "is the rod that connects man to the stars." After sexual intercourse, a healthy couple should experience something of the "oceanic feeling" that characterizes mysticism, and this oceanic feeling is an intuition of the godlike, not the demonic. If Huysmans's diabolists had possessed any powers of self-observation, they would have noted that they experienced a sense of release, of "cosmic consciousness," after their orgy and that this is inconsistent with their professions of diabolism. Diabolism is an artificial antithesis, conjured into existence by bigotry and frustration—not a genuine expression of man's revolt against the godlike.[28]

There was a lot of "ordure and dirt" that night in Miami among the half-naked women present in the crowd, though none ever made it onto the stage. At the end of the concert:

... the floor was carpeted with clothing—dresses, pants, swimsuits, socks, shoes, shorts, shirts, blouses, stockings, bras and panties." [Ray noted] "Jim's audiences were always a major part of his performance, his "theater," and he instinctively sensed that these exploding young bodies were clamoring for more. So, he pushed them and lured them into pushing him. It was an unbelievable dance they did together ... People were just going *insane*, man. The whole thing was just madness. John, Robby, and I kept playing, keeping it going, keeping the madness going, "Light My Fire" on and on and on." Robby [agreed]: "It looked like a scene from that movie *The Snake Pit*, where people were rushing around in endless waves. I don't know what Ray did, but finally, John and I scooted off the stage because someone was yelling that it was about to collapse.[29]

We have assembled inside this ancient and insane theater
To propagate our lust for life
And flee the swarming wisdom of the streets[30]

Jim wrote a term paper while attending FSU on Dutch-Netherlandish painter Hieronymous Bosch (1450—1516 AD), Jim's favorite artist—

Jim stood looking for hours at Bosch's triptych *The Garden of Earthly Delights* in the Museo del Nacional Prado when he visited Madrid in 1971 with Pamela—in which Jim presented Bosch as an Adamite.

> Bosch . . . viewed the world as a hell in which we pass through the devil's digestive system, and about whom almost nothing is known for sure. Jim's theory was that the artist was a member of the Adamite Sect, a group of medieval heretics.[31]

Adamites were Christians in North Africa in the second, third, and fourth centuries CE who wore no clothing during worship. It's as if the concert that night progressed through scenes in *The Garden of Earthly Delights* with Jim the Adamite in the middle of an "ancient and insane theater" of his own making (at one point holding a lamb), his thoughts and fantasies coming to life in performance, teasing the audience that he was going to pull out his cock, "the rod that connects man to the stars."

There are no laws, there are no rules, just grab your friend and love them.[32]

Figure 18.2. Hieronymous Bosch (1450—1516), *The Garden of Earthly Delights*, triptych (1503—1515), Museo Nacional del Prado, Madrid, Spain.

After the show, before making his exit, Jim would look upon the chaos he created from a balcony overlooking the floor of Dinner Key Auditorium.

Jim gave the audience a chance to rebel against "the cleanliness" society demands of them so they could have a fun time together feeling wicked "wallowing in the dirt." Creating concert venue chaos that felt like being in a sinful, beautiful, terrifying, and ecstatic Bosch painting was one of Jim's original visions he'd once dreamed of achieving as a filmmaker. The Doors were just as much Bosch-rock as they were Artaud or acid-rock. The Living Theater came along to show Jim how he could push it to the limit. *Paradise Now* was Jim's inspirational icing on the cake.

In a 1970 interview with American rock music journalist Salli Stevenson, Jim said:

I was just fed up with the image that had been created around me . . . which I sometimes consciously, most of the time unconsciously, cooperated with. It just . . . it got too much for me to really stomach and so I just put an end to it in one glorious evening.[33]

Miami blew my confidence
but really I blew it
on purpose
The Decency Rally
"And away we go."
The Jury—Sniffing the Witnesses
Trying the Devil in Florida[34]

19

There's a Killer on the Road

We need less perfect but more free films.

—JONAS MEKAS

As the fallout from the Miami show mounted, Jim engaged himself with other creative projects back home in Los Angeles. As far as acting, he didn't have much luck in Hollywood, not surprising since Jim thought the commercial film industry was "a bunch of bullshit," "syrup for the masses." Jim was even turned down by American actor Steve McQueen for a part in the film *Adam at 6 A.M.*[1]

So Jim returned to his original ambition, experimental filmmaking. Jim formed his own production company, HWY Productions, to shoot his 1969 experimental-independent film *HWY: An American Pastoral,* codirected with UCLA film school friends Paul Ferrara, Babe Hill, and Frank Lisciandro. Shot in the Direct Cinema method, *HWY* is about a drifter named "Billy" and based on a ten-page screenplay Jim wrote called *The Hitchhiker.* In an interview, Jim stated: "Well, it's about a hitchhiker who—essentially it's just a movement from a state of nature gradually to city."[2] *HWY* is a generous vision of Jim's love for Southern California's desolate natural beauty, and it contains many scenes that also capture Jim's mysteriousness and erotism. In a broad sense, *HWY* also parallels Gebser's stages of consciousness.

HWY begins by portraying the birth of the shaman's spiritual life. The opening scenes were shot in Tahquitz Canyon, a place of great significance to the Cahuilla people that's part of the Agua Caliente Indian

Reservation in Palm Springs, California. Jim's shamanic life journey, his fascination with the dark side of life, and Tahquitz Canyon's native history made this area the perfect location for *HWY's* opening scenes:

> The canyon is home to *Tahquitz*, the first shaman created by *Mukat*, the creator of all things. Tahquitz had much power, and in the beginning, he used his power for the good of all people. Tahquitz became the guardian spirit of all shamans, and he gave them power to do good. But over time, Tahquitz began to use his power for selfish reasons. He began to use his power to harm the Cahuilla People. The people became angry, and they banished Tahquitz to this canyon that now bears his name. He made his home high in the San Jacinto Mountains in a secret cave below the towering rock known today as Tahquitz Peak.[3]

Eliade states in *Shamanism*: "The grant of shamanic powers occurs after a deliberate quest . . . candidates withdraw to mountain caves or solitary places and seek, by intense concentration, to obtain the visions that can alone determine a shamanic career."[4]

> *To come of age in a dry place*
> *Holes and caves*[5]

Figure 19.1. Jim Morrison in *HWY: An American Pastoral, released October 20, 1969.*
Directors: Jim Morrison, Paul Ferrara, Babe Hill, Frank Lisciandro.

We hear sirens over the opening credits of *HWY* and see a descending shot from a half-moon to the canyon pond surface. Right away, the Hermetic dictum "as above, so below" is invoked. Then a sound like that of a shofar is heard, an instrument used by the ancient Israelites as a battle signal, perhaps reflecting Jim's view that we're at war with "the robot" and those stuck in ordinary consciousness.

Jim emerges with leather pants on, no shirt, his arms swaying, like a newborn pony gently struggling to free itself at birth. There's a slow zoom on a peace symbol that's carved into a tree. This scene has the atmospheric feel of the beginning of time, "the archaic stage of consciousness" as the practice of shamanism is tens of thousands of years old. Jim then puts on his shirt and boots before venturing off into the wilderness.

> *The killer awoke before dawn*
> *He put his boots on*[7]

Wilson writes in The Occult: "Magic shares another fundamental principle with mysticism: the notion 'as above, so below' (attributed to Hermes Trismegistus). In mysticism, this means that the soul and God are the same."[6]

At a critical point in *HWY*, Jim rock hops a stream and begins ascending a mountain trail. At the top, Jim stops to take in the view from an overlook. This is significant in terms of the history of consciousness. The Italian poet Petrarch's ascent of Mount Ventoux in France on April 26, 1336, to take in the view from the top marked the beginning of "the deficient mode of the mental-rational stage of consciousness." Lachman writes in *The Secret Teachers of the Western World* that:

> This ability of the Renaissance artist to imbue inanimate objects with a strange, powerful life—which remains as vital today as when it first appeared—is a clear example of the new confidence in man's own godlike powers, symbolized by Petrarch's ascent of Mount Ventoux.[8]

At the top of Mt. Ventoux, Petrarch experienced a shift in perspective that shattered his view of life. He would later write about the guilt he felt for having enjoyed the *worldliness* of the vast and beautiful scenery that he saw. But Petrarch couldn't help how he felt:

> Petrarch's trepidation in gazing on the "wide expanse" that left him "dazed" was, we've seen, informed by his conscience as a good Christian. But it was also informed by his awareness that with his ascent of Mt. Ventoux, he had cut loose his moorings and was now adrift. It was as if some figure in a medieval tapestry suddenly found that he could step out of the fabric of his world and move about at will. Or as if we found ourselves able to move about freely in a film . . . With Petrarch's ascent of Mount Ventoux, human consciousness, at least in the West, became aware of distance, depth, and all that we take for granted as "empty space." We had detached ourselves from our ground and were now floating freely . . . Although the separation of consciousness from the world began, Gebser believed, around 1225 [BCE] with the rise of the mental-rational structure of consciousness, it did not reach its peak until the emergence of the "perspectival age." It was at this point that the separation of consciousness from the world—and, according to Gebser, from its unmanifest source, "Origin"—became complete.[9]

Seen through the lens of the Western esoteric tradition, the screen's fading to black can be interpreted as the rejected knowledge being driven underground in the early seventeenth century. Jim's waking up from what appears to be a nap evokes the first popular spiritual/occult awakening that explodes across the West in the 1960s.

Jim then makes his way down to a desert highway. Here we see Jim the killer. The setting of *HWY* also changes from one of being immersed in the primitive world of nature—the *archaic*, the *magical*, and the *mythical*—to the decaying *mental-rational* world of modern civilization in its *deficient mode*. After several minutes of trying to hitch a ride, Jim draws a V-shaped face in the sand with eyes, hinting that the veil separating him from the spirit world is thin.

Jim finds a ditched station wagon, circles it, and smashes a rock on the windshield, showing his disdain for the fragility of material things, partaking in an "activity that seems to have no meaning." This part of the film goes on for several minutes with Jim walking the highway's edge while thumbing for a ride to Los Angeles.

> *The grand highway*
> *is*
> *crowded*
> *w/*
> *lovers*
> *&*
> *searchers*
> *&*
> *leavers*
> *so*
> *eager*
> *to*
> *please*
> *&*
> *forget.*
> **Wilderness.**[10]

Jim gets picked up. Then, there's a sudden shot of Jim driving, no longer the hitchhiker. Later in a phone booth scene Jim tells a friend he's committed a murder (the victim is the owner of the Shelby GTO). Jim sublimates the murderer within himself into the character of the American hitchhiker, "the killer on the road."

> *If you give this man a ride*
> *Sweet family will die*[11]

Jim encountered a dying coyote while filming *HWY,* triggering his memory of the New Mexico accident. It was a poignant moment; Jim's life had come full circle. He was reminded that what happened was "not just a ghost story," but his Faculty X being activated again. Wilson stated in an interview:

Figure 19.2. Jim Morrison in *HWY: An American Pastoral,* released October 20, 1969. Directors: Jim Morrison, Paul Ferrara, Babe Hill, Frank Lisciandro.

The example I've always been given [of Faculty X] is that of Proust who in *Swann's Way* describes how his hero, coming in very tired one day, had taken a little cake called a madeleine and dipped it in herb tea, and as he tasted it suddenly experienced a wonderfully ecstatic sense of happiness, which he was able to pin down to the fact that the madeleine brought back his childhood with great clarity—he'd always been offered a madeleine when he came back from a long walk every Sunday by his Aunt Leone. In other words, the madeleine made Proust suddenly aware of the reality of his past.[12]

The dying coyote had a similar effect on Jim in reminding him of his past. Watching the coyote take its last breaths caused Jim to wonder, "Is death where it's at or is it not where it's at? That's what I want to know,"[13] leaving it hanging as a question like the philosopher Jim was.

Jim stops the Shelby GTO he's stolen, gets out, looks up and around, becomes lost in thought, then gets back in and drives off. He dances among children in a sunset desert scene. Then it's night.

> *You know the day destroys*
> *the night*
> *Night divides the day*[14]

Car headlights illuminate a map of Southern California that Jim steps on and then looks over. He walks around in the darkness and then drives away. It's day again at a gas station. Jim twirls a book rack (scouring the paperbacks), gets a light for his cigarette, and finds a big stick in the passenger side footwell. After shots of gas station attendants, Jim waves goodbye and drives off.

Jim continues to head west through downtown Los Angeles and then through the fifteen miles of neighborhoods to Venice. The passing houses filmed through the car's window recall an observation Jim makes in *The Lords: Notes on Vision*:

> Modern life is a journey by car . . . we slice through cities, whose ripped backsides present a moving picture of windows, signs, streets, buildings.[15]

Made the scene from week to week
Day to day, hour to hour[16]

Jim walks back outside and converses with strangers, saying, "Nice night," "Got any groovy pussy in this joint?" "Any LSD?"

Inside the nightclub, someone says "Get him a table, would ya please?"

Jim shows us his home at *HWY's* end. We see sunset evening views of Jim's West Hollywood neighborhood where he lived in the Alta Cienega Motel, all within walking distance of The Doors offices and his favorite bars like Barney's Beanery.

Motel money murder madness[17]

✳

Jim had another kind of home within himself and with his close friends. He found a definition for this in twentieth-century German author Hermann Hesse's 1932 novel *The Journey to the East*. Jim told his friend Phil O'Leno, "Just read it. It's got the whole key to everything right there."[18]

Jim shared with writers like Hesse an intuitive knowing that humanity is at long last "coming home:"

> I realized that I had joined a pilgrimage to the East, seemingly a definite and single pilgrimage—but in reality, in its broadest sense, this expedition to the East was not only mine and now; this procession of believers and disciples had always and incessantly been moving towards the East, towards the Home of Light. Throughout the centuries it had been on the way, towards the light and wonder, and each member, each group, indeed our whole host and its great pilgrimage, was only a wave in the eternal stream of human beings, of the eternal strivings of the human spirit towards the East, towards Home. The knowledge passed through my mind like a ray of light and immediately reminded me of a phrase that I had learned during my novitiate year, which had always pleased me immensely without my realizing its full significance. It was a phrase by the poet Novalis, "Where are we really going? Always home!"[19]

In *The Secret Teachers of the Western World*, Lachman quotes Ouspenky in his:

> search for the miraculous, [when]. Ouspenksy had met people who were interested in the same ideas that interested me, that spoke the same language that I spoke, people between whom and myself there was instantly set up an entirely distinctive understanding.[20]

Jim found this camaraderie in friends like Ray Manzarek. Jim called his inner circle "a feast of friends," preferring them "over the giant family," some of them spiritual seekers like Jim who were much like Hesse's characters found in *The Journey to the East*:

> a procession of believers and disciples that had always and incessantly been moving towards the East, towards the Home of Light. . . a wave in the eternal stream of human beings, of the eternal strivings of the human spirit towards the East, towards Home.[21]

Bolen provides another view of what coming home means in *Gods in Everyman*.

It's possible to come home. "Home" is a psychological destination where we connect with a spiritual center, just as in Ancient Greece, home was a sacred place of homecoming because Hestia was there. As a symbol of the Self, or the center of the personality, we experience our own "Hestia" as an inner still point associated with a sense of wholeness. We find Hestia whenever we enter a sanctuary and find a welcoming hearth. It may literally be home, or a place of solitude and peace, or in the arms of another person, or at play, or at work, or in a place of worship, or in nature. Wherever and whenever we find ourselves "at home," we also find harmony and bliss, and we are living our personal myth.[22]

When knowledge of the mythic dimension comes into your possession, it can help you find your bearings and a path that is true for you; one that reflects who you authentically are, which makes life meaningful.[23]

The most important kind of freedom is to be what you really are . . . There can't be any large-scale revolution until there's a personal revolution, on an individual level. It's got to happen inside first.[24]

20
Death Makes
Angels of Us All

The only thing he ever did was buy himself a car, a Mustang GT 500, license number VRD 389. And he bought Pamela a Porsche. He truly had no interest in physical possessions. He was a Zen master in a way. He was unlike any person I'd ever met and to this day he is unlike any person I've ever met. His concerns were of another world, not mine.

—BILL SIDDONS

In his memoir *The Seven Pillars of Wisdom*, T. E. Lawrence stated: "I don't value material things much. Sensation and mind seem to me much greater."[1] Sensation, mind, and the creative, mystical impulse were of absolute preeminence to Jim the rockstar warrior-poet. Much more so than the modern occultist's more will-to-power-driven aims.

In *The Occult Explosion*, Freedland quotes twentieth-century Oriental philosopher and author Alan Watts, another writer Jim gravitated to, in making an important distinction between occultism and mysticism:

Occultism and mysticism are two different things. Occultism without mysticism simply deals with learning how to manipulate the future—it's a power game. But the mystic seeks a basic understanding of the universe and identification of universal realities. This has to be achieved by full involvement with the eternal present.[2]

Wilson makes a similar distinction in *The Occult* between the masses and the poet:

> The characteristic of the everyday personality is its will-to-power: the desire for money, possessions, sexual conquest, position. The mystical urge, on the other hand, transcends all these. A poet enchanted by the freshness of an April shower experiences strange longings, something bursting and struggling inside them, a feeling of the richness and mysteriousness of the universe that makes the ambition of ordinary persons seem stupid and mistaken.[3]

Christina and Stanislav Grof write in *The Stormy Search for the Self*:

> "The mystical teachings of all ages," revolve around the idea that the exclusive pursuit of material goals and values by no means expresses the full potential of human beings. According to this point of view, humanity is an integral part of the creative cosmic energy and intelligence and is, in a sense, identical to and commensurate with it. Discovery of one's divine nature can lead to a way of being, on both an individual and a collective scale, that is incomparably superior to what is ordinarily considered the norm.[4]

Ray Manzarek said this in an interview:

> Topping the charts is not the point of it. Topping the charts is numbers, man. The point of it is not numbers. The point of it is not how much money you'll make, what chart position you make, how many cities you have on your tour, how many people come to see you when you play, that's not the point. That's numbers . . . numbers are not the point of it. VIBRATION—I'm going to talk to you like a hippie now—VIBRATION is the point of it. Are you in harmony with the planet? Or are you out of phase with Mother Nature? If you can put yourself into harmony, man, you don't need a nickel. The great mystic from the Middle East, Jesus, the Christ said, you know, it's all about the VIBRATION, you don't need money, that's

what He was talking about, the mystical Christ . . . you don't need money. You don't need money. You need a couple of bucks to buy something to eat, pay your rent, get a little car, a little roof over your head, that's all you need. If you're in harmony with the planet—and that's what opening the doors of perception are all about—if you had the courage to open the doors of perception, you're gonna find a whole new world inside of you, man. Numbers and money? Poof, out the window.[5]

"Mysticism, then," writes author D.J. Moore in his 2006 book *Mystical Discourse in Wordsworth & Whitman*, "is the perception of the universe and all of its seemingly disparate entities existing in a unified whole bound together by love."[6]

> *I promised I would drown myself in mystic heated wine*[7]

Jim lived on the fringes to remain in touch with the "new, alien and *other*," both within and around him just as his heroes Jack Kerouac, Charles Baudelaire, Arthur Rimbaud, Friedrich Nietzsche, and Antonin Artaud did before him. During his last days with The Doors in Los Angeles, Jim lived off and on in a seedy West Hollywood motel, the Alta Cienega, which was within walking distance of his favorite bars, restaurants, and The Doors offices. For a time he became the rock and roll Beat version of Huysmans's character Des Esseintes in his 1884 novel *À Rebours*. Wilson describes him in *The Occult* as "a rich young man, Des Esseintes, who detests the banality of everyday life, and locks himself inside his villa, surrounded by exquisite food, liqueurs, pictures and books to live a life of the imagination and senses."[8]

> *Urge to come to terms with the "Outside,"*
> *by absorbing, interiorizing it.*
> *I won't come out, you must come into me.*
> *Into my womb-garden where I peer out.*
> *Where I can construct a universe within the skull,*
> *to rival the real.*[9]

Jim's heroes met tragic ends after leading lives often filled with terrific disappointments, long periods of grinding poverty, and devastating health issues. After years of financial hardship, Charles Baudelaire suffered a terrible stroke in 1866, spending the remainder of his life in a semi-paralyzed state in a few *maisons de santé* in Brussels and Paris, where he died in 1867 at age forty-six. Following a lifetime of heartbreak and a mental breakdown, Friedrich Nietzsche spent his last ten years incapacitated while being cared for by his sister. Nietzsche died of pneumonia in 1900 at the age of fifty-five. After being taken into custody by French authorities following a wild trip around Ireland to await the Apocalypse while traveling with his "walking stick of St. Patrick," Antonin Artaud suffered in mental asylums from 1943 up until he died in 1948 at age fifty-one due to the lethal dose of a sedative, chloral hydrate. (Nietzsche used to write out his own prescriptions for chloral hydrate, signing off on them as "Dr. Nietzsche," and William S. Burroughs, while living at the Los Alamos Ranch School for Boys, one day walked into a drugstore in Santa Fe to buy chloral hydrate. When the druggist inquired why he wanted to buy "knockout drops," in a "sepulchral voice" Burroughs answered, "to commit suicide." Days later, Burroughs came close to joining Artaud when he almost died himself from a near-lethal dose of the chloral hydrate he'd bought.[10]) In 1969, while taking care of his mother, a bitter Jack Kerouac complained that the only ones interested in reading his novels were the teenagers shoplifting them. Kerouac died at age forty-seven in St. Petersburg, Florida, from an esophageal hemorrhage due to cirrhosis from alcoholism. And Arthur Rimbaud, who detested his mother, renounced writing poetry at the ripe old age of twenty-one. Rimbaud never got to enjoy the money he'd worked hard to save while toiling away in Africa's perilous gun trade, passing away at age thirty-seven in 1891 in a hospital in Marseilles following a leg amputation.

Jim on the other hand led a lifestyle of fame and fortune that Baudelaire, Nietzsche, Artaud, Kerouac, and Rimbaud could never imagine. After graduating from UCLA, Jim was living an impoverished, homeless existence in Venice. But with the commercial success of The Doors less than two years later, Jim came into a lot of money. Never before in the history of the Western esoteric tradition had a secret teacher poet done so well following their creative, mystical impulse. Maynard writes in *Venice West*:

> Whatever else it may have been, the phenomenon of which they became a part was an example of something real merging with something fabricated to produce something totally unforeseeable: a new branch of popular culture dedicated to the rejection of popular culture.[11]

> Part of the significance of the Beat Generation was that it proved rebellion sells, and Venice West, even without its cooperation, helped provide one of its earliest examples of how the culture of perpetual dissatisfaction could be profitably turned back on itself.[12]

Jim became the sole beneficiary Venice Beat poet (albeit unwittingly) in what turned out to be the most marketable and profitable rebellion in history, courtesy of the West's first occult/spiritual awakening conjoined with a mass appetite for all that was "new, alien and *other*." Jim also understood the sociology of his time helped to make his rise to fame possible:

> The hippie lifestyle is really a middle-class phenomenon, and it could not exist in any other society except ours when there's such an incredible surfeit of goods, products, and leisure time . . . The generations preceding ours had world wars and depressions to contend with, and for the last ten or fifteen years in this country there's been time enough, and there's been money enough, to live kind of a flagrant outrageous lifestyle, which was impossible before.[13]

Jim left us timeless songs and poetry that sprang from his understanding of universal realities, and accomplished by his "full involvement with the eternal present." Jim was also of the spirit to pull some really fucking crazy shit. He "tested the bounds of reality" in his grand *poète maudit* style, like vomiting all over the front entrance to your record company president's Manhattan apartment building, or getting drunk with porn actors and disrupting commercial airline flights. (Jim and his drinking buddy Tom Baker were both arrested at the gate by FBI agents in Phoenix following this stunt.) Jim was indeed—"a very old soul stuck in an immature incarnation,"[14]—sometimes living on the edge of Dionysian madness.

This brings us to Jim's drinking. If there was ever an artist more deserving of compassion regarding their struggle with alcohol, it was Jim. Between the combination of his Dionysian archetype's compulsion to heighten experiences with alcohol, the terrific energy happening all around him, the exciting and exuberant feelings of being young and sexy in a successful rock band, and the tremendous spiritual electricity coursing through him night after night before thousands of people . . . we can forgive Jim for seeking fun and relief in a bottle. Krieger in *Set the Night on Fire* writes about an intervention attempt to get Jim to cut down on his drinking. Krieger remembers Jim was able to stay dry for only a couple of weeks, but made a good point that in the late 1960s, there didn't exist a multi-billion-dollar drug treatment industry. Getting Jim real professional help was next to impossible. His bandmates tried to "chaperone" Jim through persons such as Tony Funches, but Krieger writes they just ended up drinking *with* him.[15]

> *It's like gambling somehow. You go out for a night of drinking and you don't know where you're going to end up the next day. It could work out good or it could be disastrous. It's like the throw of the dice.*[16]

Jim once told his friend Frank Lisciandro he drank to shut the demons up, or what in ancient Greek belief are called *daemons,* defined in the Oxford Languages dictionary as "a divinity or supernatural being of a nature between gods and humans." Twentieth-century American novelist Henry Miller states in his 1956 work *The Time of the Assassins: A Study of Rimbaud,* "All the great artists of the modern age have struggled to demagnetize themselves. All were annihilated by Jovian bolts. They were like inventors who, having discovered electricity, knew nothing about insulation. They were attuned to a new power which was breaking through, but their experiments led to disaster."[17] This same spiritual electricity Hamlet felt after his visitation with the Ghost.

Perhaps the same can be said about Jim. Lead vocalist Ian Astbury of the late twentieth-century British rock band The Cult—who performed over one hundred and fifty shows with *The Doors of the 21st Century* in the 2000s—stated in an interview:

> I can understand—I have a perspective now, on why perhaps the pressures pushed [Jim] in a position where he lost his life at a very early age. Because—there was so much *voltage* put through that human being.[18]

American spiritual teacher Ram Dass compares such a person to a toaster, and his or her reaction to "sticking your plug into 220 volts instead of 110 volts and everything fries."[19] Conway's words in *Magic: An Occult Primer* echo Ram Dass's words:

> The power that is used in magic is derived from forces . . . from within and outside ourselves. It is formed by linking one aspect of the magician's personality with a corresponding aspect of the cosmic mind. This at once sets up a current of power that the magician can draw upon for his own purposes. It is not unlike flicking a switch to turn on the electric light. However, just as electricity requires an efficient wiring system, so magical power always needs a suitable conductor through which to flow. This conductor is established by the performance of an appropriate ritual, every detail of which contributes to the final influx of power. It is because each detail is so important that [rituals] must be scrupulously followed. This is not only because the success of the whole operation will depend on it, but because, as in the case of electricity, magic can be dangerous when tampered with.[20]

As The Doors began raking it in, Jim set out to have a once-in-a-lifetime blast with his cash. The homeless poet who once roamed the beaches and streets of Venice with nothing but the clothes on his back had won the Mystic Powerball Rock 'n' Roll Lottery. Jim insisted the band's earnings be split four equal ways between the other three Doors and himself. He created a joint bank account with Pamela and racked up enormous bar tabs with his drinking buddies, dined at high-end restaurants with friends, bought himself quality black leather pants and a Mustang, paid weekly motel room rates, and rented apartments and homes for Pamela and himself in hip Los Angeles neighborhoods such as Laurel Canyon. Jim also spent a fortune on his film projects and legal problems. The Miami trial alone cost The Doors a cool million. Jim also put up $300,000 for Pamela's West Hollywood clothing boutique, Themis.

Jim was the consummate artist. The vision, the voice, the lyrics, the music, the drama—the whole experience had to be just as unforgettable as a film like *Lawrence of Arabia* or a triptych like *The Garden of Earthly Delights,* a work of art that would stand out for all time. Jim was much inspired by Nietzsche's existential aesthetics, as stated in *The Joyous Science*, in making his life into a work of art*:*

> To give style to one's character—that is a grand and rare art! He who surveys all that his nature presents in its strength and in its weakness, and then fashions it into an ingenious plan, until everything appears artistic and rational, and even the weaknesses enchant the eye—exercises that admirable art.[21]

But the body of this once powerful butterfly-stroke swimmer, through whom had coursed so much spiritual voltage onstage while being persecuted offstage, had succumbed to the decadence of his fast and excessive rock and roll lifestyle. Jim crammed what would be for the rest of us decades of living into just a few short years.

In the last few weeks of his life, Jim lived with Pam in an apartment in the 4th *arrondissement* of Paris. Jim died there on July 3rd, 1971, the day after Rear Admiral Morrison gave a speech at the decommissioning ceremony aboard his first command, the USS *Bonhomme Richard*, the aircraft carrier where Jim and The Commander last spent time together.

> *Death makes angels of us all*
> *And gives us wings*
> *Where we had shoulders*
> *Smooth as raven's claws*[22]

Retire Now to Your Tents & to Your Dreams

Jim Morrison helped trailblaze the way for us to validate our firm persuasions regarding the mystical or paranormal experiences that we feel carry real meaning for our lives, imparting the knowledge that's beyond what is "material, tangible, and measurable." This is what the ancients did in *ages of imagination* when "the truth of correspondences was common knowledge." This is the strange divine coming through our "instinctive desire to believe in the unseen forces, the wider significance," giving us purpose and vitality. None of us are "contingent, mediocre, accidental or mortal," as Wilson stated, so we shouldn't allow ourselves to become incapable of "a firm persuasion of anything."

Stanislav Grof wrote back in 1990 that:

Three decades of detailed and systematic studies of the human mind through observations of non-ordinary states of consciousness in others and myself have led me to some radical conclusions. I now believe that consciousness and the human psyche are much more than accidental products of the physiological processes in the brain; they are reflections of the cosmic intelligence that permeates all of creation. We are not just biological machines and highly developed animals, but also fields of consciousness without limits, transcending space and time.[1]

Maybe primitive people have less bullshit to let go of, to give up. A person has to be willing to give up everything— not just wealth. All the bullshit they've been taught—all

> *society's brainwashing. You have to let go of all that*
> *to get to the other side. Most people aren't*
> *willing to do that.*[2]

Prepare for the coming integral stage of consciousness. Archaic, magical, mythical, and mental-rational consciousness are coming together. At the same time, a world more "new, alien and *other*" beyond our wildest imagination is being born all around us. We're going to need a strong dose of Lawrence's funny sense of fun.

> *Strange days have found us*
> *Strange days have tracked us down*[3]

In the nineteen sixties, it took the direct, gut-level energy of artists like Jim Morrison to begin pushing us out of the deficient mode of the mental-rational stage of consciousness. Though in making our way into this new integral stage of consciousness, let's keep in mind Gary Lachman's words in *Beyond the Robot*:

> Though stingy, the life force is not an absolute miser, and occasionally it allows us to experience a fuller, broader, deeper consciousness. These are our poetical and mystical experiences, the "all is good" feeling that brings a sense of "absurd affirmation." For some reason, during them, our blinders are temporarily removed and reality is let in. Our doors of perception are opened, but only for a moment. Then they shut again. Yet these moments tell us that reality *is not* meaningless. In fact it is dripping with meaning, so much meaning that if we experienced it in full, we would most likely blow a psychic fuse; any number of accounts of mystical experiences suggest this. This tells us two things. One is that the world we perceive most of the time is not the world as it really is, but a highly edited version of it. The second is that our doors of perception are not permanently locked. They can open. The question then becomes, how can we open them just enough to allow more reality into consciousness, so we are not taken in by gloomy pronouncements about its meaninglessness, but not so much that we are overwhelmed by it and our will inhibited?[4]

So cast out all those smaller meanings holding you captive to that partial amnesia as Jim Morrison and Colin Wilson once did. With the rise of AI, the stakes are going to become super high. Jim foresaw the challenges of our time when he stated:

> There does seem to be a trend of a more primitive outlook on life, a more tribal attitude. I think it's a natural reaction to industrialization. Unfortunately, it's kind of naive. The future is going to become increasingly mechanized—computerized, and I don't think there's any turning back. It's just figuring out a way to survive and thrive in that kind of society.[5]

Let's not just survive but learn to thrive in this increasingly cold, digitized world by engaging our precious glimpses into this immense-meaning universe with a fierce intent to create something unique and relevant. It could be anything. Abraham Maslow writes in *The Third Force* that:

> Spontaneity, also, is also synonymous with creativity. Self-actualizing people are less inhibited; and therefore more expressive, natural, and simple. They do not usually feel it necessary to mask their feelings or thoughts or play artificial roles. Creativity requires courage, the ability to stick one's neck out, to be able to ignore criticism and ridicule; and the ability to resist the influence of one's culture. "Every one of our great creators . . . has testified to the element of courage that is needed in the lonely moment of creation, affirming something new (contradictory to the old). This is a kind of daring, a going out in front all alone, a defiance, a challenge. The moment of fright is quite understandable, but must nevertheless be overcome if creation is to be possible."[6]

In the meantime, the new technology is there to serve us, not us for it. No matter how lightning-fast the AI machines of the near future may be, they will never be able to attain cosmic consciousness, nor feel the rush of purpose and vitality that can only come from spiritual awakening and wonder, that life-changing "give it welcome" excitement that's given birth to renaissances throughout human history. AI will never be able to know the truth of all the as-yet-to-be-discovered mysteries that our secret teachers can through gnosis.

The catch is, as technology becomes more outrageously advanced, our capacity for gnosis will become maimed if we fall prey to the ever-increasing temptation to become mere creatures of convenience. This is how, as Lachman writes, civilization will "slide into the gulf" if we're not more careful and aware. "Technology alone is not enough," declared Apple founder Steve Jobs, "It's technology married with liberal arts, married with the humanities, that yields us the result that makes our heart sing."[7]

We need to keep our minds firing on all cylinders through active reading, critical thinking, and communicating openly with each other on a consistent basis. We have to put down the smartphone, fold up the laptop—and perhaps soon turn off the implant—and take a long walk in nature to allow our minds to connect the dots, listen to what's in our hearts, and learn what our souls are meant to discover. We should strive to become that higher type of person with a "new unity of purpose," as Jim once said: "The answer is for everyone to stand up and say *I'm me* and be fully aware of that fact and to let everyone else know that you're yourself and express it."[8] But to do this, you have to be fully in touch with your *authentic self* and be *fearless* about it; achieving a truly confident level of self-knowledge and awareness takes effort as well as leaving behind what you know has made you too comfortable in life, bringing you into stagnation, perhaps even desperation. Sometimes getting your real self back means you must "live dangerously" for a time.

Find out which sign your north node is in, learn everything you can about this direction, and follow it without compromise. And remember what Wilson states with life-saving conviction in *The Occult,* that:

[Human beings] need a sense of meaning to release [these] hidden energies . . .[because they] live and evolve by 'eating' significance, as a child eats food. The deeper [a human being's] sense of wonder, the wider [their] curiosity, the stronger [their] vitality becomes, and the more powerful [their] grip on [their] own existence.

Release the hidden energies of all the gods and myths of the ages within you. Celebrate your firm persuasions and peak experiences, your glories, "the mother of all creativeness," and your madness, that "veritable manna from heaven," with as much creative fun as Jim Morrison had with The Doors.

> *Tomorrow we enter the town of my birth.*
> *I want to be ready.*[9]

Notes

PREFACE. 1717

1. *The Thin Red Line.*
2. *The Thin Red Line.*
3. *The Thin Red Line.*
4. *The Thin Red Line.*
5. Nicholson, "Interview with Jim Morrison's father and sister." "Poor interpreter" quote found at 04:42. YouTube video accessed on January 21, 2024.

INTRODUCTION. THIS IS THE STRANGEST LIFE I'VE EVER KNOWN

1. Lachman, *The Secret Teachers of the Western World*, 2–3.
2. Lisciandro, "From the Tape Noon Journal," "The Long Sweep," verse 23, lines 4–7, *The Collected Works of Jim Morrison*, 141.
3. Corsini and Auerbach, *Concise Encyclopedia of Psychology*, 627.
4. Grof, *The Stormy Search for the Self*, 90.
5. Grof, *The Stormy Search for the Self*, 90. (Quote from Boehme, Jacob. *Aurora: Dawning of the Day in the East*.)
6. Steinbeck, *East of Eden*, 130.
7. Maslow, *The Third Force*, 58.
8. Kerouac, *Windblown World*, 369.
9. Wilson, *Beyond the Occult*, xxii.
10. Lachman, *Beyond the Robot*, 87.
11. Wanis, "Jim Morrison thoughts on freedom—Lizzie James interview," website, accessed on April 2, 2023.
12. Cinetropic, "Interview with Jim Morrison," website, accessed on April 2, 2023.

13. Manufacturing Intellect, "Harold Bloom interview on Hamlet (2003)," video, accessed on February 11, 2023.
14. Mack, *A Prince of Our Disorder*, xvii-xix.
15. Wilson, *Rasputin & The Fall of The Romanovs*, 13.
16. Lisciandro, "An American Prayer," lines 26–29, *The Collected Works of Jim Morrison*, 103.

CHAPTER 1. IT'S NOT A GHOST STORY

1. Grof, *LSD: Doorway to The Numinous*, 7.
2. Rhodes, *The Making of The Atomic Bomb*, 453.
3. Morgan, *Literary Outlaw*, 53.
4. Atomic Heritage Foundation, "Native Americans & The Manhattan Project," website, accessed on September 5, 2020.
5. Durham, "Dawn's Highway," video, accessed on May 2, 2020.
6. The Dutch Guy, "Dawn's Highway Told by Frank Lisciandro and Jim Morrison at the HWY office," video, accessed on September 2, 2022.
7. Nietzsche, *Twilight of the Idols*, 80.
8. Seligmann, *The History of Magic & the Occult*, 49.
9. Morrison, "Peace Frog," lines 24-28, *The Collected Works of Jim Morrison* 510.
10. Durham, "Dawn's Highway," video, accessed on May 2, 2020.
11. Durham, "Dawn's Highway," video, accessed on May 2, 2020.
12. Blake, *The Marriage of Heaven & Hell*, xxi.
13. Shakespeare, *Hamlet*, 1.4. 39–82.
14. Wilson, *The Occult*, 178.
15. Bloom, *Hamlet: Poem Unlimited*, 98.
16. Bloom, *Dramatists & Dramas: Bloom's Literary Criticism 20th Anniversary Collection*, 64.
17. Morgan, *Literary Outlaw*, 55.
18. Periodic Presidents, "What is Tecumseh's Curse?" website, accessed on January 21, 2023.
19. Bloom, *Hamlet: Poem Unlimited*, 24.
20. Shakespeare, *Hamlet*, 3.1.187.
21. Shakespeare, *Hamlet*, 1.5.166.
22. Shakespeare, *Hamlet*, 1.5.65.
23. Empty Mirror, "Jim Morrison and Jack Kerouac" website accessed January 14, 2024.

24. Lisciandro, "An American Prayer" lines 32-33, *The Collected Works of Jim Morrison*, 103.

CHAPTER 2. FACULTY X

1. Lachman, *Beyond the Robot*, 159-160.
2. Wilson, *The Occult*, 322.
3. Wilson, *The Occult*, 59-62.
4. Wilson, *The Occult*, 91.
5. Bloom, *Bloom's Major Literary Characters: Hamlet*.
6. Wilson, *Beyond the Occult*, xxxii.
7. Wilson, *Beyond the Occult*, 321.
8. Wilson, *The Occult*, 579.
9. Wilson, *The Occult*, 146.
10. Wilson, *The Occult*, 21.
11. Lisciandro, "The Celebration of The Lizard," line 15, *The Collected Works of Jim Morrison*, 33.
12. Wilson, *The Occult*, 21–22.
13. Wilson, *The Occult*, 580.
14. Wanis, "Jim Morrison thoughts on freedom—Lizzie James interview," website, accessed on April 2, 2023.

CHAPTER 3. A SPIRITUAL AWAKENING

1. Lisciandro, *Friends Gathered Together*, Chapter 2, 41–71.
2. Lisciandro, *Friends Gathered Together*, Chapter 2, 41 of 41.
3. Grof, *The Stormy Search for the Self*, 48.
4. Ratazzura, "Jim Morrison & Tony Thomas 1970 Interview," video, accessed on November 21, 2022.
5. Grof, *The Stormy Search for the Self*, 2.
6. Grof, *The Stormy Search for the Self*, 5.
7. Bolen, *Gods in Everyman*, 6.
8. Bolen, *Gods in Everyman*, 251–55.
9. Wilson, *The Occult*, 192.
10. Grof, *The Stormy Search for the Self*, 199.
11. Mack, *A Prince of Our Disorder*, 226–242.
12. Wanis, "Jim Morrison thoughts on freedom—Lizzie James Interview"

(From 1981 *Creem Magazine* edition, Lizzie James, "Jim Morrison: Ten Years Gone") website accessed January 14, 2024.

CHAPTER 4. THE SECRET OF MIND-CHANGE REALITY

Epigraph: Seligmann, *History of Magic & the Occult*, 206.

1. Hopkins and Sugerman, *No One Here Gets Out Alive*, 17.
2. Hopkins and Sugerman, *No One Here Gets Out Alive*, 29.
3. Wilson, *The Occult*, 178.
4. Wilson, *Beyond the Occult*, xviii.
5. Conway, *Magic: An Occult Primer*, 39.
6. Lisciandro, "An American Prayer," line 20, *The Collected Works of Jim Morrison*, 103.
7. Ratazurra, "Jim Morrison & Tony Thomas 1970 Interview," video, accessed on March 2, 2021.
8. Pinchbeck, *Breaking Open the Head*, 5.
9. Lisciandro, "From the Tape Noon Journal," "Tunnel Where Dreams Are Born," section 10, lines 6-20, *The Collected Works of Jim Morrison*, 133.
10. Lisciandro, *The Collected Works of Jim Morrison*, 79.
11. Sparrow, "Kurt Seligmann at Home," website, accessed on April 4, 2023.
12. WOS Galerie, "Artist: Kurt Seligmann, 1900—1962," website, accessed on April 4, 2023.
13. Bloom, *Hamlet: Poem Unlimited*, 96.
14. Seligmann, *The History of Magic & the Occult*, Introductory Note.
15. Seligmann, *The History of Magic & the Occult*, 321.
16. Seligmann, *The History of Magic & the Occult*, 79
17. Lisciandro, *The Collected Works of Jim Morrison*, 29.
18. Lisciandro, "The Lords: Notes on Vision," section 35, lines 3–5, *The Collected Works of Jim Morrison*, 88.
19. Lisciandro, *The Collected Works of Jim Morrison*, 101.
20. Seligmann, *The History of Magic & the Occult*, 99.
21. Seligmann, *The History of Magic & the Occult*, Introduction, 21.
22. Blake, *The Marriage of Heaven & Hell*, Introduction, 18.
23. Blake, *The Marriage of Heaven & Hell*, Introduction, 17.
24. Kerouac, *Windblown World*, 17.

25. Nietzsche, *The Birth of Tragedy*, 66.

26. Wilson, *The Occult*, 171.

27. Conway, *Magic: An Occult Primer*, 45.

28. Seligmann, *The History of Magic & the Occult*, 206.

29. Morrison, *The Lords & the New Creatures*, 83. Lisciandro, "The Lords: Notes on Vision," section 70, lines 1-2, *The Collected Works of Jim Morrison*, 95.

30. Lisciandro, "The Lords: Notes on Vision," section 22, lines 1–12, *The Collected Works of Jim Morrison*, 86.

31. Lachman, *The Secret Teachers of the Western World*, 246–49.

32. Nietzsche, *Selected Letters of Friedrich Nietzsche*, 7.

33. Seligmann, *The History of Magic & the Occult*, 88.

34. Seligmann, *The History of Magic & the Occult*, 322.

35. Lisciandro, "The Lords: Notes on Vision," section 62, lines 1–11, *The Collected Works of Jim Morrison*, 94.

36. Lisciandro, "The Lords: Notes on Vision," section 33, line 4, *The Collected Works of Jim Morrison*, 88.

37. Bolen, *Gods in Everyman*, 267.

38. Grof, *The Stormy Search for the Self*, 38.

39. Wanis, "Jim Morrison Thoughts of Freedom—Lizzie James interview" (From 1981 *Creem Magazine* edition, Lizzie James, "Jim Morrison: Ten Years Gone) accessed January 14, 2024.

40. Lisciandro, *The Collected Works of Jim Morrison*, "The Lords: Notes on Vision," section 34, lines 1–9, *The Collected Works of Jim Morrison*, 88.

41. Antiques Roadshow, "Appraisal: 1963 Jim Morrison Inscribed Book," "The History of Magic," video, accessed on March 3, 2023.

42. Lisciandro, "An American Prayer," line 68, *The Collected Works of Jim Morrison*, 104.

CHAPTER 5. THIS IS THE LAND WHERE THE PHARAOH DIED

1. Lachman, *The Secret Teachers of the Western World*, 1.

2. Lachman, *The Secret Teachers of the Western World*, 2.

3. Lachman, *The Secret Teachers of the Western World*, 3.

4. Lachman, *The Secret Teachers of the Western World*, 42–21.

5. Wilson, *The Occult*, 30.

6. Wilson, *The Occult*, 132-33.

7. Lisciandro, "An American Prayer," lines 104-105, *The Collected Works of Jim Morrison*.

8. Lisciandro, "The Lords: Notes on Vision," section 50, lines 12–19, *The Collected Works of Jim Morrison*, 92.

9. Wilson, *The Occult* (1971 Edition), 22.

10. Freedland, *The Occult Explosion*, 17.

11. Hopkins and Sugerman, *No One Here Gets Out Alive*, 59.

12. Reed, "Rock & Roll," line 9, *Loaded*.

13. Morrison, Press Conference filmed by Granada TV, ICA Gallery, The Mall, London, England, September 4, 1968.

14. Lachman, *The Secret Teachers of the Western World*, 121.

15. Seligmann, *The History of Magic & the Occult*, 33.

16. Bolen, *Gods in Everyman*, 103.

17. Seligmann, *The History of Magic & the Occult*, 31–33.

18. Lachman, *The Secret Teachers of the Western World*, 122.

19. Lachman, *The Secret Teachers of the Western World*, 130.

20. Seligmann, *The History of Magic & the Occult*, 84.

21. Lachman, *The Secret Teachers of the Western World*, 130.

22. Lisciandro, "Orange County Suite," section 10, lines 6–8, *The Collected Works of Jim Morrison*, 375.

23. Bucke, *Cosmic Consciousness*, 17.

24. Wilson, *The Occult*, 28.

25. Maynard, *Venice West*, 11.

26. Lisciandro, "Notebook & Journal Poems," lines 13–19, *The Collected Works of Jim Morrison*, 244.

CHAPTER 6. THERE'S DANGER ON THE EDGE OF TOWN

1. Wilson, *The Occult*, 66–67.

2. Wilson, *The Occult*, 269.

3. Rawles, "Masters of Darkness: Queen Elizabeth's Magician," video, accessed on June 14, 2020.

4. Lachman, *The Secret Teachers of the Western World*, 155–56.

5. Lachman, *The Secret Teachers of The Western World*, 248.

6. Lisciandro, "Paris Journal," section 6, lines 14–18, *The Collected Works of Jim Morrison*, 193.

7. Lachman, *The Secret Teachers of the Western World*, 255.

8. Lachman, *Aleister Crowley*, 12.

9. JimJohnRayRobby[2,] "Jim Morrison—talking to an independent pastor (Fred L. Stagmeyer)," accessed on May 12, 2020.

10. Seligmann, *The History of Magic & the Occult*, 79.

11. Seligmann, *The History of Magic & the Occult*, 81–82.

12. Krieger, *Set the Night on Fire*, 273.

13. Lisciandro, "Shaman's Blues," lines 30–31, *The Collected Works of Jim Morrison*, 500.

14. Hutchinson, "Jim Morrison, a Pardon and the FBI," website, accessed on March 3, 2023.

15. Krieger, *Set the Night on Fire*, 274.

16. CBC Art News "Florida opens door to pardoning Jim Morrison," website, accessed on March 3, 2023.

17. Halperin, "The Doors' John Densmore: Jim Morrison 'Didn't' Expose Himself," website, accessed on March 3, 2023.

18. Fischer, "The Doors Don't Support Jim Morrison Pardon," website, accessed on March 3, 2023.

19. Bolen, *Gods in Everyman*, 260–62.

20. Bolen 270–71.

21. Rutazzurra, "Jim Morrison & Howard Smith—Nov 6, 1969," video, accessed on August 7, 2020.

CHAPTER 7. LESSONS OF THE ANCIENT WAR

1. Hopkins and Sugerman, *No One Here Gets Out Alive*, 17.

2. Plutarch, *Plutarch's Lives*, 431.

3. Setlowe, "The Admiral & The Poet," website, accessed on November 3, 2021.

4. Grimes, "George S. Morrison, Admiral & Singer's Father, Dies at 89," website, accessed on November 3, 2021.

5. Lisciandro, *Friends Gathered Together*, "Phil O'Leno—Little Brother," p. 12 of 41.

6. Bloom, *Hamlet: Poem Unlimited*, 4-5.

7. Bolen, *Gods in Everyman*, 22.

8. Bolen, *Gods in Everyman*, 30.

9. Bolen, *Gods in Everyman*, 32.

10. Wanis, "Jim Morrison thoughts on freedom—Lizzie James Interview" (From

1981 *Creem Magazine* edition, Lizzie James, "Jim Morrison: Ten Years Gone) website accessed January 14, 2024. website accessed January 14, 2024.

11. Lisciandro, "The End," lines 51–53, *The Collected Works of Jim Morrison*, 476.

12. Helge Nicholson, "Interview w/ Jim Morrison's Father & Sister," video, accessed on June 10, 2020.

13. Lachman, *The Secret Teachers of the Western World*, 120.

14. *Rolling Stone*, "Jim Morrison: The Rolling Stone Interview," website accessed January 14, 2024.

15. Grof, *The Stormy Search for the Self*, 1.

16. Lisciandro, "An American Prayer," lines 11–12, *The Collected Works of Jim Morrison*, 103.

17. Lisciandro, "An American Prayer," lines 54–56, *The Collected Works of Jim Morrison*, 109.

18. Smith, "The Village Voice Interview," website, accessed on June 10, 2020.

19. *Rolling Stone*, "Michael McClure Recalls an Old Friend," website, accessed on June 10, 2020.

20. *Rolling Stone*, "Michael McClure Recalls an Old Friend," website, accessed on June 10, 2020.

21. Lisciandro, *The Collected Works of Jim Morrison*, 153.

CHAPTER 8. RIGHT BACK WHERE I CAME

1. Lisciandro, "An American Prayer," lines 8–10, *The Collected Works of Jim Morrison*, 103.

2. Wilson, *The Occult*, 106–107.

3. Lachman, *The Secret Teachers of the Western World*, 230.

4. Lachman, *The Secret Teachers of the Western World*, 14.

5. Shaw, "Gebser's States of Consciousness: An Overview," video, (2:54) accessed on May 20, 2021.

6. Lachman, *The Secret Teachers of the Western World*, 15.

7. Morrison, "The World on Fire," line 1, *An American Prayer*.

8. Lachman, *The Secret Teachers of the Western World*, 458.

9. Smith, "The Doors' Jim Morrison: 10 profound, bizarre, and brilliant quotes," website, accessed on February 2, 2023.

10. Gradesfixer.com, "The Main Concepts of Aristotle's Metaphysics," website, accessed on February 2, 2023.

11. Cytaty, "The Doors," European website, accessed on December 3, 2022.

CHAPTER 9. TESTING THE BOUNDS OF REALITY

1. Hopkins and Sugerman, *No One Here Gets Out Alive*, 276.
2. Elevate Society, "100 Quotes by Jim Morrison" website accessed on January 14, 2024.
3. Polcaro, Rafael, "The 10 best Jim Morrison (The Doors) quotes about life" website accessed January 14, 2024.
4. Wilson, *The Outsider*, 71.
5. Wilson, *The Outsider*, 72
6. Mack, *A Prince of Our Disorder*, 115.
7. Mack, *A Prince of Our Disorder*, 95.
8. *Lawrence of Arabia*.
9. *Lawrence of Arabia*.
10. Mack, *A Prince of Our Disorder*, 92.
11. Mack, *A Prince of Our Disorder*, 189.
12. Smith, "The Doors' Jim Morrison: 10 Profound, bizarre and brilliant quotes," website, accessed on February 5, 2023.

CHAPTER 10. A FUNNY SENSE OF FUN

1. Hopkins and Sugerman, *No One Here Gets Out Alive*, 17.
2. Schopenhauer, *The World as Will & Representation*, 154.
3. Encyclopedia Britannica, Vol. 19 (11th ed.), Cambridge University Press, p. 672.
4. Nietzsche, *The Gay Science*, 273.
5. Nietzsche, *Twilight of the Idols*, 33.
6. Nietzsche, *The Gay Science*, 223.
7. Nietzsche, *Human, All Too Human*, 174.
8. Tanos, "How Many Times Was Jim Morrison Arrested?" website, accessed on March 10, 2023.
9. Hopkins and Sugerman, *No One Here Gets Out Alive*, 36.
10. Chinaski, "The Doors: A Retrospective," accessed on March 10, 2023.
11. *South Florida Sun Sentinel*, "JIM MORRISON, when you gonna come home . . ." website, accessed on March 10, 2023.
12. Mack, *A Prince of Our Disorder*, 70.
13. *Lawrence of Arabia*.
14. Lisciandro, "Road Days," lines 8-10, *The Collected Works of Jim Morrison*, 560.

15. Manufacturing Intellect, "Harold Bloom Interview "Hamlet" (2003)," video, accessed on March 10, 2023.
16. Lawrence, *The Seven Pillars of Wisdom*, 24.
17. Lisciandro, "Road Days," lines 85–95, *The Collected Works of Jim Morrison*, 563.
18. Nietzsche, *The Birth of Tragedy*, 66.
19. Wilson, *The Outsider*, 79.
20. Krieger, *Set the Night on Fire*, 107–108.
21. Utti, "Top 22 Jim Morrison Quotes," website, accessed on March 10, 2023.
22. *Lawrence of Arabia.*
23. Krieger, *Set the Night on Fire*, 96.
24. Dahl, Danielle, *Everyday Power*, "25 Jim Morrison Quotes that Opened the Doors to His Mind" website accessed on January 14, 2024.
25. Freedland, *The Occult Explosion*, 43.
26. Grof, *The Stormy Search for the Self*, 20.
27. Grof, *The Stormy Search for the Self*, 194–96.
28. Grof, *The Stormy Search for the Self*, 113.
29. Lisciandro, "End of The Night," lines 1–2, *The Collected Works of Jim Morrison*, 473.
30. Seligmann, *The History of Magic & the Occult*, 322.
31. Blake, "Proverbs of Hell," Plates 7–10, *The Marriage of Heaven & Hell*, xviii.
32. Morrison, "The End," line 13.
33. Lisciandro, "Lament for the Death of My Cock," lines 50–52, *The Collected Works of Jim Morrison*, 382.
34. *Lawrence of Arabia.*
35. Manzarek, *Light My Fire*, 287.
36. Manzarek, *Light My Fire*, 289.
37. *Blinkist Magazine*, "The Wisdom of Jim Morrison: Top Ten Quotes to Inspire and Enlighten," website accessed January 14, 2024.
38. Academy of Ideas, "Abraham Maslow: The Jonah Complex and The Fear of Greatness," website, accessed on March 11, 2023.
39. *Lawrence of Arabia.*
40. Bolen, *Gods in Everyman*, 4.
41. Lisciandro, "An American Prayer," section 2, lines 19–22, *The Collected Works of Jim Morrison*, 108.
42. Nietzsche, *The Gay Science*, 228.
43. Wilson, *The Outsider*, 71.

44. Lisciandro, "Shaman's Blues," lines 1–5, *The Collected Works of Jim Morrison*, 500.

45. Wilson, *The Occult*, 22.

46. Mack, *A Prince of Our Disorder*, Introduction, 25.

47. Utti, Jacob, *American Songwriter*, "Top 22 Jim Morrison Quotes" website accessed January 14, 2024.

48. Kennedy, "Remarks at a Close & Circuit Television Broadcast on Behalf of the National Cultural Center," website, accessed on March 11, 2023.

49. Sudo, *Zen Guitar*, 81.

50. Lisciandro, "Take It as It Comes," lines 19–22, *The Collected Works of Jim Morrison*, 473.

CHAPTER 11. I'LL NEVER LOOK
INTO YOUR EYES AGAIN

1. Cosgrave, *Love Her Madly*, 50-53.

2. Grof, *The Stormy Search for the Self*, 49.

3. Lisciandro, *The Collected Works of Jim Morrison*, 29.

4. Lisciandro, "Orange County Suite," section 10, lines 5–6, *The Collected Works of Jim Morrison*, 375.

5. Bolen, *Gods in Everyman*, 260.

6. Grof, *The Stormy Search for The Self*, 19.

7. Matyas and Jones, *Chasing the Blues*, 8.

8. Lisciandro, "When the Music's Over," lines 19–20, *The Collected Works of Jim Morrison*, 489.

9. Morrison, *The Collected Works of Jim Morrison*, line 60, 489.

10. Cosgrave, *Love Her Madly*, 53.

11. Hopkins and Sugerman, *No One Here Gets Out Alive*, 53.

12. Cosgrave, *Love Her Madly*, 54.

13. Cosgrave, *Love Her Madly*, 50.

14. Turgenev, *First Love*, 193–196.

15. Hopkins and Sugerman, *No One Here Gets Out Alive*, 25.

16. Grof, *The Stormy Search for the Self*, 61. 17American Film Institute, "Martin Scorcese on LAWRENCE OF ARABIA," video, accessed on June 21, 2023.

17. Morrison, "The End," line 8.

18. Lisciandro, "Orange County Suite," section 9, lines 4-13, *The Collected Works of Jim Morrison*, 375.

CHAPTER 12. THE PATH OF THE SUN

Epigraph: Grof, *The Stormy Search for the Self*, 116. Quote cited by Grof from *Ecstatic Religion* by I.M Lewis, page 32.

1. Cosgrave, *Love Her Madly*, 64.
2. Manzarek, *Light My Fire*, 183 (poetry lines contained in quote are from Jim Morrison's poem "The Celebration of the Lizard").
3. Krieger, *Set the Night on Fire*, 170.
4. Yogatherapymallorca.com, "Persephone—Daughter & Goddess of The Underworld." website, accessed on January 10, 2023.
5. Altman, *Magick Tarot*, 38.
6. Goodreads, website, accessed on January 10, 2023.
7. Seligmann, *The History of Magic & the Occult*, 87.
8. Lisciandro, "The End," lines 9–13, *The Collected Works of Jim Morrison*, 476.
9. Riordan and Prochnicky, *Break on Through*, 69.
10. Cosgrave, *Love Her Madly*, 35.
11. Lipton, "Bruno in Venice West," lines 1-25, *Bruno in Venice West & Other Poems*.
12. Blair, Robert, *Tenement TV*, "The Enduring Wisdom of Jim Morrison: 46 Years On" website accessed January 14, 2024.

CHAPTER 13. A VAST, RADIANT BEACH

1. Hopkins and Sugerman, *No One Here Gets Out Alive*, 43.
2. Grof, *The Stormy Search for the Self*, 93.
3. Hopkins and Sugerman, *No One Here Gets Out Alive*, 58.
4. Bremner, *Hermetic Philosophy & Creative Alchemy*, 85.
5. Eliade, *Shamanism*, n13 xii in the foreword.
6. Lisciandro, *The Collected Works of Jim Morrison*, 101.
7. Grof, *The Stormy Search for the Self*, 146.
8. Grof, *The Stormy Search for the Self*, 145.
9. Utti, Jacob, *American Songwriter*, "Top 22 Jim Morrison Quotes," accessed website on January 14, 2024.
10. Maynard, *Venice West*, 1.
11. Maynard, *Venice West*, 13.
12. Lipton, *Holy Barbarians*, 15.

13. Wilson, *Beyond the Occult*, xxii.

14. Grof, *The Stormy Search for the Self*, 1.

15. Grof, *The Stormy Search for the Self*, 44.

16. Grof, *The Stormy Search for the Self*, 64.

17. Morrison, *Wilderness,* 22.

18. Maynard, *Venice West*, 13.

19. Maynard, *Venice West*, 11–12.

20. Helge Nicholson, "Interview with Jim Morrison's father and sister," video, accessed on January 12, 2023.

21. Wilson, *The Occult*, 24.

22. Hopkins and Sugerman, *No One Here Gets Out Alive*, 58.

23. Bolen, *Gods in Everyman*, 261.

24. Nietzsche, *The Birth of Tragedy*, 17-18.

25. Wilson, *The Occult*, 110.

26. Bloom, *Hamlet: Poem Unlimited*, 154.

27. Bolen, *Gods in Everyman*, 257.

28. Lisciandro, "Peace Frog," line 35, *The Collected Works of Jim Morrison*, 510.

CHAPTER 14. WHO ARE OUR FRIENDS?

1. Riordan, *Break on Through*, 60.

2. Lachman, *The Secret Teachers of the Western World*, 424–25.

3. Riordan and Prochnicky, *Break on Through*, 59, 63.

4. Manzarek, *Light My Fire*, 90.

5. Bloom, *Hamlet: Poem Unlimited*, 15.

6. Seligmann, *The History of Magic & the Occult*, 5.

7. Manufacturing Intellect, "Harold Bloom Interview on "Hamlet" (2003)," video, accessed on February 11, 2023.

8. Krieger, *Set the Night on Fire*, 86.

9. Bolen, *Gods in Everyman*, 257.

10. Nietzsche, *The Birth of Tragedy*, 43.

11. Blake, *The Marriage of Heaven & Hell*, Introduction, 23.

12. Hopkins and Sugarman, *No One Here Gets Out Alive*, 142.

13. Riordan and Prochnicky, *Break on Through,* 77.

14. Grof, *The Stormy Search for the Self,* 1.

15. Riordan and Prochnicky, *Break on Through*, 60–61.

16. Maynard, *Venice West*, 2.

17. Kerouac, *On the Road*, 5.

18. Kerouac, *On the Road*, 8.

19. Riordan and Prochnicky, *Break on Through*, 92.

20. Schmidt, *Arthur Rimbaud: Complete Works*, 113.

21. Fowlie, *Poem & Symbol*, 71.

22. Fowlie, *Rimbaud*, 377.

23. Smith, Thomas, *New Music Express*, "The Doors' Jim Morrison: 10 Profound, Bizarre, and Brilliant Quotes," website accessed January 14, 2024.

24. Bolen, *Gods in Everyman*, 103.

25. Bolen, *Gods in Everyman*, 99.

26. Lisciandro, "Not to Touch the Earth," lines 50-51, *The Collected Works of Jim Morrison*, 492.

CHAPTER 15. AN INTENSE VISITATION OF ENERGY

1. Grof, *The Stormy Search for the Self*, 67.

2. Lisciandro, *Friends Gathered Together*, "Phil O'Leno—Little Brother" chapter.

3. Blake, "The Doors Ray Manzarek Talks Jim Morrison in Rare Interview with Barry Roskin Blake 1991," video, accessed on March 15, 2023.

4. Cosgrave, *Love Her Madly*, 103.

5. Cosgrave, *Love Her Madly*, 59.

6. Morrison, *Wilderness*, 78.

7. Grof, *The Stormy Search for the Self*, 83-84.

8. Wilson, *The Occult*, 75.

9. Grof, *LSD: Doorway to the Numinous*, 18.

10. Grof, *LSD: Doorway to the Numinous*, 158.

11. Grof, *LSD: Doorway to the Numinous*, 3.

12. Hopkins and Sugerman, *No One Here Gets Out Alive*, 93.

13. Grof, *LSD: Doorway to the Numinous*, 157-9.

14. Grof, *The Stormy Search for the Self*, 62–63.

15. Grof, *The Stormy Search for the Self*, 81–82.

16. Grof, *The Stormy Search for the Self*, 49.

17. Morrison, *Wilderness*, 36.

18. Morrison, *Wilderness*, 37.

CHAPTER 16. THE CALL OF THE WILD

1. Campbell, *The Hero with A Thousand Faces*, 188.
2. Grof, *The Stormy Search for the Self*, 157-158.
3. Wilson, *The Occult*, 146.
4. Malagon and Berlin, Chicago Tribune, "Inspirations Behind the Design of a Chicago Police Cruiser? Jim Morrison and a retro sensibility," website accessed January 14, 2024.
5. Bolen, *Gods in Everyman*, 277.
6. Eliade, *Shamanism*, 4.
7. Bolen, *Gods in Everyman*, 256–59.
8. Eliade, *Shamanism*, 388, 401.
9. Bolen, *Gods in Everyman*, 258.
10. Eliade, *Shamanism*, 109.
11. Lisciandro, "The Lords: Notes on Vision," section 83, lines 1–9, *The Collected Works of Jim Morrison*, 98.
12. Conway, *Magic: An Occult Primer*, 38.
13. Lisciandro, "The Lords: Notes on Vision," section 22, lines 1–4, *The Collected Works of Jim Morrison*, 85.
14. Lachman, *The Secret Teachers of the Western World*, 330.
15. Lisciandro, "Soul Kitchen," line 19, *The Collected Works of Jim Morrison*, 468.
16. Fowlie, *Poem & Symbol*, 9.
17. Fowlie, *Poem & Symbol*, 5.
18. Lachman, *The Secret Teachers of the Western World*, 330-331.
19. Demilo, "Allen Ginsburg: Mindbreaths in the Night," website, accessed on January 10, 2023.
20. Lachman, *The Secret Teachers of the Western World*, 331.
21. Chris K, "John Dee—Masters of Darkness," "the primal essence of things" quote found at 22:30, "barbarous, rich sounding language" quote found at 22:38, YouTube video accessed on January 21, 2024.
22. Durham, "Dawn's Highway," video, accessed on October 11, 2021.
23. Rawles, "Masters of Darkness: Queen Elizabeth's Magician," video, accessed on October 11, 2021.
24. Nietzsche, *The Birth of Tragedy*, 47.
25. Hopkins and Sugerman, *No One Here Gets Out Alive*, 98.
26. Sontag, *Antonin Artaud*, Introductory essay, liii.

27. Kerouac, *Windblown World*, 252.

28. Lisciandro, "The WASP," lines 42–43, *The Collected Works of Jim Morrison*, 527.

29. Lisciandro, *The Collected Works of Jim Morrison*, 79 (from an interview with Bob Chorush, *Los Angeles Free Press*, January 15, 1971 issue, website accessed January 18, 2024).

30. Pogson, "Death in The Desert," website, accessed on January 15, 2023.

31. Stevenson, "Circus Magazine Interview," website, accessed on January 15, 2023.

32. Grof, *LSD*, 175.

33. Seligmann, *The History of Magic & the Occult*, 4.

34. Seligmann, *The History of Magic & the Occult*, 90.

35. Lisciandro, "Notebook and Journal Poems," "The Universe," section 1, lines 1–7, *The Collected Works of Jim Morrison*, 309.

36. Bolen, *Gods in Everyman*, 261–62.

37. Wilson, *The Occult*, 178.

38. Lisciandro, "The End," lines 30–31, *The Collected Works of Jim Morrison*, 476.

CHAPTER 17. AND WE'RE ON OUR WAY

1. Wilson, *The Occult*, 40.

2. "FL Probation Dept Letter & Reply from Adm. Morrison | TheDoors4 Scorpywag "Other Voices": Doors Talk Forum"

3. Bolen, *Gods in Everyman*, 263–64.

4. Bolen, *Gods in Everyman*, 267.

5. Bolen, *Gods in Everyman*, 39.

6. Hopkins and Sugerman, *No One Here Gets Out Alive*, 40–41.

7. Manzarek, *Light My Fire*, 271.

8. *The Oxford Dictionary of Quotations*, 533, website accessed on January 14, 2024.

9. Lisciandro, "When the Music's Over," lines 57-59, *The Collected Works of Jim Morrison*, 489.

10. Bolen, *Gods in Everyman*, 283.

11. Lisciandro, "The End," lines 54–55, *The Collected Works of Jim Morrison*, 476.

12. Eliade, *Shamanism*, 13.

13. Lisciandro, "Paris Journal," section 7, lines 9-14, *The Collected Works of Jim Morrison*, 194.
14. Lisciandro, "The Lords: Notes on Vision," section 41, *The Collected Works of Jim Morrison*, 89.
15. Lisciandro, "The Lords: Notes on Vision," section 20, *The Collected Works of Jim Morrison*, 85.
16. Hopkins and Sugerman, *No One Here Gets Out Alive*, 84.
17. Krieger, "Light My Fire," *The Doors.*

CHAPTER 18. PARADISE NOW

1. Hopkins and Sugerman, *No One Here Gets Out Alive*, 220.
2. Fong-Torres, "The Doors at the Bowl: Mick, LSD, and a Moth," website, accessed on April 20, 2023.
3. Utti, Jacob, *American Songwriter*, "Top 22 Jim Morrison Quotes," website accessed on January 14, 2024.
4. Grof, *The Stormy Search for the Self*, 70.
5. Laing, *The Politics of Experience*, 108–14.
6. Bolen, *Gods in Everyman*, 259.
7. Lisciandro, "The Celebration of The Lizard," lines 29–32, *The Collected Works of Jim Morrison*, 33.
8. Laing, *The Politics of Experience*, 116.
9. Lisciandro, "The Lords: Notes on Vision," section 42, *The Collected Works of Jim Morrison*, 89.
10. Lisciandro, "Notebook Journal and Poems," "The Universe," section 12, lines 1–6, *The Collected Works of Jim Morrison*, 315.
11. Alice & Books, "The best Thus Spoke Zarathustra quotes," website accessed on January 14, 2024.
12. Hopkins and Sugerman, *No One Here Gets Out Alive*, 40.
13. Krieger, *Set the Night on Fire*, 72.
14. Sontag, Antonin Artaud, Introductory essay, xlvii–xlix.
15. Bolen, *Gods in Everyman*, 274.
16. Bloom, *Hamlet: Poem Unlimited*, 53.
17. JimJohnRayRobbie2, "Jim Morrison—talking to an independent pastor (Fred L. Stagmeyer)," video, accessed on May 12, 2020.
18. James, Lizzie, *Creem Magazine*, "Jim Morrison: Ten Years Gone" website accessed on January 14, 2024.

19. Sontag, Antonin Artaud, Introductory essay, xxxiii.

20. James, Lizzie, *Creem Magazine*, "Jim Morrison: Ten Years Gone" website accessed on January 14, 2024.

21. Wolfsonarchive, "Jim Morrison Interview in Miami August 12, 1970" (found at 0:24) YouTube video accessed January 14, 2024.

22. Bolen, *Gods in Everyman*, 272.

23. Bolen, *Gods in Everyman*, 251.

24. Jerónimo Oscar Alende. "The Doors Miami 1969 Full Audio Concert," accessed on February 14, 2023.

25. Bolen, *Gods in Everyman*, 267.

26. Hopkins and Sugerman, *No One Here Gets Out Alive*, 10–11.

27. Lisciandro, "Lament for the Death of My Cock," lines 1–7, *The Collected Works of Jim Morrison*, 381.

28. Wilson, *The Occult*, 344–45.

29. Riordan and Prochnicky, *Break on Through*, 301–2.

30. Lisciandro, "An American Prayer," lines 46–50, *The Collected Works of Jim Morrison*, 104.

31. Hopkins and Sugerman, *No One Here Gets Out Alive*, 38.

32. Utti, Jacob, *American Songwriter*, "Top 22 Jim Morrison Quotes" website accessed on January 14, 2024.

33. Stevenson, "Circus Magazine Interview," website, accessed on March 3, 2023.

34. Lisciandro, "As I Look Back," lines 51–63, *The Collected Works of Jim Morrison*, 562.

CHAPTER 19. THERE'S A KILLER ON THE ROAD

1. Hopkins and Sugerman, *No One Here Gets Out Alive*, 267.

2. Zevallos, "Interview with Jim Morrison," website, accessed on March 22, 2023.

3. TahquitzCanyon, "The Legend of Tahquitz," website, accessed on March 22, 2023.

4. Eliade, *Shamanism*, 101.

5. Lisciandro, "Orange County Suite," section 5, lines 9–10, *The Collected Works of Jim Morrison*, 370.

6. Wilson, *The Occult*, 232.

7. Lisciandro, "The End," lines 38–39, *The Collected Works of Jim Morrison*, 476.

8. Lachman, *The Secret Teachers of the Western World*, 242.

9. Lachman, *The Secret Teachers of the Western World*, 229.

10. Lisciandro, "From the Tape Noon Journal," "The Long Sweep," section 8, lines 1–16, *The Collected Works of Jim Morrison*, 137.

11. Lisciandro, "Riders on the Storm," lines 12–13, *The Collected Works of Jim Morrison*, 527.

12. Lorberer and Everding, "Beyond the Outsider: An Interview with Colin Wilson," website, accessed on February 25, 2023.

13. Durham, "Dawn's Highway," video, accessed on February 25, 2023.

14. Lisciandro, "Break on Through," lines 1–3, *The Collected Works of Jim Morrison*, 467.

15. Lisciandro, "The Lords/Notes on Vision," section 56, lines 1, 5–6, *The Collected Works of Jim Morrison*, 93.

16. Lisciandro, "Break on Through," lines 27–28, *The Collected Works of Jim Morrison*, 467.

17. Lisciandro, "L.A. Woman," line 30, *The Collected Works of Jim Morrison*, 520.

18. Lisciandro, *Friends Gathered Together*, "Phil O'leno—Little Brother" chapter, p41-42 of 91.

19. Hesse, *The Journey to the East*, 12–13.

20. Lachman, *The Secret Teachers of the Western World*, 437.

21. Hesse, Hermann, *The Journey to the East*, 12.

22. Bolen, *Gods in Everyman*, 294.

23. Bolen, *Gods in Everyman*, 286.

24. Wanis, Patrick, "Jim Morrison thoughts on freedom—Lizzie James Interview" (From 1981 *Creem Magazine* edition, Lizzie James, "Jim Morrison: Ten Years Gone") website accessed on January 14, 2024.

CHAPTER 20. DEATH MAKES ANGELS
OF US ALL

1. Mack, *A Prince of Our Disorder*, 189.

2. Freedland, *The Occult Explosion*, 17.

3. Wilson, *The Occult*, 156.

4. Grof, *The Stormy Search for the Self*, 40.

5. Barry Roskin Blake, "The Doors Ray Manzarek Talks Jim Morrison in Rare Interview with Barry Roskin Blake," video, accessed April 2, 2023.

6. Moore, *Mystical Discourse in Wordsworth & Whitman*, 36.

7. The Doors, "Yes, The River Knows," line 15.

8. Wilson, *The Occult*, 342.

9. Lisciandro, "The Lords: Notes on Vision," section 71, lines 1–5, *The Collected Works of Jim*, 96.

10. Morgan, *Literary Outlaw*, 48.

11. Maynard, *Venice West*, 13.

12. Maynard, *Venice West*, 20.

13. Rutazzurra, "Jim Morrison & Tony Thomas 1970 Interview," video, accessed on January 23, 2023.

14. Lisciandro, *Friends Gathered Together*, "Phil O'leno—Little Brother" chapter.

15. Krieger, *Set the Night on Fire*, 268–70.

16. *Harper's Bizarre*, "Promises: Roll the Dice" website accessed on January 14, 2024.

17. Miller, Henry, *The Time of the Assassins*, 113–14.

18. Schichter, "Ian Astbury on singing Jim Morrison's songs with The Doors," video, accessed March 17, 2023.

19. Grof, *The Stormy Search for the Self*, 85.

20. Conway, *Magic: An Occult Primer*, 40.

21. Nietzsche, *The Gay Science*, 232.

22. Lisciandro, "An American Prayer," lines 154–58, *The Collected Works of Jim Morrison*, 107.

EPILOGUE. RETIRE NOW TO YOUR TENTS & TO YOUR DREAMS

1. Grof, *The Stormy Search for the Self*, 33.

2. Wanis, Patrick, "Jim Morrison thoughts on freedom—Lizzie James Interview" (From 1981 *Creem Magazine* edition, Lizzie James, "Jim Morrison: Ten Years Gone") website accessed on January 16, 2024.

3. Lisciandro, "Strange Days," lines 1–2, *The Collected Works of Jim Morrison*, 483.

4. Lachman, *Beyond the Robot*, 110–11.

5. Rutazzurra, "Jim Morrison & Tony Thomas 1970 Interview," video, accessed on April 12, 2023.

6. Maslow, *The Third Force*, 26–27.

7. Ziller, *Steve Jobs*, 3.

8. Rutazzurra, "Jim Morrison & Tony Thomas 1970 Interview," video, accessed on April 12, 2023.

9. Lisciandro, "The Celebration of the Lizard," lines 138–139, *The Collected Works of Jim Morrison*, 37.

Bibliography

Academy of Ideas. "Abraham Maslow: The Jonah Complex and the Fear of Greatness." March 18, 2015. Academy of Ideas website. Accessed Jan. 7 2024.

Akil, Fadi. "Human All Too Human: Friedrich Nietzsche | BBC 1999." 21 June 2021. YouTube website. Accessed Jan. 7 2024.

Alice & Books. "The best Thus Spoke Zarathustra quotes." Published September 2, 2021. Alice & Books website. Accessed January 14, 2024.

Altman, Magick. *Magick Tarot: A Journey of Self-Realization*. San Francisco: Magickal Times Books, 2016.

American Film Institute. "Martin Scorcese on LAWRENCE OF ARABIA." Posted on December 20, 2011. YouTube website. Accessed Jan. 7 2024.

Antiques Roadshow PBS. "Appraisal: 1963 Jim Morrison Inscribed Book, 'The History of Magic,'" February 12, 2014. YouTube website. Accessed Jan. 7 2024.

Artaud, Antonin. *Antonin Artaud, Selected Writings*. Edited by Susan Sontag, Berkeley, University of California Press, 1988.

———. *The Theater & its Double*. New York: Grove Press, 1958.

Atomic Heritage Foundation. "Native Americans and the Manhattan Project–Nuclear Museum." *Atomic Heritage Foundation*. June 28, 2016. Nuclear Museum website. Accessed Jan. 7 2024.

Barry Roskin Blake. "The Doors Ray Manzarek Talks Jim Morrison in Rare Interview with Roskin Blake 1991." September 13, 2011. YouTube website. Accessed Jan. 7 2024.

Baudelaire, Charles. (tr. Richard Howard). *The Flowers of Evil*. Jaffrey: David R. Godine, Publisher Inc, 1982.

Blair, Robert. *Tenement TV*. "The Enduring Wisdom of Jim Morrison: 46 Years On." Published July 3, 2017. Tenement TV website. Accessed on January 14, 2024.

Blake, William. *The Complete Poetry and Prose of William Blake*, edited by David Erdman. Berkeley, University of California Press, 2008.

Blake, William. *The Marriage of Heaven & Hell*. Oxford: Oxford University Press, 1975.

———. *The Complete Poems of William Blake*. Edited by Alicia Ostriker, Harmondsworth ; New York, Penguin, 1977.

Blinkest Team, The. *Blinkest Magazine*. "The Wisdom of Jim Morrison: Top 10 Quotes to Inspire and Enlighten." Published December 5, 2023. Blinkist Magazine website. Accessed January 14, 2024.

Bloom, Harold, ed. 2004. *Bloom's Major Literary Characters: Hamlet*. Chelsea House Publishers.

———. *Dramas & Dramatists: Bloom's Literary Criticism 20th Anniversary Collection*. New York: Chelsea House Publishers, 2006.

———. *Hamlet: Poem Unlimited*. New York: Riverhead Books, 2003.

Bolen, Jean Shinoda. *Gods in Everyman: A New Psychology of Men's Lives & Loves*. New York: Harper Collins, 1989.

———. *Goddesses in Everywoman: Powerful Archetypes in Women's Lives*. New York: Harper Paperbacks, 2014.

Bremner, Marlene Seven. *Hermetic Philosophy & Creative Alchemy*. Rochester: Inner, 2022.

Brinkley, David, ed. 2004. *Windblown World: The Journals of Jack Kerouac, 1947–1954*. Viking Penguin.

Bucke, Richard Maurice. *Cosmic Consciousness: A Study in the Evolution of the Human Mind*. New York: Arcana, 1991.

Campbell, Joseph. *The Hero with a Thousand Faces*. Novato: New World Library, 2008.

CBC Art News. "Florida opens door to pardoning Jim Morrison." December 4, 2010. CBC website. Accessed Jan. 7 2024.

Cherry, Jim. "Jim Morrison and Jack Kerouac." *Empty Mirror* website. November 4, 2013. Accessed January 14, 2024.

Chinaski, Bill. "The Doors: A Retrospective." January 28, 2019. *Alternative Reel* website. Accessed Jan. 7 2024.

Chris K. "John Dee—Masters of Darkness." YouTube website, October 9, 2012, accessed on January 21, 2024.

Conway, David. *Magic: An Occult Primer*. London: Aquarian Press, 1988.

Corsini, Raymond J., and Alan J. Auerbach, eds. *Concise Encyclopedia of Psychology*. New York: John Wiley & Sons, 1998.

Cosgrave, Bill. *Love Her Madly: Jim Morrison, Mary & Me*. Toronto: Dundern Press, 2020.

Cytaty. The Doors. Doors European website.

Dahl, Danielle. *Everyday Power.* "25 Jim Morrison Quotes that Opened "The Doors" to His Mind." Everyday Power website. Published August 10, 2022. Accessed January 14, 2024.

Dee, John. *The Private Library of Dr. John Dee: and the catalogue of his library manuscripts, from the original manuscripts in the Ashmolean museum at Oxford, and Trinity college library, Cambridge.* New York: AMS Press, 1842.

Demilo, David A. "Allen Ginsburg: Mindbreaths in the Night." *The Harvard Crimson.* February 4, 1978. The Harvard Crimson website. Accessed Jan. 7 2024.

Densmore, John. *Riders on the Storm: My Life with Jim Morrison & The Doors.* New York: Dell Publishing, 1990.

Dj Barker. "(Jim Morrison) on Nudity in the Arts." YouTube website, Dec. 31 2017, Accessed Jan. 8 2024. Originally recorded in August 12, 1970. Channel 4, WTVJ, Miami.

Durham, Brad. "Dawn's Highway FINAL." YouTube website. July 31, 2016. Accessed Jan. 7 2024.

Dutch Guy, The. "Jim Morrison 1947 Dawn's Highway Accident. Docu, Interviews." YouTube website. Oct. 19, 2021. Accessed Jan. 8 2024.

Elevate Society. "100 Quotes by Jim Morrison." By AJ. Elevate Society website. Accessed January 14, 2024.

"FL Probation Dept Letter & Reply from Adm. Morrison." TheDoors4Scorpywag "Other Voices." Doors Talk Forum website.

Fear & Loathing in Las Vegas. Directed by Terry Gillam, performances by Johnny Depp and Benicio del Toro, Summit Entertainment/Rhino Films/ Shark Productions/Fear and Loathing LLC, 1998.

Fong-Torres, Ben. "The Doors at the Bowl: Mick, LSD and a Moth." The Stingray Blog. June 11, 2020. Stingray Blog website. Accessed Jan. 8 2024.

Fowlie, Wallace. *Poem & Symbol: A Brief History of French Symbolism.* University Park: The Pennsylvania State University & Press, 1990.

———, tr. *Rimbaud: Complete Works, Selected Letters.* Chicago: University of Chicago Press, 1967.

Frankl, Viktor E. *Man's Search for Meaning.* Boston: Beacon, 2017.

Freedland, Nat. *The Occult Explosion.* New York: Putnam, 1972.

Freeman, Philip. *Alexander the Great.* New York: Simon & Schuster, 2011.

Goble, Frank G. *The Third Force: The Psychology of Abraham Maslow.* New York: Pocket Books, 1971.

Grimes, William. "George S. Morrison, Admiral & Singer's Father, Dies at 89." December 8, 2020. *The New York Times* website. Accessed Jan. 8 2024.

Grof, Stanley. *LSD: Doorway to the Numinous.* Rochester: Park Street Press, 1975.

Grof, Christina, and Stanley Grof. *The Stormy Search for the Self: A Guide to Personal Growth Through Transformational Crisis.* Los Angeles: Jeremy P. Tarcher Inc., 1990.

Halperin, Shirley. "The Doors' John Densmore: Jim Morrison 'Didn't' Expose Himself." *The Hollywood Reporter.* December 2, 2010. Hollywood Reporter website. Accessed Jan. 8 2024.

Harper's Bizarre. "Promises: Roll the dice." Published October 8, 2017. Harper's Bizarre Wordpress website. Accessed January 14, 2024.

Hesse, Hermann. *The Journey to the East.* London: Vision Press, 1933.

———. *The Journey to the East.* New York: The Noonday Press, 1968.

Hopkins, Jerry, and Danny Sugerman. *No One Here Gets Out Alive.* New York: Warner Books Inc., 1980.

Hutchinson, Lydia. "Jim Morrison, a Pardon & the FBI." *Performing Songwriter.* December 9, 2010. Performing Songwriter website. Accessed Jan. 8 2024.

HWY: An American Pastoral. Directed by Jim Morrison, Babe Hill, Paul Ferrara & Frank Lisciandro, performance by Jim Morrison, HiWay Productions, October 20, 1969.

James, Lizzy. "Lizzie James—Interview with Jim Morrison." Cinetropic website. Accessed Jan. 8 2024.

JimJohnRayRobby[2]. "Jim Morrison—talking to an independent pastor (Fred L. Stagmeyer)." December 8, 2011. YouTube website. Accessed Jan. 8 2024.

Kennedy, John F. "Remarks at a Close & Circuit Television Broadcast on Behalf of the National Cultural Center. |The American Presidency Project." presidency.ucsb.edu, 29 Nov. 1962. Accessed Jan. 8 2024.

Kerouac, Jack. *On the Road.* New York: Viking, 1979.

Knowles, Elizabeth M., Ed. *The Oxford Dictionary of Quotations.* Originally appeared in an edition of *Time* on January 24, 1968. Accessed January 14, 2024.

Krieger, Robby. "Light My Fire." Track #6, *The Doors.* Elektra. Released on *The Doors* on January 4, 1967.

———. *Set the Night on Fire: Living, Dying, & Playing Guitar with The Doors.* Boston: Little, Brown & Company, 2021.

James, Lizzie. *Creem Magazine*. "Jim Morrison: Ten Years Gone." Published in 1981 edition. Waiting for the Sun Archives website. Accessed January 14, 2024.

Jerónimo Oscar Alende. "The Doors Miami 1969 full Audio concert." Posted October 10, 2015. YouTube website. Accessed Jan. 8 2024.

Lachman, Gary. *Aleister Crowley: Magick, Rock and Roll, & the Wickedest Man in the World*. New York: Jeremy P. Tarcher/Penguin, 2014.

———. *Beyond the Robot: The Life & Work of Colin Wilson*. New York: Tarcher/Perigee, 2016.

———. *The Secret Teachers of the Western World*. New York: Jeremy P. Tarcher Inc./Penguin, 2015.

Laing, R.D. *The Politics of Experience & the Bird of Paradise*. New York: Penguin, 1967.

Lawrence, T.E. *The Seven Pillars of Wisdom*. New York: Anchor, 1991.

Lawrence of Arabia. Directed by David Lean, performances by Peter O'Toole and Omar Sharif, Horizon Pictures, 1962.

Lewis, I.M. *Ecstatic Religion: A Study of Shamanism & Spirit Possession*. New York: Routledge, 2003.

Lipton, Lawrence. *Bruno in Venice West & Other Poems*. Van Nuys: Venice West Publishers, 1976.

———. *The Holy Barbarians*. Mansfield Center, CT: Martino Publications, 2009.

Lisciandro, Frank, ed. *The Collected Works of Jim Morrison: Poetry, Journals, Transcripts & Lyrics*. Harper Design, 2021.

———. *Friends Gathered Together*. McMinnville: Vision Words & Wonder, LLC, 1990.

Lorberer, Eric, and Kelly Everding. "Beyond the Outsider: An Interview with Colin Wilson." *Rain Taxi*. Vol. 2, No. 4. Winter (#8). Raintaxi website. Accessed Jan. 8 2024.

Mack, John E. *A Prince of Our Disorder: The Life of T.E. Lawrence*. Cambridge: Harvard University Press, 1976.

Malagon, Elvia, and Jonathan Berlin. *Chicago Tribune*. "Inspirations behind the design of Chicago police's new cruiser? Jim Morrison and a retro sensibility." Published March 13, 2018. Chicago Tribune website. Accessed January 14, 2024.

Manufacturing Intellect. "Harold Bloom interview on "Hamlet" (2003). *The Charlie Rose Show*. February 20, 2017. YouTube website. Accessed Jan. 8, 2024.

Manzarek, Ray. *Light My Fire: My Life with The Doors*. New York: Berkley, 1999.

Matt Schichter. "Ian Astbury on singing Jim Morrison's songs with The Doors." May 10, 2016. YouTube website. Accessed Jan. 8 2024.

Matyas, Josephine, and Craig Jones. *Chasing the Blues: A Traveler's Guide to America's Music*. Lanham: Backbeat Books, 2021.

Maynard, John Arthur. *Venice West: The Beat Generation in Southern California*. New Brunswick: Rutgers University Press, 1991.

Miller, Henry. *The Time of the Assassins*. New York: New Directions, 1962.

Moore, D.J. *Mystical Discourse in Wordsworth & Whitman*. Leuven: Peeters Publishers, 2006.

Morgan, Ted. *Literary Outlaw: The Life & Times of William S. Burroughs*. New York: Henry Holt & Company, 1988.

Morrison, Jim/The Doors. *An American Prayer*. Elektra Asylum Records, 1978.

Morrison, Jim. *The Lords & the New Creatures*. New York: Simon & Schuster, 1987.

———. *Wilderness the Lost Writings of Jim Morrison*, Vol. 1. New York: Vintage Books. 1988.

———. "A World on Fire." Track #4, *An American Prayer*. Elektra & Asylum Records. Released on *An American Prayer* on November 17, 1978.

———. "An American Prayer." Track #5, *An American Prayer*. Elektra & Asylum Records. Released on *An American Prayer* on November 17, 1978.

———. *The Lords & the New Creatures*. New York: Touchstone, 1969, 1970.

———. "Waiting for The Sun." Track #2, *Morrison Hotel*. Elektra Records. Released on *Morrison Hotel* on February 9, 1970.

Music News. "Jim Morrison Remembered." Music News. *Neuhoff Media Lafayette*, July 2, 2020. Neuhoff Media Lafayette website. Accessed Jan. 8 2024.

Nicholl, Charles. *Somebody Else: Arthur Rimbaud in Africa, 1880-91*. Chicago: University of Chicago Press, 1999.

Nicholson, Helge. "Interview with Jim Morrison's Father and Sister." August 9, 2010. YouTube website. Accessed Jan. 8 2024.

Nietzsche, Fredrich. *The Birth of Tragedy and the Case of Wagner*. Edited by Walter Kaufman, Vintage, May 5, 2010.

———. *The Birth of Tragedy Out of the Spirit of Music*. London; New York: Penguin, 1993.

———. *The Birth of Tragedy & The Geneology of Morals*. Garden City, New York: Doubleday, 1956.

———. *The Gay Science*. New York: Vintage Books, 1974.

———. *Human, All Too Human: A Book for Free Spirits*. Lincoln: University of Nebraska Press, 1984.

———. *The Portable Nietzsche*. Translated by Walter Kaufman, New York: Penguin Books. 1977.

———. *Selected Letters of Friedrich Nietzsche*. Edited by Christopher Middleton. Indianapolis: Hackett Publishing Company, 1996.

———. *Twilight of the Idols*. Translated by R.J. Hollingdale, London; New York: Penguin Books, 2003.

———. *Twilight of the Idols*. Translated by Anthony M. Ludovici, London: George Allen & Unwin LTD, 1927.

Nunamaker, Susan Sun. *Windermere Sun*. "A Friend Is Someone Who Gives You Total Freedom to be Yourself." Published February 2, 2019. Windermere Sun website. Accessed January 14, 2024.

Periodic Presidents. "What is Tecumseh's Curse?" June 11, 2013. Periodic Presidents website. Accessed Jan. 8 2024.

Pinchbeck, David. *Breaking Open the Head: A Psychedelic Journey into the Heart of Contemporary Shamanism*. New York: Random House, 2002.

Plutarch. *Plutarch's "Lives."* New York: Biblio & Tannen, 1966.

Pogson, Andrew. "Death in the Desert." *14850 Magazine* website. Accessed Jan. 8 2024.

Polcaro, Rafael. "The 10 Best Jim Morrison (The Doors) quotes about life." Published on January 4, 2021. Rock and Roll Garage website. Accessed Jan. 8 2024.

Reed, Lou. "Rock & Roll." Track #3, *Loaded*. Cotillion. Released on *Loaded* in November 1970.

Rhodes, Richard. *The Making of the Atomic Bomb*. New York: Simon & Schuster, 1968.

Rimbaud, Arthur. *Arthur Rimbaud: Complete Works*. Tr. by P. Schmidt. New York: Harper Perennial Modern Classics. 2008.

Riordan, James, and Jerry Prochnicky. *Break on Through: The Life & Death of Jim Morrison*. New York: William Morrow & Company, 1991.

Rolling Stone. "Michael McClure Recalls an Old Friend." *Rolling Stone*. Issue 88. August 5, 1971. Waiting for the Sun Archives website. Accessed Jan. 8 2024.

Rutazzura. "Jim Morrison and Ben-Fong Torres 1971 Interview." December 3, 2012. YouTube website. Accessed Jan. 8 2024.

———. "Jim Morrison & Tony Thomas 1970 Interview." November 14, 2012. YouTube website. Accessed Jan. 8 2024.

Schiller, Ferdinand Canning Scott, 1911. "Nietzsche, Wilhelm Friedrich." In Chisholm, Hugh (ed.). *Encyclopedia Britannica*. Vol. 19 (11th ed.). Cambridge: Cambridge University Press.

Schopenhauer, Arthur. *The World as Will & Representation*. New York: Dover Publications, 1966.

Setlowe, Rick. "The Admiral & The Poet." *USS Midway Veterans Association*. 2020. USS Midway Veteran's Association website Accessed Jan. 8, 2024.

Shakespeare, William. *Hamlet*. London: Penguin Books, 1994.

Shaw, Jessie. "Gebser's States of Consciousness: An Overview." March 31, 2020. YouTube website. Accessed Jan. 8 2024.

Smith, Howard. "The Village Voice Interview." *The Village Voice*. November 1970. Part 2. YouTube website. Accessed Jan. 8 2024.

Smith, Thomas. "The Doors' Jim Morrison: 10 profound, bizarre, and brilliant quotes." *New Music Express* website. Accessed Jan. 8 2024.

South Florida Sun-Sentinel. "JIM MORRISON, WHEN YOU gonna come home." Published July 6, 1986. Sun Sentinel website.

Sparrow. "Kurt Seligmann at Home: A Brave Encounter with the Unconscious." *Chronogram* website. December 1, 2012. Accessed Jan. 8 2024.

Steinbeck, John. *East of Eden*. New York: Penguin Books, 2016. First publication New York: The Viking Press, 1952.

Stevenson, Salli. "Circus Magazine Interview." October 13, 1970. Waiting for the Sun Archives website. Accessed Jan. 8 2024.

Sudo, Philip Toshio. *Zen Guitar*. New York: Simon & Schuster, 1997.

Tahquitz Canyon Palm Springs. "The Legend." Tahquitz Canyon website. Accessed Jan. 8 2024.

Tanos, Lorenzo. "How Many Times Was Jim Morrison Arrested?" Published February 15, 2022. Grunge.com. Accessed Jan. 8 2024.

The Thin Red Line. Directed by Terrence Malick, performances by Jim Caviezel and Sean Penn, Fox 2000 Pictures/Phoenix Pictures/Geisler-Roberdeau, 1998.

Thoreau, Henry David. *The Portable Thoreau*. Edited by Jeffery S. Cramer, New York, Penguin Books, 2012.

Turgenev, Ivan. *First Love & Other Stories*. New York: Oxford University Press, 1999.

Utti, Jacob. *American Songwriter*. "Top 22 Jim Morrison Quotes." Published 2 years ago as of January 2024. American Songwriter website. Accessed January 14, 2024.

Wagner, Mirjam. "Persephone—Daughter & Goddess of The Underworld." *Yoga Therapy Mallorca*. Accessed Jan. 8 2024. Research based on Jean Bolen's book *Goddesses in Everywoman*.

Wanis, Patrick Ph.D. "Jim Morrison thoughts on freedom—Lizzie James interview." *Patrick Wanis Behavior Expert Ph.D*. April 16, 2014. Patrick Wanis website. Original article, "Jim Morrison: Ten Years Gone," first appeared in *Creem Magazine*, Special Edition, 1981.

Willeford, William. "Abandonment, Wish, and Hope in The Blues," in *Music and Psyche: Contemporary Psychoanalytic Explorations*. Edited by Paul W. Ashton and Steven Bloch, 243-259. New Orleans: Spring Journal Books, 2010.

Wilson, Colin. *Beyond the Occult*. London: Watkins Publishing, 2020.

———. "Beyond the Outsider: An Interview with Colin Wilson." Conducted by Eric Lorberer and Kelly Everding. *Rain Taxi*, Vol. 2, No. 4, Winter 1997.

———. *The New Existentialism*. New York: Harper Collins, 1983

———. *The Occult*. London: Hodder & Stoughton, 1971.

———. *The Outsider*. London: Victor Gollancz LTD, 1956.

———. *Rasputin & the Fall of the Romanovs*. New York: Farrar, Strauss & Company, 1964.

———. *Rogue Messiahs: Tales of Self-Proclaimed Saviors*. Charlottesville: Hampton Roads, 2000.

Wolfsonarchive. "Jim Morrison Interview in Miami August 12, 1970." YouTube website. Accessed January 14, 2024.

WOS Galerie. "Artist: Kurt Seligmann, 1900-1962." Gallery WOS website. Accessed Jan. 8 2024.

Zevallos, Hank. "Interview with Jim Morrison." *Poppin Magazine*. March 1970. TheDoors4Scorpywag 'Other Voices':DoorsTalk Forum website. Accessed Jan. 8, 2024.

Ziller, Amanda. *Steve Jobs: American Genius*. New York: HarperCollins Publishers, 2011.

Index

Page numbers in *italics* indicate illustrations.

BOOKS OF RELATED INTEREST

The Occult Sylvia Plath
The Hidden Spiritual Life of the Visionary Poet
by Julia Gordon-Bramer

The Mirror of Magic
A History of Magic in the Western World
by Kurt Seligmann

Into the Mystic
The Visionary and Ecstatic Roots of 1960s Rock and Roll
by Christopher Hill

Hermetic Philosophy and Creative Alchemy
The *Emerald Tablet*, the *Corpus Hermeticum*, and the Journey through the
Seven Spheres
by Marlene Seven Bremner

The Hermetic Marriage of Art and Alchemy
Imagination, Creativity, and the Great Work
by Marlene Seven Bremner

Women of Visionary Art
by David Jay Brown and Rebecca Ann Hill

Moksha
Aldous Huxley's Classic Writings on Psychedelics
and the Visionary Experience
by Aldous Huxley
Edited by Michael Horowitz and Cynthia Palmer

Net of Being
by Alex Grey
With Allyson Grey

INNER TRADITIONS • BEAR & COMPANY
P.O. Box 388
Rochester, VT 05767
1-800-246-8648
www.InnerTraditions.com

Or contact your local bookseller